W9-CPB-849
AntonioElmaien.com
UncoveringTheCivilWar.com

UNCOVERING
— *the* —
CIVIL
WAR

UNCOVERING

the

CIVIL
WAR

CONVERSATIONS CONNECTING
OUR PAST, PRESENT, AND FUTURE

VOLUME I

Antonio Elmaleh

Copyright © 2021 Antonio Elmaleh

All rights reserved. Published in the United States by Redwood Publishing, LLC., and distributed worldwide. No part of this book may be used or reproduced or transmitted in any form or by any means electronic or mechanical, including photocopy, recording, or any information storage and retrieval system now known or to be invented, without permission in writing from both the publisher and author, except by a reviewer who wishes to quote brief passages in connection with a review written for inclusion in a blog, website, magazine, newspaper, broadcast, or digital media outlet; and except as provided by United States of America copyright law.

Published by 21 Cent Imprints, LLC

ISBN 978-0-9906406-1-5 (hardcover)
ISBN 978-0-9906406-3-9 (paperback)
ISBN 978-0-9906406-4-6 (ebook)

Cover Design: Heather Parlato
Interior Design: Ghislain Viau

Printed in the United States of America

10 9 8 7 6 5 4 3 2 1

CONTENTS

A NOTE FROM
THE CO-PRODUCERS

It was during a random phone call in the summer of 2017 that an idea began to form. Antonio Elmaleh, author of *The Ones They Left Behind*, and major Civil War buff, was talking about how the American Civil War has been given short shrift in our schools, in our media, and in our pop culture. He was also disturbed that many Americans could not see the direct links between the Civil War and what was happening in our country today – and more importantly, were unaware of the fact that our Civil War has never really ended.

We decided to find a way to engage Americans in this course-altering event in a new way. The *Uncovering the Civil War* podcast series was our solution.

We discussed, at length, the topics we might (un)cover, and our "dream team" of experts we would approach to appear on the podcasts. The lists for both began to grow exponentially until we decided that we should "crawl before we walk," and narrow the initial list down to a manageable number. Which is exactly what we did.

The topics chosen were, to us at least, interesting, unusual, revealing, enlightening, fun – or all of the above. The guests, all of whom we owe an enormous debt of gratitude, were all experts in their respective fields, engaging, articulate, ridiculously intelligent, and just a whole lot of fun to work with. Each gladly shared their precious time and expertise to illuminate many little-known aspects of our Civil War. From a sunken ironclad in Georgia to food of the time; from medicine to weapons; and from reenactors to pornography, we covered and uncovered a plethora of unusual and important information about the Civil War. Because our guests shared so much fascinating information, we decided to split the content into two volumes in such a way as to illustrate the depth and breadth of these discussions.

History is constantly revealing itself as new information comes to light and historical dots are connected, reevaluated, and reframed in wider contexts. The conversations contained in this book took place between the fall of 2017 and spring of 2019. The information our guests shared with our audience was information known to be accurate at the time they were recorded. As you read these transcripts, some of this information may be seen in a different light today, so please don't blame the experts for any inaccuracies; blame history for taking its own sweet time to reveal itself in greater detail.

In putting the transcripts together, we wanted to keep the feeling of the podcast. Each episode truly is an interesting conversation between new friends, not a doctoral thesis. The ideas discussed are presented in a much more informal and, we hope, accessible way – just as they actually happened. If you have ever done a live interview for 90 minutes or two hours (which is incredibly difficult!), you know it is absolutely impossible to not trip over your tongue or lose your train of thought a few times for that long of a stretch. We have done some light editing for the sake of clarity, but have been careful to avoid changing the content being presented. People speak differently than they write, and since you are reading this without the benefit of hearing the speaker's tone of voice or inflection, some minor editing needed to be done just so you could continue to follow-the-thread, so to speak.

It bears repeating that the generosity of our guests to share their time and expertise is the real reason for the success of *Uncovering the Civil War* podcasts. We cannot thank all of them enough for helping us uncover more about our Civil War. Each of these wonderful people are the kind of people you would want riding shot-gun next to you on a long, cross-country road trip. There would never be a dull moment, that is for sure.

Unfortunately, Antonio passed away before this book was completed. We hope that he would be proud of the final result. We were proud to have worked beside him on this project that was so dear to his heart. More importantly, we are proud to have called him a dear friend.

We hope you will find these conversations enlightening and entertaining.

As Antonio always said, "Stay safe, and do good."

Joe Marich
Chandra Years
Co-Producers, *Uncovering the Civil War*
January 2020

P.S. If you would like to hear the original podcast version of these discussions, visit the Uncovering the Civil War website for links at UncoveringTheCivilWar.com.

INTRODUCTION

Welcome to our program, everyone. This is Antonio Elmaleh, your host in a series of conversations in which my guests, all experts in their respective fields, help us to uncover new or little-known information and offer fresh insight into our Civil War and Reconstruction. Through these conversations I hope to uncover why our war has affected them so deeply and instilled a commitment to honor, preserve, and separate myths from our understanding of the most profound period in our history.

ONE

UNCOVERING THE SECOND GREAT AWAKENING

Guest: Dr. Ronald White

Antonio Elmaleh: Greetings everyone, welcome to another episode of *Uncovering the Civil War*. Today, I'm especially excited to welcome back Dr. Ronald C. White. Ron is the author of New York Times' Bestselling biographies of Abraham Lincoln and Ulysses S. Grant; he's currently writing a biography of Joshua Lawrence Chamberlain, the hero of Little Round Top at Gettysburg. Welcome back, Ron.

Ron White: Thank you, very good to be with you again.

Antonio Elmaleh: Before we begin, I must happily declare my right to break one of the cardinal rules of historians, which is to avoid "what if" suppositions. I will invoke this right at the end of the program. Today, we're going to be discussing one of the great friendships of American history, that of Ulysses S. Grant and Mark Twain. We will also explore the resonances and repercussions this friendship inspired in American literature. Ron, would you comment on how some history has created myths about both Grant and Twain? I speak first of Grant's reputation

1

as a butcher, a drunk, and a personification of the corruption of the Gilded Age. Do you agree with this?

Ron White: I do not, and of course neither did Mark Twain. Mark Twain called himself "Grant-intoxicated," an interesting metaphor, but he was enormously attracted to Grant long before they developed a relationship in terms of Grant's memoirs. This story of Grant is really the product of what we would call the lost cause, the idea very quickly put into place by Southerners, generals, and newspaper editors that the only reason the South lost the Civil War was that they were overwhelmed by the numerical superiority of the Union Army, the industrial might of the North, and that butcher, Grant. That somehow he just threw his men heedlessly into battle, not aware of the casualties that they would face. Twain did not accept this; now I think we don't accept it any longer, but it was in play for a long time.

Antonio Elmaleh: Can you pinpoint when that started to take hold? It certainly didn't start right after the war, but I've always been fascinated by how some historians hijack the narrative of the war. Do you have a sense of where that really picked up momentum?

Ron White: Well, it began in the last decades of the 19th century, and yet, as I suggested in my book, *Theodore Roosevelt*, when asked in 1900 who were the greatest Americans, said, "The greatest were three: Washington, Lincoln, and Grant." Then Roosevelt went on to say, "Of second rank are Benjamin Franklin, Thomas Jefferson, Alexander Hamilton, and Andrew Jackson." So it was a mixed bag. Then in the 1930s there was a whole series of books on American Presidents. The one written about Grant continued this myth and said that, interestingly, there were no papers of Grant's, and we know that Grant, this author said, was not a good writer. Well, this was before the collection of the Grant papers and obviously he had not paid attention to Grant's memoirs.

Antonio Elmaleh: So it sounds like it was an attempt to whitewash the true reason the war was fought, mainly slavery and ...

Ron White: Yes, absolutely. This was a big part of it, that the whole meaning of the war is a fight over slavery was not there at the advent of Jim Crow towards the end of the 19th century. So, all the things that Grant did as President, namely defending the rights of African Americans, would not have held him in high regard by Americans of that day.

Antonio Elmaleh: The next myth, if you will, is a perception that Twain was always wealthy, that all his books were best sellers, and essentially, he was a happy man. Do you agree with that notion?

Ron White: Well, he made a lot of money, but he was not a good manager of money. So actually he was always in financial trouble. Even the publishing firm that published Grant's memoirs, run initially by his son-in-law, would ultimately go bankrupt more from mismanagement than from what it really could do as a publisher. So Twain was not a very disciplined person. He was a very creative person. He made a lot of money but he never was able to keep a lot of money.

Antonio Elmaleh: I always thought he was wealthy and I always thought that every book was a bestseller. Clearly that wasn't the case. In reading about him and his life, a lot of his books just fell flat or certainly did when they were published, and it took a long, long time for them to find a much wider audience.

Ron White: Well, that's true, when he came into contact with Grant as Grant was thinking about writing his memoirs, this was right at the time that Huckleberry Finn was published and it was a bestseller, it did make money. So there were moments when the books were quite successful and Twain made a lot of money. Just couldn't hold on to it.

Antonio Elmaleh: Yes. Six servants, as I recall somewhere in reading.

Ron White: Right, right, yes. He was a big spender too, yes.

Antonio Elmaleh: Can you tell us the circumstances in which Grant and Twain first met?

Ron White: Yes, they met in two different places, actually. The first was when Grant was attending a reunion of Union soldiers in Chicago and they had a whole number of speakers that evening that were slated to speak. Grant was there with Sheridan, he was there with Sherman, and the last speaker in the evening, it was about 2:00 o'clock in the morning, was Twain. Everybody had had quite a bit of alcohol, and everybody was pretty tired, but Twain, who was a terrific public speaker, kind of welcomed, and aroused the audience. When the speech was over, the two of them met. Twain said to Grant how much he admired him, and this was their first coming together. This was, I think, in 1867, so two years after the end of the Civil War.

Antonio Elmaleh: I recall somewhere it being said the thing that Grant said about Twain was, "He makes me laugh."

Ron White: That's it, but this also says something about Grant. We don't seem to have much laughter today in our politics and Grant was a person who loved a good joke, who had a wry sense of humor, and so for those reasons I think he was very much attracted to Twain because Twain had this wonderful sense of humor that Grant understood and appreciated.

Antonio Elmaleh: Do you recall the circumstances that led to Grant writing his memoirs? I think it's just an amazing story.

Ron White: It is. First of all, it's very important to know that Grant did not want to write his memoirs. He'd been asked by a newspaper reporter in St. Louis a few years after the Civil War, "Are you going to write your memoirs?" and he said, "Absolutely not." Grant believed that memoirs were egotistical, self-serving, used for settling scores, and he was not going to write his memoirs.

I often say to audiences that in the eight years of Dwight Eisenhower only one memoir was written by a member of his cabinet. Think to the eight years of George W. Bush or the eight years of Barack Obama, everybody's writing a memoir, and if you think about it, the memoirs are often self-serving, settling scores, quite egotistical. So Grant was quite critical of Sherman for writing his memoirs, but then when Grant returns from his world tour after his two terms as President, struggles to make some money, is making money, invests that money with his son, his second son, Buck, in a Wall Street firm. However, the Wall Street firm, the owner of it is really involved in a Ponzi scheme, Grant has lost everything. He retires to his summer cottage at Long Branch, New Jersey, bites into a peach, has this incredible pain that he feels in October of that year. He goes and does a biopsy with his New York doctor, and his doctor determines that what Grant has experienced is due to cancer. Now, keep in mind that there are no Presidential pensions until the year of Harry Truman, after FDR. Grant now is approached to write his memoirs and he reconsiders whether he needs to do this. Why? So that he can provide for Julia after his death.

Let me just say that the approach is done by The Century Magazine, which is a major magazine of that day. They had, in Grant's turmoil and financial distress, they had first approached him about writing essays on the great battles of the Civil War from Shiloh, Vicksburg, Chattanooga, and the wilderness. They would pay him five hundred dollars, which in today's money would be something like thirteen thousand dollars per essay, which was a lot of money. Well, Grant agrees and they're quite successful. They liked the essays and they then approached him to do his memoirs, and they offered him ten thousand dollars, which is a lot of money, but not a lot of money according to Mark Twain. When Mark Twain hears about this he rushes over to Grant's home on East 62nd Street in New York and quickly says to him, "You cannot accept this money, this is ridiculous, this is what," Twain writes later, "they would pay an unknown Comanche to write his memoirs."

Well, Grant's DNA is loyalty. He hasn't signed a contract with The Century Magazine, but he feels an obligation. He sort of verbally said, "Yes, I will do this," but now he is persuaded by his oldest son, Fred, and one of his financial advisors that he really needs to think about Twain's offer because Twain understands from the outset that he thinks Grant's memoirs could sell three hundred thousand copies. He asks Twain, "Well, what are you being offered by The Century Magazine?" and Twain says, "Well, I'm being offered ten percent," which would be standard, but a good royalty in the 19th century. Twain says, "Well, listen, I'll offer you something much better, I'll offer you seventy percent of the total proceeds of the book." Well, Grant finally changes his mind in terms of The Century, and signs to do the memoirs with Twain.

Antonio Elmaleh: Also, I want to point out to our listeners that it was sold via subscription.

Ron White: Yes.

Antonio Elmaleh: Which is a very different process of publishing. I don't know if it was experimental at that point but that was, I think, also Twain's real ace in the hole. He felt that doing it that way it would avoid a lot of pitfalls and middlemen and be the most direct financial arrangement between the consumer and the author.

Ron White: Yes, it was a somewhat standard process. What this meant was Twain hired something like, oh, at least fifteen to twenty of these persons, and they would go out across the country and they would knock on doors, and they would say, "Madam, Sir, you've heard of Ulysses S. Grant? He's writing his memoirs and I want to give you an opportunity to get on board right at the outset to buy a copy of the two-volume set," to buy the set, so it was done by subscription, yes.

Antonio Elmaleh: In the spirit of Twain's storytelling, I read a description of that scene where he bursts into Grant's office. As Twain describes it, Grant had his pen literally over the paper, hovering, and Twain said, "Wait, wait," and got him to reconsider for another day, and in that miraculous twenty-four hours, history was made. Do you think there's any truth to that, or is that, again, part of the tall tale? Spinning a good yarn.

Ron White: Well, Twain wrote several autobiographies. It's wonderful that they've come out in recent years. Obviously, he's looking back on this from several years later, but I think the kernel of the truth is there. Whether it all happened so dramatically or took more than twenty-four hours, I don't know, but Twain was a persuasive person and I think George Childs, his financial advisor who lived in Philadelphia, and son, Fred, saw that this could be a much, much better way to promote Grant's memoirs, to let Twain be the publisher.

Antonio Elmaleh: Can you describe what other factor there was in Grant writing these memoirs? What do you think inspired him to actually believe he was a writer? Because what I read is that he didn't think he was a writer at all.

Ron White: He did not.

Antonio Elmaleh: And wouldn't dare give himself permission.

Ron White: Yes, when The Century Magazine first approached him, they traveled out to his home cottage, a twenty-eight-room cottage at Long Branch, New Jersey. They said, "Would you do this?" Well, what they initially received was basically just a rewriting of his orders that he had given for a medal and it didn't have anything that was really to commend it. So, in a very tactful way they sent an editor back out to Long Branch and said, "Now, you know, you need to think about the audience that's going to read this and you need to allow them to see what went into your decision-making. What were the factors?" Grant got it and so he took some time and he rewrote the essay. It came back to the editors of The Century and it was quite good. But Grant was not sure he was a good writer and so even in the process of writing the memoirs, at one point he said to his son, "You know, Twain has not commented at all. Maybe he doesn't like it." So, the son let Twain know this and Twain came down from his home in Hartford, Connecticut, and he told Grant how terrific these were because Grant did not have a sense that he was a good writer.

I argue in my biography that great writers are invariably great readers and one thing we've missed in the Grant story is that we have failed to note, what did Grant read? He finishes twenty-first out of thirty-nine at his class at West Point in 1843, but in his memoirs, he says, "I must apologize." Well, why did he apologize? He said, "I spent most of my time reading novels." Well then he tells us the authors that he read and the novels that he read, and then you begin to understand.

Okay, well, he's been reading some pretty great writers, so whether he understood it or not, these writers were influencing his ability to be a great writer.

Antonio Elmaleh: That's interesting, very interesting. In studying Grant's memoirs and the body of Twain's work, is there any validity to the notion that they represent a kind of democratization of American non-fiction and fiction? I mean, Grant's memoirs are told with a simplicity, a humility, and a concise clarity of prose, and much of Twain's body of work is about country boys, slaves, and "Ordinary folk." Do you subscribe to the notion that this was a democratization of literature that took place, I think in large part, because of the Civil War and the mingling of all these different classes of people?

Ron White: I do. I think that American culture, American literature, was very much a kind of a hand-me-down for a long time of British culture or European culture and writing. You don't really have remarkable American writers until you get to the 19th century. So, Twain is, even beyond the early American writers, he does represent what you call, what others have called the democratization of American writing. He writes in vernacular language, he writes clearly, he tells stories that come out of American culture. So, I think this is one reason he found himself so appreciative of Grant, that Grant did not write the sort of high-toned literature or writing, but very direct, straight, simple, clean prose. It's why Twain admired Abraham Lincoln, who wrote in the very same way. Lincoln's second inaugural address is seven hundred and one words. Five hundred and five are one-syllable, just straightforward, what would be called the Saxon language; it's direct, strong verbs and Grant wrote in very much the same way.

Antonio Elmaleh: Not like John Steinbeck.

Ron White: No hoop-de-doodle in this writing, no, not at all. So, I think it is fair to say that there's a similarity of Twain and Grant, not that Grant was thinking about this, but in a kind of direct democratization of American writing.

Antonio Elmaleh: In reading your biography and also in other accounts of the writing of this book, I don't get a clear sense of what process Grant followed: sometimes he's dictating, other times he's writing. Obviously, he's doing a ton of reading and taking massive numbers of notes, but do you have a handle on what was his actual process? Did he start with the dictation? Because I also noticed that there's a strong sense that he wrote the way he spoke, or spoke the way he wrote, or either way.

Ron White: Well, he was writing in his home in New York, just writing it on a little table on the second floor. He used his son, Fred, as kind of a researcher. He asked Fred to bring to him various records so that he could, in a sense, refresh his memory. So that was the way he wrote. He wrote remarkably fast for someone who was already beginning to go downhill, in terms of his physical strength, due to the cancer. He wrote with Adam Badeau, who was his assistant in this writing, this would ultimately produce a conflict, which we might mention later. But one thing he does begin to do, which he didn't do in his writing as general, is he becomes his own editor. You see in the memoirs, which interestingly were published this last fall by Harvard University Press in a new annotated version, you see that he is striking out, writing over, he's editing his work.

In the evening he would often read it, the day's work, to Julia. Here again, this is something we've lost in our culture, the idea of reading something out loud, that you hear something in that process that you do not get if you're reading it silently to yourself, which is our process of reading. In the 19th century people read out loud. Lincoln read out loud. Grant read out loud and he heard something, so he would be editing even that evening as he heard his words read to his wife. So, he did have a process that's pretty straightforward. Now the process will change, and we can get to that in a minute, as his illness progresses. So, for example, Twain hires a stenographer, to help Grant in the process, so Grant now can dictate. So, Grant says out loud to the stenographer, who writes it down, but even again Grant would then look at it that evening and edit it and come back the next morning.

Antonio Elmaleh: And let's just remind our audiences that the man is suffering from cancer of the tongue, which is spreading quite aggressively, which means that his tongue and his throat are swelling and speaking becomes increasingly more difficult to the point where it's almost like a whisper. How was he able to talk or dictate? Or did that stop entirely as it got really clear that he was in agony all the time. Do you have any ideas on that?

Ron White: Yes. Well, he got to the point where he was afraid he might die by choking to death, so he began to sleep sitting up in a chair. He didn't even want to sleep in a bed, he thought this could become too dangerous for his health. So yes, pretty soon the stenographer no longer works, so now Grant begins to, he's still writing, but he begins to communicate with his doctors or even Twain, when Twain stops in for a visit, by writing on little slips of paper. I have held in my hand those slips of paper at the Library of Congress. For example, he writes to his doctor, Dr. John Douglas, he writes on one little slip of paper, which we have, he says, "With every line I write, I know I'm driving another nail into my coffin." Another nail into my coffin. His doctors believed that the only reason he was still alive was the memoirs, that he had to complete the memoirs and he had to complete the memoirs to provide for Julia. This was the basic reason, this was the income that would be received from the memoirs so that she could live her life.

Antonio Elmaleh: I read, and I'm not sure exactly where, I think you might have written this, but he also wrote a passage to his doctors, they didn't lie to him but they didn't come right out and say, "General, you're going to die." I believe that he wrote somewhere, "I'm going to die of three things." One was, "I'm going to choke", then "I'm going to starve", or I forget what the third was. Do you recall that? Him writing that?

Ron White: Yes, well at first, he didn't know how to tell Julia, so Julia went to the doctor herself. Although she heard from the doctor that this was what we would say terminal, yet as his wife she could never quite believe that he really was going to die. So, at the very end he writes a note to her and pins it inside his coat, believing that he could not actually say this to her and she could not bear to hear it. The note is just absolutely profound. He just says to her, in effect, he said, "I'm going to die and I hope our children will go on in the moral life to which we have trained and nurtured them. I would not be upset if they were to die from physical death. I would be upset if they were to depart from the morality, which you and I have nurtured them in." But he can't even say that to her and he doesn't think she can hear it, so he pins it inside his coat and she finds it after his death. This is now spring of 1865.

Antonio Elmaleh: '85, isn't it?

Ron White: 1885, pardon me, 1885, right. Now we have newspaper reporters who are just hovering in his home on East 66th Street. "Grant is dying" headlines the March 1st The *New York Times*, but then at the end of March it appears that Grant really is dying. He's experienced a violent choking fit on the evening of March 30th and Julia's sitting there by him, holding his hand. Everybody expects him to die that evening, but he does not.

I'm really struck, I want to read this, on April 4, Mark Twain wrote in his notebook, Twain is in Hartford, "General Grant is still living this morning. Many a person between the two oceans lay hours awake last night listening for the booming of the fire bells that should speak to the nation in simultaneous voice and tell of its calamity." Twain specified, "The bell strokes are to be thirty seconds apart and there will be sixty-three, the General's age. They will be striking in every town of the United States at the same moment."

It is so important for people to understand that Grant was not simply appreciated or respected, he was loved. There was an incredible affection for this man, and Twain, the way he describes this, "Every single town in America, the bells will be rung." Boy, this is the way Grant was understood and appreciated in his day.

Antonio Elmaleh: To that point, I just want to mention to our audience, and you can please feel free to comment, that at the funeral procession, the President ordered sixty thousand soldiers to march down Broadway. They estimated the crowds in the hundreds of thousands. And guess who didn't participate? There was Twain from a window watching from above. I always wondered when I read that, was that a disconnect, or was he just trying to get a larger perspective on the incredible spectacle that was unfolding before him? What's your impression of that moment?

Ron White: I don't know whether Twain might have felt that he would have been mobbed as kind of a celebrity and everybody knew of his role with Grant. I don't know. I don't know what this really says about him as a person.

Antonio Elmaleh: Okay, that's one of those suppositions.

Ron White: Yes.

Antonio Elmaleh: Let's turn to Huck Finn. What parallels, if any, do you see between Grant's greatest victory, the Vicksburg campaign, which in military history is considered certainly one of the greatest military campaigns ever waged, and Huck and Jim's journey down the Mississippi.

Ron White: It's a fascinating question. I'm certainly not an expert on Twain. Both understood the importance of the Mississippi, which we don't understand today. During the Civil War, Lincoln understood that whoever controlled the Mississippi would control the heart of the nation, and could divide the Confederacy in half. Abraham Lincoln took two trips down the Mississippi from his homes in Indiana where he saw for himself the horror of slavery as he got to the docks of New Orleans. He saw men and women separated from each other, husband and wife separated from each other by the river. So, Twain, who grows up on the Mississippi River, who had been a pilot himself, he makes this story, the Mississippi River is really the interstate highway of that day, the sort of central metaphor by which he tells the story of Huckleberry Finn. So until you asked the question, I can honestly say I'd never quite thought about the parallel, but obviously there are parallels and Twain sees the parallel in his appreciation of Grant.

Antonio Elmaleh: Let me point out to you what I picked up in reading, there's a couple of great questions: why did Huck go south to free a slave? That's counterintuitive.

Ron White: Yes, it was.

Antonio Elmaleh: And everybody wondered, would Grant ever stop? Oh, he's going to be set back, he'll head north or he'll veer away. What's not really commonly understood is that Grant failed to take Vicksburg eight times. He crossed the river continuously, trying to get at Vicksburg from land. Well there's certainly a parallel there because I think Huck and Jim crossed that river innumerable times as well.

I think the other parallel involves, I think his name is Harrison Terrell, and what he meant to Grant? Because I think there's a parallel between that friendship and that of Jim and Huck.

Ron White: You're talking about the African American man that was an important person for Grant.

Antonio Elmaleh: Right.

Ron White: Well, and this begins to start the story, part of the irony of history and the irony of biography is that Grant's family was strongly anti-slavery in Ohio, but Julia, his wife's family, was strongly pro-slavery in Missouri. Grant's family would not come to the wedding when they were married because he was marrying into a slaveholder's family; Julia's father gave her four slaves as a wedding dowry. And yet Grant does not appear to be anti-slavery in the early part of the Civil War, he says he will carry out whatever order comes from Abraham Lincoln about slavery. He's very deferential to civilian power and leadership, but then the further South he travels, as African Americans begin to come into the Union lines, he becomes more and more empathetic to their plight and his whole attitude toward them changes.

I think a great quality of leadership, of Presidential leadership, is the capacity for empathy. You might take someone like Franklin Delano Roosevelt who's a very, very wealthy man and yet he had a remarkable capacity for empathy. So Grant's empathy for the African American, as he travels further south, as Jim and Huck travel further south, will finally show itself when he becomes President and he steps forward to defend the rights of African Americans, even as his own Republican party steps back from their defense of African Americans.

Antonio Elmaleh: And getting back to Terrell.

Ron White: Yes.

Antonio Elmaleh: How did he meet him? What was their relationship like?

Ron White: Well, he met him in his journey south and came to know him and respect him. Maybe this is, I guess you could argue, one of the first friendships that he developed in relationship with African Americans. If I might build on this and say that, for the audience, if you have the opportunity you want to visit the so-called Ulysses S Grant National Historic Site which is right outside of St. Louis. It's where Grant met Julia, Julia's family's country home was there. Ultimately they bought the country home years later, but when Grant struggled after his time at West Point and posted to the Pacific Coast and resigned from the military, he comes back and one of those slaves, well the four slaves were given to Julia but Julia's father gave him a slave named William, William helped him try to make a living as a farmer.

In 1859, when things are not going well for Grant financially at all, in the most amazing act he does, this is the film that you will see if you visit the Grant Historic Site, he frees William. He walks into St. Louis and signs emancipation papers and frees William. William was probably in his early thirties, and would have been worth a thousand dollars to Grant, who was desperate for money, but he frees William.

Antonio Elmaleh: I wanted to double-back on a point you made about Grant's split family and correct me if I'm wrong, but when Grant was elected President, both his father and his father-in-law lived in the White House and they would daily refight the Civil War.

Ron White: Well, yes, it's interesting. The father-in-law did not want Julia to marry Grant because Grant was a kind of a soldier, a kind of a nomadic person; he wanted her to marry a businessman or a lawyer, someone of much more substance and money. So at first it was a very difficult relationship and both Julia's mother and Mary Robinson, the chief female slave, were very impressed with the way Grant would listen to old man Dent and not try to contradict him, and yet hold his ground and make his own point. But years later, yes, the father-in-law lived in the White House, terribly proud of his son-in-law. Sometimes Grant's father also lived in the White House. I don't know how much they refought the Civil War, but they lived there together, yes. Yes.

Antonio Elmaleh: One big happy family.

Ron White: Right, right, right. [Laughter]

Antonio Elmaleh: It says a lot about Grant's ability to contain a lot of different opposites and find a way to work through stuff.

Ron White: I think it does, I think it does, absolutely. Good point, yes.

Antonio Elmaleh: I also want to point out a little vignette that I read to our listeners, which is that, and this is in relation to Terrell, that during the campaign South, it was a common sight to see thousands of slaves training behind the Union columns. As they conquered Southern territory and towns and everything, slaves would just realize, "This is our opportunity to get out of here," so they were trailing behind the columns. I think it was Sherman who was sitting with Grant by the side of the road as the Union troops were marching and this column of really pathetic people, with everything they own on their backs, is trudging behind them. Grant turns to Sherman and says, "I really don't know these people." It's a strange comment, isn't it?

Ron White: It is. It's a very honest comment.

Antonio Elmaleh: It is.

Ron White: It's a very honest comment. I don't hear it as a deprecating comment at all.

Antonio Elmaleh: Not at all.

Ron White: But, "I don't really know these people." And of course, this is the question that emerges for both Lincoln and Grant. For Lincoln, it's did he sign the Emancipation Proclamation simply as a political, military move, but had no real sympathy for these people? I don't think that's true. I think he did have sympathy, and I think Grant's the same way. I think he came to know these people, they came to him in the White House ultimately, but initially he didn't really know these people. He understood that many of the Union soldiers were not at all sympathetic to these people coming into the Union lines, so that's why it's all the more remarkable to me, his own journey and how he comes to know these people and comes to be the advocate for their cause.

Antonio Elmaleh: Yeah, it's remarkable to me, but as we've outlined in our discussion you can see the seeds of his perception of tolerance and his kind heart. That's another thing that seems to always emerge is his fundamental kindness coupled with his will of steel. It's a fascinating, fascinating combination and I think really two of the most necessary attributes of great leadership.

Ron White: Well, I think so, too. I think one of the missing parts of the Grant story that I try to lift up in my biography is where does this attitude come from? I think a lot of this attitude does come from his Methodist upbringing. Methodism was strongly anti-slavery. His mother taught him values, especially of humility and self-effacement, and giving credit to others. So, these are qualities that are deeply part of Grant's personality. You always have to ask where did they come from? It's not easy to answer that question, but I think his Methodist background had a lot to do with the values that shaped him.

Antonio Elmaleh: Well, let's make a plug for our earlier program in which you talked at great length about the Second Great Awakening. I wonder whether that's exactly what you're really referring to, that he grew up in the so-called west, where all this started, and he believed that faith without good works is empty.

Ron White: Yes, I think sometimes I worry that we sort of say, "Well, that was the 19th century, people were religious," but we don't go any further than that to say, what was the meaning of their religion? How did it shape their lives? I think it shaped their lives in very profound ways and I think this was true for Grant.

Antonio Elmaleh: Can you recall, in your distinguished career as a historian, does something compare to this friendship in terms of two people of incredibly different backgrounds united around this very creative interaction, inspiring each other, etc. etc. Do you recall anything that resembles anything like this friendship in your studies?

Ron White: That's a great question. I might not use the word friendship, but I would, as I thought about this in terms of Lincoln, two people come to mind. First is Walt Whitman. We're not sure they ever met, I don't think they did, but Whitman observed Lincoln when Lincoln came on his tour to become President, he stopped in New York City and Whitman was in the crowd. Then Whitman, you may remember, was operating as a kind of a nurse in Washington D.C. On a number of occasions he observed Lincoln with great appreciation. Of course, after Lincoln's death, then he writes some poetry that really lifts up Lincoln, so Whitman was not a friend but an observer.

The other would be Harriet Beecher Stowe, who does visit the White House. We don't know whether these are the exact words, but she comes, she's now very famous, she's written Uncle Tom's Cabin, and when she's ushered into Lincoln's office, he says, "Oh," he says, "you're the little woman that started this big war." So again, not that it was a friendship, but he knew who she was and she wasn't exactly sure who he was, in the sense that she was a little concerned whether he was, at that point in time when she visited, strongly enough an abolitionist or at least anti-slavery? So, she comes away later offering quite a strong comment in commendation of Lincoln. But that conversation, we don't know the substance of it. It was probably critical for her changing her mind about him. She came to view Lincoln as much more strongly anti-slavery than she had thought he was.

Antonio Elmaleh: Here's a supposition. Some people maintain that each man, Grant and Twain, saw something in the other they never believed in themselves, i.e., Grant never believed he was a writer and Twain never thought of himself as a soldier, he was a Confederate deserter and detested authority. So, here's Grant writing one of the greatest works of nonfiction and Twain serving his Commander-in-Chief with a loyalty and an adoration that any commander would ever wish of any soldier under his command. Is that leaping too far? Or do you find the grains of truth in that?

Ron White: No, I think that's a fascinating suggestion. So, when we say Twain is Grant-intoxicated, well, why is he intoxicated with Grant, what does he see in Grant? Well, obviously he sees a man of integrity that he admires, but is there anything else that he sees in Grant? It very well could be that he admires Grant the soldier, as you suggested, that Twain is not a soldier, he's a deserter, in a way.

Antonio Elmaleh: Right.

Ron White: But he sees in Grant someone who he very much admires. On the other hand, when Grant starts off on his world tour, he reads one of Twain's books as a way of trying to understand what it would be like to travel the world. So here again, why is he caught up in the Twain book? I said earlier that he was caught up with reading novels, all the way back to his days at West Point, this was extremely important to him. He would have been a ready and willing reader of Twain's work. This would not have been something that would have been strange or different to him. He would appreciate Twain from the beginning.

Antonio Elmaleh: I think that there is always some truth in what attracts people, what makes for a truly great connection, is when someone inspires someone else to be better than they are. To want to be better than they are, and I think that I was trying to point to that as a route of this mutual affection and respect that each had for the other.

Since your recent biography, what things did you learn about U.S. Grant you never knew before?

Ron White: This is a great question, too, because one of the real joys for me in doing a book tour is precisely what you're suggesting, to learn things that you never knew before. Probably the most major thing that I've learned was at the very end of the publication of the book I'd heard that General David Petraeus was a great fan of Grant. So, I said to the publisher, let's reach out to him, perhaps he would be willing to give us a blurb for the book. Well, he did, to my surprise and delight, and then he wrote to me and said, "Let's do some events together." So, we have done three events together.

The most recent one was an opening convocation at West Point. He interviews me, but then he tells the audience, in this case the cadets at West Point, why he believes Grant is the greatest American general, without question. He says, "There's three ways by which you observe or assess a general's greatness." The first is what he calls a sort of strategy, which is both political and military. Some general understands the largest dimensions of the military campaign in which he's involved. The second was Grant's ability to oversee, at the end, five different Armies fighting simultaneously. Before Grant took command in March of 1864, these Armies were really fighting independently, there was no coordinated strategy. Before the Civil War the largest American Army was fourteen thousand, led by Winfield Scott in the war with Mexico. So, Grant has the capacity to coordinate five Armies. Then finally is the tactical, fighting one particular battle. David Petraeus would point out that Dwight Eisenhower, another great general, never had a tactical command, he wanted one in World War I, but he did not. So, here's something that I didn't know. I struggled in my own way to write military history, but here's a great military leader giving his assessment of Grant. That's been a real revelation to me and to the audience where we've spoken together.

Antonio Elmaleh: There was one particular feature of the cover of your book that just really got to me and that was his eyes.

Ron White: Yes.

Antonio Elmaleh: I wanted to ask you, obviously I know, I'm sure you poured through, I don't know, dozens of pictures of Grant and came to this one. Could you tell our listeners what you saw in his eyes? Or what you saw in that photograph that captured, for you, the essence of who this man was?

Ron White: Well, I have the privilege, and I will underline privilege, of being published by Random House. So, I have to give credit to the fact that Random House put their wonderful designers on this project. They read the manuscript and they came to the conclusion that what I was attempting to do was, I call what I write "from the inside out", I was trying to describe the character, as it were, the soul, the spirit of Grant. So, they found, I didn't find, they found an 1864 photograph of Grant, which they colorized and yes, as you say correctly, the way they bring it into focus on the cover, a reader is drawn to the eyes of Grant. It's like you're looking into the eyes of this man, and that's what makes Grant so wonderful, he was called the quiet man. I call him introverted if we would have had that term in the 19th century, and yet if you take the time to get next to him, you will see here's a man of great depth and substance and integrity. That colorized photograph communicates that to the reader.

Antonio Elmaleh: Well, and I also want to add, that for me, what was quite moving is that there's sadness. There's kindness.

Ron White: Oh, yes.

Antonio Elmaleh: A deep well of experience. There's no bitterness. I mean, this is 1864, he's in the middle of the bloodiest war, the wilderness and all these horrific campaigns, and yet there is a kindness that still resides in the midst of this slaughter, which I find absolutely extraordinary.

Ron White: Well, and what we need to hear today especially, there's no self-adulation, no self-adulation, Grant will never put himself forward. If other people want to offer praise for him, all right, but he is not going to say, "Look how great I am."

Antonio Elmaleh: If you could leave our listeners with one prevailing thought or an image, or even a question about this remarkable friendship, what would it be?

Ron White: Appreciation, deep appreciation. Two very different individuals: Grant is, in many ways, quite conservative in his lifestyle; Twain is very flamboyant in his lifestyle; and yet these two men, so different, come to a deep appreciation of each other. Grant is almost bowled over that Twain appreciates him and his writing, it's very important that Twain steps into this story and says, "Grant, you are a great writer. I want you to know that." So listening to Twain, the greatest American writer, tell him this, this buoys Grant's confidence that what he's doing is worthwhile and might ultimately succeed, but on the other hand, I think Twain is just buoyed by the fact that here this, the greatest American of his day, is offering him praise and appreciation and respect. Twain is a big figure, he's a big personality, he's got all kinds of fame, but the fact that Grant offers him this commendation is very meaningful to Twain.

Antonio Elmaleh: Allow me to read the prologue to Huckleberry Finn to our listeners. "Notice: Persons attempting to find a motive in this narrative will be prosecuted; persons attempting to find a moral in it will be banished; persons attempting to find a plot in it will be shot. By order of the author, Per G.G., Chief of Ordnance." It's well known that Twain never explained this riddle, nor ever let on who G.G. was. Now here comes the supposition behind my disclaimer. Would you like to take a crack at who is G.G.?

Ron White: Well, I think you're so suggestive here. G.G.: General Grant.

Antonio Elmaleh: Yes.

Ron White: Because he is finishing up the publishing process for Huckleberry Finn just at the moment that he is now entering into this conversation and publication of Grant's memoirs. Hey, very suggestive, very possible.

Antonio Elmaleh: It seems likely to me. I'm sorry, but I have to get into the power of that acknowledgement.

Ron White: Yes, sure, yes.

Antonio Elmaleh: Why he never wanted to mention it, that's a whole other, I don't know that, I have not a clue.

Ron White: Sure, sure, yes, I don't either. Right, right.

Antonio Elmaleh: Well, I'm afraid we're out of time. I'm really, really quite thrilled that you came on the show again. I'd like to remind our listeners that they can also hear you and I discussing the Second Great Awakening on another episode of this show. And I want to thank you...

Ron White: Well, thank you so much.

Antonio Elmaleh: Oh, great pleasure.

Ron White: And of course, it's my delight, yes.

Antonio Elmaleh: Thank you, thank you. Before we go, tell our listeners about your new book so we can look it up.

Ron White: Ah, yes, yes, I am writing a biography. I've finished chapter four of the biography of Joshua Lawrence Chamberlain. Chamberlain has been rediscovered in recent decades, first through the novel, The Killer Angels, then through the movie, Gettysburg, the Civil War documentary by Ken Burns. Chamberlain is the man who grew up in Maine, graduate of Bowdoin College, went to Bangor Theological Seminary, then began to be a teacher at Bowdoin at age thirty-two against the wishes of his wife. The college offered him a two-year sabbatical in Europe, he volunteers to serve in the Union Army. At West Point, at Gettysburg, the second day of the battle, the far-left line, he is defending Little Round Top. His men have run out of ammunition, he tells them to fix their bayonets and they charge down the hill en route to the 20th Alabama. Now, Little Round Top, because of Chamberlain's reemergence as an American hero, is the most visited place at Gettysburg. After Gettysburg he moves on to become the governor of Maine four times, president of Bowdoin College.

I'm heading to Maine in two weeks to spend the first of four weeks there doing research this summer. I think it's a remarkable story. I don't want it to be what I call hagiography, but he's a man that has no contradictions and I want to explore that and I think it's a story that I'm really enjoying working on.

Antonio Elmaleh: I want to also ask you quickly to describe the moment when Lee's troops are surrendering and they're filing past the columns of Union and the Union soldiers start to cheer. What happens next?

Ron White: Well, Grant tells the Union soldiers not to cheer, but in terms of Chamberlain, Grant gives Chamberlain the command to receive the Confederate troops. As he marches forward, he does something that will become very controversial, he salutes the Confederate commander. I think it's very much, again, a kind of a Chamberlain moment, that he does this out of great respect. That's part of the Chamberlain story.

Antonio Elmaleh: Well, I'm looking forward to it. Do you have any idea when it will be published? Have they given you a publishing date?

Ron White: I'd like to publish it, not in 2020 when we're going to have quite a tumultuous election, but the fall of 2021.

Antonio Elmaleh: Okay.

Ron White: In three years, yeah.

Antonio Elmaleh: And you have no title as of yet?

Ron White: No, I don't.

Antonio Elmaleh: Any notion?

Ron White: The title may simply be *Joshua Lawrence Chamberlain* because I think those involved and interested in the Civil War know who this man is. Maybe there'll be a subtitle, I'm not necessarily in favor of a subtitle. It might just be *A Life*, or *A Biography*, or something, but that's to be determined as we move down the road.

Antonio Elmaleh: Great. Looking forward to it. Ronald White, Doctor Ronald White, thank you for joining me on the show and, as usual, for a wonderful, illuminating, and stimulating, and moving, I hope, discussion. It's been a great pleasure.

Ron White: It's been my privilege. Thank you again.

Antonio Elmaleh: And to all our listeners, thank you for taking the time and having the curiosity to listen in. Please come back for another episode of *Uncovering the Civil War*. Until then, be safe and do good.

TWO

FOLLOW THE MONEY: UNCOVERING HOW BANKING FINANCED SLAVERY

Guest: Dr. Sharon Ann Murphy

Antonio Elmaleh: Hello everyone. Today I am privileged to have as my guest via telephone Professor Sharon Ann Murphy. Professor Murphy is a professor at Providence College. She received her PhD from the University of Virginia and is an associate editor of Enterprise & Society: The International Journal of Business History, published by Cambridge University Press. She is also the author of *Investing in Life: Insurance in Antebellum America*, from the Johns Hopkins Press, which was the winner of the 2012 Hagley Prize for the Best Book in Business History; and *Other People's Money: How Banking Worked in the Early American Republic*, again, Johns Hopkins Press. Her research focuses on why financial institutions emerged, how they were marketed to and received by the public, and the reciprocal relationships between those institutions and the public. Her latest project is an investigation of the relationship between Southern banks and American slavery, and particularly the use of slaves as loan collateral.

Welcome to *Uncovering the Civil War*, Professor Murphy.

Sharon Ann Murphy: Thank you for having me.

Antonio Elmaleh: My pleasure. I'd like to start with a general comment or rather a question. Given the powerful and provocative nature of your current area of study, do you have a sense of why so little scholarship has been devoted to this subject so far?

Sharon Ann Murphy: There have been a couple of small studies done, but financial history itself is a relatively small field and tends to focus on financial institutions in the North, which were a lot more prominent, a lot larger. But it is kind of an interesting question since so much of slavery has been explored in so many different angles. When I was writing my last book, *Other People's Money*, I had a section in there in which I'd planned to discuss the relationship between banks and slavery, and I actually was shocked myself at how little had been written on this relationship. That's what actually got me started on this project; I started looking into, thinking, "Well, is there anything there?" And I did just a little bit of digging and started finding a lot very quickly. So, I think it's just the youth of the field of financial history, mainly, is at play here. But otherwise I can't really explain it.

Antonio Elmaleh: The conspiratorial mind starts to think, well, it's so profoundly upsetting and brings into stunning relief so much about the system of slavery and how it was supported. You've got people who really didn't want to go near it, but I suppose that's just pure conjecture and we will leave that alone for the moment. [Laughter]

Sharon Ann Murphy: Well, I will add that there are people that are dealing with this in the area of government, in fact. There were several laws passed in 2001 in California and Illinois requiring financial institutions to go back into their records and look for linkages between their institutions and slavery. And insurance companies had to do this, banks had to do this, and so there is actually a database of companies that found this in their records. The problem is most companies that existed during the time of slavery no longer exist, and so this law only applied to current companies and so they would go back and these are mostly companies they acquired over the years. For example, the Citizens Bank of Louisiana still exists as part of another modern bank, it was taken over and so they had to report their, I believe it was JP Morgan, had to report their relationship.

So that has come up, but I think the lack of records and these banks, most of them no longer exist, so getting to those records is also a little bit problematic. But there is a question a lot of companies do not want to have it out there that they had any relationship with slavery, even if it was extremely remote and something that they had no power over, being an acquired company that they were not a part of when they were part of slavery. Companies do not want this stain on them.

The *New York Times* just recently had a big article about New York Life Insurance Company and its relationship with slaves, and the company was pushing back quite a bit on that article as well, so I do think there is pushback from companies that they don't want to be associated with this.

Antonio Elmaleh: You've outlined several financial vehicles that Southern banks used to finance plantation owners' operations. Can you briefly name a few and describe how they worked?

Sharon Ann Murphy: Banks are the most obvious, and there's several different types of banks. Your typical state bank would be chartered by the state and they would permit slaveholders to use their slaves, not all of them but some of them, would permit slaveholders to use their slaves as collateral when they were taking out loans. You have the First and Second Bank of the United States, which were national banks that existed for part of this period, and they each, I'm not as sure about the First Bank, the Second Bank I definitely have evidence that certain branches engaged in this and were involved in this.

You also have insurance companies, they engaged in slavery in a very different way. Life insurance companies and fire insurance companies would insure the lives of slaves, and it's interesting that you have fire insurance companies engaging in this because this indicates the question, "Are slaves people or property?" since fire insurance was only on property and life insurance was only on people. So, they were both engaged in insuring slaves, even though those slaves tended to be not plantation slaves but rather highly valued slaves with skills, highly skilled slaves, domestic slaves, slaves engaged in industrial areas rather than your typical plantation slave who was easily replaceable. So, these would be slaves that were less easily replaceable.

And then you also had plantation banks, which is a slightly different type of bank that had a brief period in the South. And these were banks that very specifically were designed to securitize slaves and plantations and create, very similar to the securitization that occurred in the housing industry at the end of the 20th century, and they would securitize these slaves and then sell them as bonds to the North or to foreign investors to raise funds.

So those are the main financial institutions that would be involved in slavery at this time.

Antonio Elmaleh: Just to double back for a second, the First and Second US Banks, were they federally chartered?

Sharon Ann Murphy: Yes. The First Bank had a federal charter from 1791 to 1811, and the Second from 1816 to 1836.

Antonio Elmaleh: So actually, the federal government, in effect, was underwriting portions of the Southern banking system. As the growth of slave-based loan collateral grew, so did the slave appraisal business, I would presume. Can you tell us when this business started, and briefly describe to our listeners how the appraisal system for slaves worked?

Sharon Ann Murphy: Well, the appraisal system predates all of this. I am dealing mainly with financial institutions such as banks who were directly involved in using slaves as loan collateral, but the idea of using slaves as collateral existed long before we have these institutions. Two people, one person selling a slave to another person, can engage in a credit relationship, and so there is credit relationships that predate this.

Appraisals, and obviously slave sales, predate this. Appraisals exist pretty much for as long as we have slavery in the United States, someone needed to be able to value the slaves. It tended to be other slaveholders doing it because they're the ones who have the most at stake in this, the most knowledge of the system, so it is a little bit of an insider business. When I'm looking at my appraisal list it's often another slaveholder that is doing the appraisal for the bank, and so they were ...

Antonio Elmaleh: And they might have a vested interest? Would they potentially have a conflict of interest or a vested interest in valuing a slave lower so that they could essentially snap him up out of the market? Or were they trying to be as arm's length as possible?

Sharon Ann Murphy: It's hard to tell, but these are supposed to be third parties, so even if they're slaveholders themselves they are not directly engaged in the transaction. So, it would be in their best interest, especially if they're doing it for a bank, it would be in their best interest to do it honestly, because if the bank got wind that they're constantly giving bad appraisals they won't pay them to do this anymore. So, they're not directly involved, but there certainly could be a conflict of interest that if they're a slaveholder they're more likely to not want the value of slaves to be seen as dropping, because if they own slaves they want their slaves to maintain that value. But it's hard to tell if they were, this is still going to be dictated much by supply and demand overall, but it's hard to tell if people were completely honest brokers in the appraisal process.

Antonio Elmaleh: Kind of reminds me of 2008 and the credit wrapping fiasco of the ratings agency.

Sharon Ann Murphy: Yeah.

Antonio Elmaleh: Some things never change, right?

Sharon Ann Murphy: Right.

Antonio Elmaleh: You referred in your work to the Panics of 1819 and 1837 as important turning points in our financial history. Can you describe them briefly and what their impacts were on Southern banking specifically as it related to the slave trade?

Sharon Ann Murphy: Before the panic you have a rapid expansion of the economy, so again this is sounding a lot like 2008. Panic of 1819 happened after the end of the War of 1812, the War of 1812 ends in 1815. The opening up of the American west, and cotton prices globally are going up so people are trying to acquire land to grow more cotton, they're acquiring a lot of this land on debt to acquire bigger pieces of land, they're going into more debt to buy more slaves, so prices of land and slaves went through the roof in the late 1810s.

And then in 1819 you have a variety of factors coming together. There's still some debate over what exactly caused the Panic of 1819, but a variety of factors including things like a collapse in the global price of cotton, which caught a lot of people who were in debt to pay off their land no longer able to pay this off, they started defaulting on loans. A lot of people blamed the banks for overextending on loans, for being too permissive in extending these loans, and so you have a collapse of land prices, a collapse of slave prices, and the first depression that really touches a wide swatch of the economy, because it affected people in cities, as well.

1837, a similar series of events of rapid expansion of the economy in the 1830s. You also have the Bank War when Andrew Jackson attacked the Second Bank of the US and was determined to destroy it, and so some people argue that some of his policies toward the bank and getting rid of the bank helped fuel the problems that led to the collapse. There are other global problems such as global specie flows, Mexican silver, Chinese opium, all sorts of connections that are affecting the American economy. We are attached to the global economy even in this early period, and so in both cases you do see a rapid increase in the price of land and slaves leading up to it, and then a collapse of those in the aftermath.

There's the Panic of 1837, a brief recovery, and then another downturn in 1839, and that downturn lasted until 1843. A really horrific downturn for the country and people were very desperately affected.

And so, a lot of my evidence comes from court cases where people are disputing debts. They dispute those debts when they need to foreclose on them. A lot of my foreclosures occur after 1819 and after 1837, so that provides very valuable primary source material for me after those panics.

Antonio Elmaleh: Doubling back to the Panic of 1819, you mentioned that the global price of cotton fell through the floor. Does that suggest that cotton was that big of an industry and so powerful even by that date that Southern planters just flooded the market irresponsibly? Was that your point?

Sharon Ann Murphy: Yes. I'm not sure they flooded the market irresponsibly, but because of the global demand for cotton, the price of cotton dropped, and it's mostly due to British industry in 1819 and in 1837, mainly the British textile industry. There are other sources of cotton around the world, but at this time the U.S. South is the main source. By the late 19th century, by the Civil War, there are competing sources that enable the British to tap into other sources when the supply is disrupted during the war. This is a major industry and it has a major effect. The American economy is highly defined by the cotton trade, and not just the Southern economy, so the trade in cotton is one of the main proponents of the propellers of the American economy even at this early date.

Antonio Elmaleh: Yes, I think you're mentioning the other places where cotton might have been grown. There's a little place called India that I think the English controlled and they might have turned their sights on India.

Sharon Ann Murphy: Certainly by the Civil War.

Antonio Elmaleh: Yes. My next question has to do with the banking system. There's a relationship to the regulatory body that oversees it in any banking system. Can you tell us a little bit about the role the state governments played in supporting the Southern banking system, specifically aimed at the slave trade and the mortgaging of slaves as collateral and debt obligations? And as a follow-up question, if you can remember this, did banks own slaves outright?

Sharon Ann Murphy: I'll answer the second one first. Yes, banks did own slaves outright, mostly as a result of foreclosure proceedings. So, if they foreclosed on a slave, just like any other foreclosure proceeding, they own that property then and have to decide: Do they dispose of it immediately or do they hold onto it, especially during a downturn? And so, for example, the Citizens Bank of Louisiana often would foreclose on a property and then hold it, and sometimes even hire someone to run it. And this would be a plantation and one hundred slaves, and they would hire someone to run the plantation until prices improved and then they would sell it. Or they would send the property to auction with very explicit instructions for the representative, "If it doesn't get this minimum price, do not sell. We will hold it until we can get the price we want." So yes, they did own slaves, usually as a result of these foreclosure proceedings.

The first question on regulation all depended on who formed the bank. So, state banks were regulated by the state. In this early period we have most of the regulation done through the chartering process. When the bank received their charter, the charter gave explicit instructions and restrictions on what they could and could not do. However, as I look at these charters, most of them did not have a specific reference to slaves. They did often talk about what types of collateral could be accepted, but it would be in vaguer terms. Sometimes they did specify real estate, but not always, and so it was more of a passive regulation that came through the chartering process.

Later in the century, as we get to mid-century, 1850s, 1860s, you do start getting state banking commissions that have a little more active regulatory oversight on these banking institutions, but not too active. The plantation banks are also state chartered, however they actually have a unique relationship with the state in that initially these plantation banks, when they tried to collateralize the slaves and sell bonds, they find that they don't have a lot of people willing to invest in those bonds because they don't trust that they're going to be able to pay out on these bonds over time.

And so these banks, they turn to the state, Alabama, Louisiana, they turn to the state and say, "Can you help us on this? Can you claim these bonds as state bonds and sell them as state bonds? For example, Louisiana, they will sell bonds in the name of the state of Louisiana that are collateralized by these plantations and slaves, but sell them as Louisiana state bonds. Bondholders are much more likely to buy those because they are essentially backed by the taxpayers and they believe that the state will not default on those, and so that's how these plantation banks actually end up selling their bonds.

Interestingly, when many of the defaults that occur in the state financial system, after the Panic of 1837, in the early 1840s, several states, many of them in the South, default on their state bond obligations. And many of the Southern states who default, it's these bonds that they're defaulting on that they can't pay back and it becomes a real stain on the American financial institutions when, in the 1850s, the states start trying to sell bonds again and a lot of foreign investors feel burned and it forces up interest rates and it makes them a lot less popular.

Antonio Elmaleh: Was that a liquidity crisis in effect?

Sharon Ann Murphy: Yes, absolutely. They're unable to keep up the payments on the coupons on these bonds and this is completely because of the downturn. They just don't have the cash to pay them back and so they end up defaulting, some of them partially default, some of them fully repudiate, some of them partially repudiate, some of them later come back and pay back some of them, but it makes for a very poor financial relationship with European investors.

Antonio Elmaleh: Yes, you've mentioned one bank that actually went under, technically or informally, and yet was still chartered and in operation through the 1950s. I forget which one it was. I mean, that's a peculiar case, isn't it?

Sharon Ann Murphy: Yes. That was the Citizens Bank of Louisiana. This is one of those plantation banks. It technically failed and yet it still continued in operation despite the failure throughout the 1840s. Then in 1852, Louisiana re-charters the same bank or re-institutes the charter for this bank. It's supposed to change over from collateral based on plantations and slaves, to turn that over into cash collateral. In a traditional bank the stockholders buy the stock with actual specie, gold and silver. The plantation banks, the stock has been bought by collateral, plantations and slaves. So, they're supposed to convert over to a specie-based stockholder system; it's unclear to me, looking at their records, how far they get in actually converting, they are still dealing very heavily in plantations and slaves up through the Civil War. They're one of the few Southern banks that actually survive the Civil War, and they continue in operation until the 1920s when they start getting bought out by other bigger banks. It's one of the few Southern banks to actually survive the system.

But yes, they operate under the radar. Even though clearly, Louisiana, the state politicians, they know that they're still in operation. This is not a secret, they're just operating. You do not have to have a charter to operate, technically, what's known as private banks. The lingo gets a little confusing, a private bank is actually a bank that just doesn't have a state charter.

Antonio Elmaleh: Would that be a merchant commercial bank? Is that what you mean?

Sharon Ann Murphy: It could be a merchant bank, yes, a merchant bank could be that and early investment banks tend to operate as private banks. They tend to not have charters, as well. But there's crossover, so you can be a merchant bank and still then get a charter. Whether or not you're chartered is not clear as to what type of bank you end up being. And some states don't allow private banks, but it's hard to completely ban someone from lending money out of their store or their private fund. It's hard to ban that altogether.

Antonio Elmaleh: People have a general sense that slaveholders could do as they pleased. That's their sense, that they could dispose of slaves and acquire slaves pretty much unfettered. But were there any governmental restrictions on a slave owner breaking up a slave family? Has your research indicated that there were some possible restrictions on breaking up a slave family for whatever reason?

Sharon Ann Murphy: Technically, several states did have laws, especially about breaking up mothers and young children. It's unclear how well these laws were enforced. It's widely known that slave traders are some of the most evil people in the 19th century South, and they didn't follow many laws very closely. They very often broke up families.

What's interesting to me, and what I'm hoping to find out a little more about, is whether slaves that were part of a financial institution in some way, like a bank, whether that relationship forced the bank to enforce some of these rules a little better. A bank doesn't want to get caught being outside of the law because they could have their charter revoked. There's definitely evidence that these banks are grouping these slaves in family groups when they talk about them, and often do sell them as family groups when they're selling them. I'd like to investigate more deeply whether that relationship is actually helping to maintain those slave families by preventing the slave traders from going outside the law. Not all states had as strict laws, some were stricter than others. I believe Louisiana had a law that it couldn't be under the age of ten. I could be wrong on that detail, but I think they had one of the stricter sets of laws. But again it's widely known that it was violated. It's interesting to me, does the connection with a formal institution force more of an enforcement of this law?

Antonio Elmaleh: Please describe to our listeners the process of packaging slaves in lots and how that might have made the process more efficient for both borrowers and the banks.

Sharon Ann Murphy: What I've found in most of these situations is that when they're getting a loan, it's often on a full plantation's worth of slaves. Going through the records in New Orleans I'll see just a list of one hundred slaves on a plantation and all of them are being included in this loan collateral. So there often is just the plantation itself, but there's also individuals that are being pulled in and out of this, which is interesting to me as well. Where certain slaves will be listed as specifically excluded from the mortgage or the loan, or certain slaves will be in and then they'll request from the bank, "Please remove these two slaves from the mortgage and add in these two slaves instead." Oftentimes that's because they want to sell certain slaves and so they can't be part of the mortgage, because the mortgage would restrict their ability to sell them because the bank has a claim on them.

So they will be moving slaves in and out of the mortgage, but oftentimes it's the whole group together, but then when they list them they often list them in, sometimes not, sometimes they list them purely by age from oldest to youngest, but oftentimes it's clear they're listing them in family groups. And they'll talk about them in these family groups, which is why I think they're selling them in these family groups, they'll talk about the mother and two children or spouses, and the like.

Antonio Elmaleh: Interesting. As in any human endeavor the potential for defrauding any system is endemic. It seems like we're hard-wired certainly to be tempted to figure out a way to game the system. So it was, I think, with mortgage lending and borrowing with slaves as collateral. Would you be able to describe a typical way a borrower might defraud a lender?

Sharon Ann Murphy: I'm not sure if anything's typical, but I can tell you a couple ways that they could do it. One obvious way is slaves are liquid and so you can turn around and sell slaves that are otherwise being used as collateral, and if the person buying does not check in to that ... All of these are recorded, that's why I have this information ... It's like looking for a needle in the haystack, but when you find the haystack it's really quite amazing. They had to record these mortgages so that if you had a mortgage on a slave, someone else doesn't want to have a mortgage on them as well, because then you have competing claims. And that's the same for any property, any property you mortgaged you had to record that mortgage.

But you could potentially sell the slave. I have court cases where slaves are removed from the area, completely sold outside of the state to get them away. The slaves aren't always clearly the collateral, if you have a debt to the bank, the bank could foreclose on you and just foreclose on everything you own. So, what would happen sometimes is if a debtor knows that the bank's going to foreclose on them soon, they can try to hide as many assets as they can. It's hard to hide your land, it's hard to get rid of that, but you can hide your slaves. So cases of people "selling" their slaves to their brother-in-law, who doesn't actually pay them any money for it, but he takes them in trust, and then when the bank goes after him he says, "No, I don't own those slaves anymore, my brother-in-law owns them, I sold them to him." Even though in the course of the case it becomes very clear that he was just trying to hide these assets.

Hiding them with their wife is another way, putting something in trust for a spouse or a child, they can try to do that to hide these assets. It's a little harder to do when you have a specific collateral relationship, so when they recorded mortgages on specific slaves they actually listed them by name and age, so that's harder to run away from. But in cases where you just had a general debt that the bank was going to foreclose on whatever property you had, they could try to sell the slave out of state, put them in someone else's hands, or some other way to keep them away from the hands of the bank.

Antonio Elmaleh: It kind of sounds like a free-for-all in effect. Well, I mean, there's no way to regulate, we all know that there's plenty of ways to game the system, but they seem to be tried and true. There was a legal case adjudicated in, I think, 1832, 1837, that foreshadowed the infamous U.S. Supreme Court Dred Scott decision twenty years later. Would you tell us what that case was, how it was resolved or wasn't, and why it was so significant?

Sharon Ann Murphy: This was a case of a slave named Milly. I'm trying to find out more about her, but unfortunately Milly is a very common slave name, and I have no other information on her. But she was owned in Kentucky by a man named David Shipman, and he conveyed her to another man by the name of Smith as security for a debt, and this debt happened to be owed to the Commonwealth Bank in Kentucky, so this is how the bank got involved in it, it was kind of a three-way debt. So, Shipman, even though he had put Milly up as collateral for the debt, he still kept her, you usually keep your collateral when you put something up for a debt. But he was soon so far underwater that he knew there was no way he was going to be able to pay his debts, so he decided to flee. He fled the state, he took Milly with him, he took several other slaves with him, and he went to Indiana, which was a free state. And while in Indiana he emancipated his slaves even though they were technically collateral for this debt. Milly, he kept for himself. It's unclear the relationship with Milly.

Obviously, this is a very contentious area because, on the one hand it could have been a consensual relationship with her, on the other hand he does have a heck of a lot of power over her. So, the issue of consent with power, as we well know today, is always a very contentious one.

So, she was living with Shipman at this point in Illinois. Smith comes along and grabs her and says, "You're a part of this debt that Shipman owes me. You need to come with me." And so, Smith takes Milly away from Shipman and brings her back to Kentucky. At this point, Milly sues for her freedom from Smith, both on the basis of the deed of emancipation that Shipman had issued for all of the slaves, and also her extended residence in the free states. This is where Dred Scott comes in. This is in the late 1820s at this point, twenty years before Dred Scott, the court's trying to determine first of all who's the rightful owner? Does Shipman even have the right to emancipate a slave that is collateral for a debt? The mortgage law is unclear on this. The mortgage law is state law, it depends on the state. And all the states have different laws in this area, and the law in Kentucky was not clear on this point.

So, property offered as collateral, is that legally the property of the creditor, even if it remains in the possession of the debtor? Or is it just a lien on the property, preventing it from being sold? It was a question of possession here, and it goes through several court cases in the Supreme Court of Missouri. This gets complicated, we're skipping a lot of states around here, but in the end the court decided that Milly remained Shipman's property until Smith forecloses. That means Shipman can do whatever he wants with her, including emancipate her. But then the court also ruled that even without the deed of emancipation, just by living in Illinois, Milly was now free. Which is pretty amazing seeing as Dred Scott's going to be decided completely the opposite of that. However, they called her freedom sub modo, which is Latin for she's only free until Smith decides to foreclose on her.

She has this kind of limbo position where, "Yes, you are free, but you are still collateral for a loan, and if he decides to foreclose then you become his slave." He can't kidnap her as he did, but he could foreclose on the debt and claim her as property. And the court says, "Well, this isn't open forever." So, it's this undefined length of time where Smith could foreclose on Milly and take her as property, but not forever. So she's left with this kind of amorphous short-term freedom, but who knows what's going to happen in the longer term for her?

Antonio Elmaleh: What state adjudicated that case? Given the fact that they were moving around between Kentucky, Illinois – you also, I think, mentioned Indiana at one point.

Sharon Ann Murphy: It ended up being the Supreme Court of Missouri that adjudicated it.

Antonio Elmaleh: Was it a fact that he was just looking for a friendly court that might rule on his behalf?

Sharon Ann Murphy: I think after he kidnapped her he must have brought her back to Missouri, because she's the one who filed suit for her freedom and she filed in the Supreme Court of Missouri.

Antonio Elmaleh: Emancipation began in 1863. Great numbers of slaves simply walked away from their owners and attached themselves to occupying Union armies. Can you describe the effects of emancipation on the financing of slavery?

Sharon Ann Murphy: Emancipation added a new wrinkle to all of this, because when you have emancipation, of course, emancipation was very clear that we were not going to be paying off slaveholders; you own a slave, that slave is now no longer your own and you have no claim on the government for the value of that slave. However, when you have these debt relationships, the question is, "Well, do you still owe the debt?" And it takes a couple of different forms. If you were using slaves as collateral for a debt, do you still owe that debt even though the collateral no longer exists? And debtors will argue, "No, you don't have a collateral claim on me, so I don't owe you anything." Creditors of course say, "Well, no, you just use different collateral, you still owe the debt. The debt still exists."

A slightly different version of this is, what if it's the slave him or herself who was purchased on credit? And so, if the debtor buys the slave but only pays a portion of that price, do they still have to pay the rest of the price once emancipation occurs? And it's really a question of who's going to take the hit for emancipation. Is it the debtor who entered into this relationship and promised to pay, or the creditor who was willing to finance this relationship and not take the money upfront? And so that's actually a very contentious issue. That's not something that's clearly defined in emancipation, and the legal standards are not clear. And the people at the time dispute which is the more logical result, which is the more legal result, which is the most sympathetic to emancipation? The Louisiana Supreme Court ruled that the minute you have emancipation, all contracts that deal with slaves cease to exist because emancipation assumes that slavery was a condition that was wrong, and so any debts that are related to a wrong condition don't exist. And that obviously favors debtors because now they no longer have to pay it back. However, it's favoring debtors on a kind of a more law-of-nature kind of argument, as opposed to a debtors-versus-creditors argument. Other people will argue that the debt still exists. It doesn't matter whether or not slaves were used as collateral, the debt still exists, so you still need to pay it back, and that favors creditors. You have a really thorny issue that gets brought up with emancipation that you don't often think about with the Civil War and emancipation. You usually just think about these slaves that get freed.

Another added wrinkle to all of this is, prior to 1863 there are a lot of people who are fully aware that emancipation could happen. And so what do you do if you're a slaveholder during 1861 to '63, especially as Union Armies are coming through? A lot of areas where the Union Army was about to take over, slaveholders would often sell their slaves to other areas that are still under Confederate control. There were discussions of, "Should we get rid of these slaves right away? Should we hold on to them? What is the price that's going to be paid?"

For slaves that were bought and sold during the Civil War years, a lot of people argued, "Well, you, the debtor and the creditor knew what you were getting into. You knew that you were entering into a risky relationship." And so that was baked into the price, so they would say, "The debtor still owes that money because the debtor got a better price." The price of slaves often would drop with the uncertainty, the debtor got a better deal so they better pay off the rest of this debt. That uncertainty was baked into the price and so you have people engaging in kind of gaming the system. "What's going to happen? Should I buy up a bunch of slaves cheap because I have confidence the Confederacy's going to win and I'm going to end up with a really good deal afterwards? Or do I sell my slaves now, while I can get money from them because I think emancipation's going to happen, and if I get rid of them now, I might get some cash for them?" There's a lot of examining, assessing what they think is going to happen with the Civil War, and then planning accordingly regarding their slaves.

Antonio Elmaleh: It just occurred to me that an interesting wrinkle is also the fact that after the war started were they trading in Confederate dollars?

Sharon Ann Murphy: Yes.

Antonio Elmaleh: Because they cease to have any real value. It was very clear by 1863, not very clear, but it was certainly up for grabs that the Confederate currency was going to be undervalued, like a wheelbarrow might buy you a loaf of bread. So how did the effect of the valuation or the iffy underlying value of Confederate currency affect the monetizing of this financing system? That was one thought that I would add in there. I don't know if there's an answer to it, but I wanted to also ask you this question, which had to do with the omission for who eats the loss. Would you tell our listeners a little bit about the 1871 US Supreme Court decision that supposedly rectified it?

Sharon Ann Murphy: Sure. Taking your questions in order, as far as Confederate currency, absolutely, that is adding a whole other wrinkle into all of this. There's actually a graduate student working on a dissertation specifically on these slave sales during this questionable time period, so he might actually have a better answer for you than I do. I'm not entirely sure how they're valuing them, if they're valuing them in Confederate currency, obviously it's going to be changing rapidly. The Confederate currency took hits in chunks, and tended to respond to how the war was going. So, when the war was going better for the Confederacy it tended to stabilize, and then if they had a bad run it would drop off. So, I think during more stable times, certainly, they could value it in Confederate currency.

There is evidence of Southerners valuing things in greenbacks, Union money, because it was more stable, even though that was technically illegal to do that. But there is some evidence that they did do that to some extent, so they certainly could have been using that. However, I'm not entirely sure how they were valuing it in those terms. But that is absolutely a great question...

Antonio Elmaleh: I wonder if they knew something that their fellow slave owners didn't know. What was their thinking? How solidly were they behind the cause if they're actually trading in federal dollars for something that's so underpinning a uniquely Southern institution?

Sharon Ann Murphy: The question of how these debt contracts are going to be resolved first takes place in the state courts. And different states resolve it in different ways, so there's competing answers in different states. Some side with the creditor, some side with the debtor. As I said, Louisiana sides with the debtor, but does it in a way that is very sympathetic to the issue of slavery, so less about contract law and more about natural law regarding slavery. Several states, then, with their new state constitutions, actually barred the enforcement of any debts that involve slave property. And so again this is favoring the debtor, even though a lot of people argued in the states that that violated the Constitution since the Constitution says that no state is allowed to impair the obligation of a contract. So, by putting these clauses in, technically, you are impairing that contract.

This finally made it up to the US Supreme Court, and in 1871 the Court decided, in the case of Osborn v. Nicholson, that while emancipation ended slavery and all contracts directly related to slavery, so for example if you had a contract to hire out a slave to work in your tobacco factory for a year, that hiring contract is canceled once slavery no longer exists, it doesn't affect debt contracts. And so emancipation does not resolve you from the debt, which now favors the creditor. Debtors were still obligated to fulfill these contracts, even if they no longer had the property of the slave. And this was controversial, a lot of people disagreed with this, especially people who were supporters of the freed slaves. And so, a lot of freed blacks who had been elected to Southern legislatures, and Supreme Court Justice Salmon Chase, all disagreed. Chase actually wrote a very prominent dissent in the Osborn v. Nicholson decision, saying that by enforcing these contracts you are essentially endorsing slavery as institution, with this conclusion. It was a controversial case.

Oftentimes when we have contract law and cases dealing with debtors and creditors, a lot of times it's coming down to, oftentimes it comes up in economic downturns like the Panic of 1819 or 1837, it comes down to debtor relief, trying to help debtors who are being burdened. In these cases, though, we don't have poor debtors and rich creditors. It's rich slaveholders who are selling their slaves, and rich slaveholders who are buying the slaves who are involved in these contracts, so it's a very different kind of debtor/creditor relationship even though their wealth has been wiped out in all cases anyway. But it's a different conversation than we normally see around, say, bankruptcy law, which often pits poor debtors against wealthy creditors. This is more equal, with the question of who's going to take the hit for emancipation? But the Supreme Court eventually comes down on the side of the creditors.

Antonio Elmaleh: You've several times alluded to these different regulations favoring debtors. It strikes me as ironic that you'd have consumer-based system of laws that have a populist leaning to them, yet what the population are supporting is not exactly a model for how to get along with everybody. But that's a whole other conversation. We're all familiar with the phrase, "Follow the money," from *All the President's Men,* the movie. Have you focused any work on, for example, the aftermarket for plantation bank bonds? And specifically, what institutions were actually, was there an aftermarket for these bonds that were collateralized by slaves?

Sharon Ann Murphy: That is something I would love to pursue, especially because it would probably require me to go to Europe to do a little research. [Laughter]

They're mostly being sold to Europeans at this time, especially we're talking in the 1820s and '30s. Most of our wealthy investors are going to be European, which is fascinating because Britain emancipated their slaves in 1833-34, and yet I am positive that many British investors are buying these bonds. So, there's two questions that that raises. One, do they actually know what these are collateralized by? I have a hard time believing that they did not know that they're basically buying into the slave system. And then that begs the question of, do they have any moral qualms about doing this?

There are some Northern investors in this, and there is evidence that, after the Second Bank of the US loses its federal charter it continues in existence as a state bank, it receives a charter from Pennsylvania and so it becomes the Bank of the US of Pennsylvania. During this time period Nicholas Biddle is still president of the bank. It actually does invest in some of these bonds. There's some evidence that when it goes under, the Bank of the US of Pennsylvania goes bankrupt in 1841-42, that it's partially because of the repudiation on these bonds that it has over-invested in. So, it is also part of this system, but I'd love to follow the money more. At this point I think that may have to be a next project after this project, because I think this project is already big enough in and of itself, especially if it requires me to go to Amsterdam and look at some records there.

Antonio Elmaleh: By extension, numerous industries, notably transportation, textiles, and commodities, they all benefited hugely from the underlying savings that using slave labor had on pricing of their goods and services. And again, you've I guess answered my question, but I'll ask it anyway. What evidence do you have, if any, that Northern and European banks were lending directly to those industries, and by extension, underpinning the system of slavery as a powerful economic engine for the growth of American capitalism? It's not a subject that has been raised too frequently. I think it certainly is, to me, a really important one, whether or not you see any preliminary indication that transportation, textiles, and commodities all benefiting from the growth of cotton, and by extension, slave labor, were actively being financed by European and Northern banks. Because to me, we're all in this together; no one has an exclusive right to a higher standard of morality, to me, when it came to this issue of following the money.

Sharon Ann Murphy: Yes. There's actually been quite a bit of recent work on this topic by a number of great scholars. And basically the conclusion is the entire system was underpinned by slavery. Northerners can't get out of it, there's just too much overlap, whether it is Northern companies selling slave cloth to Southern plantations, or selling other manufactured goods to be used on plantations, Northern textile mills are buying the cotton to use in its products. So, there is a direct relation, but also indirectly as well. I think the consensus among historians at this point is that the North is absolutely complicit in all of this, even if they sometimes turn a blind eye, but sometimes they knew exactly what was going on. They knew what they were selling when they're selling slave cloth. This was a type of textile that was actually labeled slave cloth. It was a very subpar cloth. I'm not just making up that term, they actually had that, and they would manufacture a very specific subpar type of cloth that they sold in the South. So, I believe that they knew what they were involved in.

Antonio Elmaleh: It strikes me that the political implications of that support had to be a powerful deterrent for Northern opposition to the war. I'm hoping to do another program or maybe a series of programs in which we talk about just how popular was the Civil War and the effort amongst the Northern population. I think we Northerners have, again, this kind of smug, hermetically sealed assumption that we were just the good guys and the plantation owners were the bad guys, and it's just not that way to me. And so, I'm just by extension wondering what the political opposition of these very powerful different industries would have been to effectively killing the golden goose.

Sharon Ann Murphy: You have to remember that initially the Civil War for Northerners was not about ending slavery. For Southerners, Southerners were fighting to defend their slaves from the beginning, their fear is of the end of slavery. Northerners, initially, were fighting to preserve the Union, which fits this idea of the South being an essential part of not just the political union but the economic union. Northerners initially are fighting to preserve the sanctity of the Union itself. It's not until 1863 or 1862 at least that we get towards the idea of emancipation being something that should be an essential part of this war, and that's something people have to slowly come on board with. Of course, abolitionists and radical republicans were there from the beginning, and free blacks were there from the beginning, but for the majority of the Northern population the war was not about ending slavery from the beginning. And, in fact, if that had been what the war was initially about you probably would have gotten a lot more pushback against fighting this war.

The North is fighting to preserve the Republican experiment that's been going on for almost one hundred years and it can't be proved a failure at this point, you can't have this falling apart. And if the South is able to leave, what prevents the next group from being able to leave? There's all sorts of issues involved in that. The South is always fighting to preserve slavery, so I want to make that clear, I'm not belittling that side of it.

But there is a sense, you can see there's all sorts of economic connections between the North and the South that will get severed during this war, and if the Confederacy is allowed to exist will be severed, and you see that right away. Both the North and the South pass laws regarding what kind of interaction you can have as a business. So my first book is on life insurance, and then I deal with life insurance on slaves, but I also talk about life insurance during the Civil War, and you have Northern life insurance companies who have policies on Southerners. So these are ongoing policies, you pay your premiums yearly and these are ongoing, well do you have a claim on that? Are you allowed to still pay premiums to a Northern company? That's sending precious Southern money outside of the Confederacy. Are you allowed to still do that? If you've had a policy for several years in a Northern company, do they owe you anything, can they dissever your policy because, "We're at war now, you can no longer have a policy with us, we don't owe you anything."

So, it's very kind of similar to the debtor/creditor questions with emancipation, you have these laws being passed by both sides forbidding money from flowing from one side to the other, especially from Southerners having money flow to the North, which is often where the flows were going. They had investments in Northern companies, and so you want to break up those relationships right away before you lose that money. So the war itself and the idea of secession is disrupting all sorts of business relationships, and so in that sense bringing the Confederacy back in and restoring the Union would probably be what most businesses would prefer. And they're not really thinking about emancipation and the effects of emancipation on that initially, because emancipation's not on the board initially. This is just about, do the Confederates get to leave or do they get forced back in?

Antonio Elmaleh: It strikes me that when we talk, that the financial confusion caused by the upsetting of the Southern banking system, however evil it might be, had to have led to the aftermath and the chaos of trying to structure a new financial system which had had, as its underpinning, a system that was now dead and gone. Maybe not necessarily dead and gone because we know Jim Crow lasted a long, long time, but at least technically and legally. And so, it seems to me that there's another factor to contribute to the general rancor around, and, by extension, misunderstanding of Reconstruction and why it's not only so critically important to understanding race relations, but just understanding our history better. Because to me, it's not taught in schools well at all, and I can see why. It's just so incredibly complicated and fraught with all kinds of ways you can go in terms of teaching it.

Is there an overriding thought you would like to leave with our listeners, some kind of an image, or what is for you the most powerful emotional thing you've learned in doing this work? I know that's a loaded question and might take a little thought.

Sharon Ann Murphy: That is a loaded question, [Laughter] I'm going to let that rattle in the back of my brain for a minute. First, I was going to make a comment on something you had said previously. You were talking about Reconstruction and banking in Reconstruction. There's an added wrinkle that comes into all of this in that during the war, when the South was not in Congress, the North actually completely restructured the banking system of the nation. And so, it's not just a matter of Southern banks no longer existing, but Southern banks have to play by extremely different rules. So, they pass several banking regulations that basically taxed state bank notes out of existence. This is the forerunner to where we get our modern currency.

Prior to the Civil War, the federal government was not responsible for paper money, so paper money was issued by the state chartered banks and the Banks of the US, but the state chartered banks, and so you had nine thousand different types of money floating around, and that's not an exaggeration. Different denominations, different names of banks, etc. And so during the Civil War they actually tried to rationalize this system and bring it under federal control, and so when they did this, they created the forerunners of our Federal Reserve Notes, obviously the Federal Reserve doesn't exist yet, but the forerunners to the Federal

Reserve Notes, and they limited how much were going to be distributed and they tended to distribute them disproportionately in the North. And so, it kind of was a double whammy on the South. Not only did they lose their existing banking institutions, but it was more difficult for them than to reestablish banking in the aftermath because of the way the system was initially structured and actually restructured to their disadvantage.

My final thought is this: I think for me this has been exciting research for me because, as I said, it's an area that doesn't seem to have a lot of people looking at it but it has a lot of potential.

One of the things when I realized while researching slavery and life insurance, is that it's not just about finding the existence of the practice, but also about finding all the ways that slavery was influenced by and influenced these financial institutions. It is fascinating to me to see the way that Southern financial institutions developed for very different reasons, and adapted it to a slave system, and how they're using banks to help sustain and support and promote their slave system in the South.

It's very interesting to me to see how is it affecting things like we were talking about earlier, like slave families, and how is it affecting whether or not slaves get sold and broken up?

And in all of this, as I'm going through and I'm looking through these records, and as I said it's often a needle in a haystack, I come across information about these slaves and I do a little happy dance when I discover them, and especially when I discovered one of the branches of the Bank of the US in Kentucky was heavily involved in this. But then you see the slaves listed by name and by age, and then you realize you're still dealing with people and these people's lives are being manipulated by this system and they're being born and dying in this system and they're pawns, they're property.

That's also kind of a weighty responsibility to try to give these people a voice, even though you think, "I do financial history, I'm not really dealing with people and humans and trying to give them voices," but trying to do them justice and not to put them through this again, even though they're dead now, but put them through this again by treating them as a statistic or property, but to actually give them a voice in the history and try to find out more about their history through their experiences in the system.

Antonio Elmaleh: Yes, that's very laudatory. It also strikes me that those folks that you mentioned who castigate the Southerners for having a primitive understanding of finance should look to, unfortunately, the model of how slavery was financed and organized, because it strikes me as a business person as a remarkably efficient process, however evil as it was. And that's one of the tragedies of it, is that something so efficient, so well organized, so well thought out, was focused on and had as an underpinning something so heinous as owning and buying and selling people as property.

Sharon Ann Murphy: That actually might get back to your first question, which was why is this so little studied? And I think for a lot, when slavery became a topic of central study in the '80s and the '90s, people were very sensitive to making sure that they're trying to bring out the voices of these slaves, and I think there may have been a sense that if you're dealing with them in a financial way that you lose that. You're buying into the system almost. You're giving too much power to the slaveholders.

I mean, one of the classic works on the economics of slavery was Time on the Cross. It's a landmark study and it was so controversial when it came out because they literally were trying to be as unbiased and just look at slavery through statistics. And even though what they were doing, the statistics weren't wrong, it was that a lot of people felt they were not treating the slaves' humanity. And so, I think there is a sense that if you lose that humanity, that's problematic, and that maybe these types of issues aren't as natural for seeking that out as other areas of slave study are. And so, I think that may be one of the reasons why this is kind of the last, I don't know if it's the last, but one of the last frontiers of the study of slavery.

Antonio Elmaleh: It seems then to shy away from that as an historian strikes me as not professional either. You can't selectively argue the morality on one point while ignoring it on another. I understand that, but when you're trying to figure out the historical realities, you have to be, I think, somewhat dispassionate. That's not to say close your heart, but it does mean you have to look at things coldly and you have to separate out, which is one of the reasons why I think this conversation has been so marvelous, is that we're able to separate out the morality and respect it and see it, and at the same time have a very thoughtful, I think, and powerful conversation about just the business of it. And historically it's valuable to have this perspective.

Which is a natural segue for me to say that I think we've run out of time. How about that? I want to thank you, Professor Sharon Ann Murphy, for joining us today, and especially salute you for the groundbreaking work you're doing to uncover, to me anyway, a profound and hitherto little-explored area of scholarship of our history. So, thank you very much, Professor Murphy.

Sharon Ann Murphy: You're welcome. I enjoyed it.

Antonio Elmaleh: And to all our listeners, I'd like to thank you for joining me today. I hope you'll come back again for another episode of *Uncovering the Civil War*. Until then, stay safe and do good.

UNCOVERING THE PRESS DURING THE CIVIL WAR, PART I

Guest: Dr. Ford Risley

Antonio Elmaleh: Hello everyone. Welcome to another segment of *Uncovering the Civil War*. Today my guest by telephone is Ford Risley. Ford is Professor of Communications and Associate Dean of the Donald Bellisario College of Communications at Penn State University. He is also the author or editor of three books, including *Civil War Journalism*, and *Abolition and the Press: The Moral Struggle Against Slavery*. His latest book, *Dear Courier: The Civil War Correspondence of Editor Melvin Dwinell* will be published this year by the University of Tennessee as part of its series Voices of the Civil War. Welcome to the show, Ford.

Ford Risley: Thank you for having me.

Antonio Elmaleh: You're very welcome. I'd like to start off with an observation made by, I think it was John Steinbeck, who talked about purple prose and what the secret of good writing is, to eliminate the "hooptedoodle." In your book I was struck by a point that you made that the actual language of reporting changed during the war. It became more concise and more precise. Why do you think this happened?

Ford Risley: Well, yes, there were several reasons. One is just the sheer requirement of having to report often on deadline, and reporting big events, meant that authors and journalists could no longer write in the essay style that had been popular for so long, they had to write in a more lean, concise style. Certainly it was still different than what we would see today if you pick up a newspaper or magazine, but newspaper writing had come a long way. The other thing that contributed to this was the birth of telegraphic reporting. Of course, the telegraph, newspapers pay for telegraph by the word and by the letter, so it was important for reporters to be as concise as possible in order not to rack up big bills.

Antonio Elmaleh: Do you think it also had to do with just the physical difficulty of the conditions they were in? They didn't have a lot of time to scratch out this purple prosey thing, but just get the events down.

Ford Risley: Absolutely yes, they were writing under some very difficult conditions in camps and on trains. There just wasn't the time, the ability to write fanciful prose that had been so popular.

Antonio Elmaleh: It was in this time that I think we can safely say that photojournalism was born, during the war. Can you tell us what the necessary tools were for a photojournalist or a combat illustrator, typically hired by one of the weekly magazines, the tools were necessary to do his job, and how he'd find ways to get the pictures back in a timely fashion.

Ford Risley: Well, timeliness was a problem, and photographs and illustrations were in no way timely, they just didn't have that value. What they did provide were the first real pictures of what a war looked like. Now, cameras could not capture action, pictures had to be posed or they focus on still-lives, nonetheless it gave people a real image of what a battlefield looked like, the aftermath of a battlefield, certainly the death and destruction that you saw in such a horrific way during the war.

Illustrations were also important. They were published by newspapers like Harper's Weekly, and they captured all aspects of camp life. Some illustrators, frankly, romanticized the war, but others really gave readers a real sense of what it was like to be in camp, to march, they gave people a picture of what battles actually looked like, the sweep of battles and of course the aftermath of battles.

Taking photographs was a cumbersome process, it was nasty, it involved chemicals, it took lots of time, it required big wagons that carried around the chemicals, it was a two-man job, but nonetheless it gave people a real picture of what the war looked like.

Antonio Elmaleh: Now, as a student of the war I've often been struck by Jefferson Davis's apparent tone deafness around military commanders, specifically Braxton Bragg. And also, his tone deafness around the subtleties and the necessity for diplomacy in the European capitals, thinking that the South was too good for negotiating. Let's apply that to the value of using newspapers. Why do you think he was so tone deaf, at least initially, to the value of using newspapers to promote the government's case to prosecute the war and its narrative of it? If you remember the rest of the question, can you contrast this with Lincoln's approach which seems remarkably adept and modern?

Ford Risley: Yes, I'll start with Lincoln if it's okay.

Antonio Elmaleh: Sure.

Ford Risley: Because I think he was really the first President who really grasped the press for what it had become and the potential it had as a tool for reaching the public. Lincoln had always been interested in newspapers, he had written for newspapers as a young lawyer in Illinois and he really grasped what a newspaper could do for him as President. He courted reporters, he welcomed them into his offices, he spoke with them relatively freely without certainly sharing military secrets, but he was accessible. Then he also wrote editorials and wrote pieces that were published in newspapers that were friendly to him, he was really masterful at dealing with the press.

Contrast that with Jefferson Davis who really had no experience and no real appreciation for what newspapers could do for him; he really had no use for newspapers, didn't know reporters. That did not serve him well because the press in the South was willing to be behind Jefferson Davis, was willing to support him, but he didn't really do anything to court the press.

Antonio Elmaleh: As a follow-up, it just struck me that when Lincoln was writing his editorials, did he publish them under his own name or did he use some kind of pseudonym?

Ford Risley: No, he did not publish them under his own name, but many people kind of figured out who was writing them.

Antonio Elmaleh: I think we're all familiar with the phrase habeas corpus. Lincoln suspension of it. I think it was in response to the fact that the war must have triggered just incredibly violent opinions and borderline treason and all this.

Ford Risley: Certainly, that prompted widespread outrage by the press, and as a result Lincoln shut down newspapers and went to war in many ways with the Copperhead press, shutting down newspapers, editors were arrested. So that produced a great deal of criticism.

Antonio Elmaleh: Do you have any evidence that any reporters were ever executed for publishing stories that were considered treasonous?

Ford Risley: No, there was none of that. Reporters were jailed or editors were jailed, but there was nothing like that. Of course, there's the famous incident of William Sherman seeking to court-martial a reporter, which got a lot of attention.

Antonio Elmaleh: In your book, again as a follow-up, you talk a lot about how the invading Union Army went and made it a point to destroy newspapers in every town that they occupied. Can you comment on that?

Ford Risley: Yes, of course. The Army recognized the role that newspapers in the South had played in really whipping up anti-Union sentiment, so newspapers were a target for soldiers and the Armies when they captured a city. Newspapers were occupied, in some cases taken over, in some cases soldier newspapers were published using the equipment that was left behind, then when the Armies left they would often wreck the newspaper and just leave it a total mess.

Antonio Elmaleh: I think a lot of listeners may be familiar with the publication Stars and Stripes, which I believe got its birth during the Civil War, and which is to this day our military newspaper, the newspaper of the Armed Forces. Did Lincoln use the Army's own publications like Stars and Stripes to forge public support for prosecuting the war?

Ford Risley: He really didn't use soldier newspapers, because soldier newspapers were primarily put out by the individual units and not by the government. What Lincoln did use, were his friends at newspapers like The *New York Times* and The *Chicago Tribune* and The *Springfield Republican*, editors that were staunch Republicans, who were sympathetic, and supported Lincoln at every turn. So he could count on them for support. When he wanted a message or wanted something to get out he would use them to help deliver a message.

Antonio Elmaleh: In your book you've mentioned the phrase, which struck me again as very interesting, "The inner life of the Army." Can you describe to our listeners what's meant by that phrase and why it was so important for newspapers to get behind that as a factor in reporting?

Ford Risley: Yes. I think the best journalists wanted to show Army life for what it was, that it was not just battles, that there was so much else that went on. Like the way soldiers lived, and the way they drilled, and the way they spent their idle time, and the way they held religious services, and entertained themselves, and all of these things. The best reporters gave people a picture of what that was like, and some of the best illustrations showed camp life and gave people a real picture of what it was like. So sometimes I think we focus more on the battles and the reporting of battles and what else went on. But of course, that's just a small part of any army's life. Far more time is spent drilling and downtime and marching and all of these things. The best journalists, the best reporters, the best publications gave people a real picture of that kind of thing.

Antonio Elmaleh: We've talked so far primarily about newspapers, but I also remember you talking in your book about the growth of weekly magazines like *Harper's Weekly*, I forget some of the other titles. In fact, I have in my office several copies, reproductions of *Harper's Weekly*. Can you tell us a little bit about why those magazines grew? You even mentioned something like three thousand by the end of the war. What was specifically different about a magazine, a weekly magazine, and let's say a daily paper?

Ford Risley: Yes, well the big thing were the illustrations. These magazines were much like *Time* and *Newsweek* in their heyday. They were weekly publications that sought to capsulize and summarize the week's news, but they were also heavily illustrated. They were recognition that people wanted to see the news of the war that they read about. So you had sketch artists who would follow the Army around, sketching all sorts of scenes, battles, camp life, you name it. They sent these sketches back to New York where an artist then turned these sketches into beautiful illustrations, and then these illustrations were, through a long process of engraving, put into magazines like *Harper's Weekly* and *Leslie's Illustrated*. So these publications were just chock full of page after page of illustrations. They were just enormously popular because people could see the war, they could see what was happening. They covered other events as well during this time, it wasn't exclusively the war, but the war dominated the pages of these newspapers. It was an enormously costly and time-consuming process to produce those illustrations, but they were so popular with readers and I think they really gave us an indication of just how popular pictures would be and as a way of reporting the news.

Antonio Elmaleh: In that light, was there the same level of urgency, of timeliness that there would have been for a reporter trying to get a breaking story over the telegraph?

Ford Risley: Right, yes, I mean that was so hard. The artist in the field, they sent their sketches back as quickly as they could, but then it would take a week or so to finally get the illustration into print. They weren't timely, certainly, in the modern sense of the term. A big battle like Gettysburg or Antietam, you could see pictures of that within a couple weeks after the battle was fought.

Antonio Elmaleh: Can you describe the physical layout of one of the magazines?

Ford Risley: Yes, they were a combination of newspapers and magazines. They weren't published in color obviously. They weren't published on heavy paper, they were published on newsprint. They were tabloid in size, they weren't the big folio-size paper that newspapers were published on, so they could be folded and stuck in a bag and carried about. They were easily read, more like magazines than newspapers, and as I said they were just enormously popular because they gave people a real sense of what the war looked like.

Antonio Elmaleh: And in that light can you describe some of the physical challenges of these artists? Were they under fire?

Ford Risley: Yes.

Antonio Elmaleh: Winslow Homer. Alfred Waud. All these folks became quite wonderful painters in their own right, but can you describe what kind of dangers they went through to get the drawing, to get the visual depiction of what was going on?

Ford Risley: Yes, just like reporters, they suffered under really difficult working conditions. They followed the Army around, often on horseback or by train or whatever means possible. When a battle began they got as close as they could while still trying to maintain some level of safety. They suffered under some really difficult conditions, they were troopers, they were away from home for long stints and just lived under, in many ways, the same conditions that the soldiers themselves did. It was a tough life, most did not last the entire four years of the war.

Alfred Waud was one of the few who lasted for most, if not all, of the war. It was difficult going.

Antonio Elmaleh: Were any journalists or illustrators killed in action?

Ford Risley: There were. I don't know of any illustrators, but there were a couple of journalists who were killed, several who were wounded, many got sick. It was a tough life, they did not have the support that the Army provided to soldiers of course, they were largely on their own. Yes, it was tough.

Antonio Elmaleh: I imagine that very toughness would have ingratiated themselves with the troops, saying, "Well, if he's brave enough to get with us under these conditions, he can't be such a bad guy." That's why the soldiers loved Ernie Pyle so much in the Second World War, that he just went down wherever they went and ultimately he was killed by a sniper. Do you think there's some truth to that? Just seeing these reporters rubbing elbows under these horrific conditions would have earned their trust.

Ford Risley: I haven't read anything of reporters talking about that or writing about that. I'm sure that happened. Folks in the Army, soldiers, officers also often viewed the press with some suspicion. They had never been around reporters a great deal. They really didn't know what they were doing. Certainly, they liked it when their unit got praise in a newspaper or got some attention, but there were other times of course when the battle went the other way. Of course, that happened a great deal in the North initially, the North was losing the war in the early years. Soldiers and officers didn't appreciate sometimes what reporters were telling their readers.

Antonio Elmaleh: Right. Shifting to another topic, have you uncovered any evidence of news editors deliberately planting false stories about the outcomes of individual battles to influence the financial markets, so they could speculate on anything from currency to whatever else, for their own personal gain?

Ford Risley: No, I don't know of anything like that. I mean certainly there were plenty of stories that were wrong, I don't know that they were deliberately wrong. In most cases they were just rushed into print or reporters didn't have all the information that they needed. I don't think there was any of that, but there were plenty of mistakes made by journalists and by editors. Remember that journalism was still a maturing profession, it didn't have the standards that we like to think of today for what journalists should strive for. It was still a maturing profession and so reporters were in no way objective. They didn't try to present both sides of a story, in most cases. So, that was a big part of also what went on.

Antonio Elmaleh: Did they at least follow the rule that you should get a couple of corroborating witnesses to an event, or they didn't even bother with that, sometimes?

Ford Risley: No, they didn't even bother with that, they often would report what they saw or what they heard from perhaps one source, one soldier, one officer, and they would go with that. So, no, the standards of accuracy were not what we like to think the best journalists are doing today.

Antonio Elmaleh: You've written in your book that about half of all Southern papers died by the end of the war. Can you tell our listeners why that occurred and what was their growth in the run up to the war, and if you have any figures like circulation totals before and after, if you could share those so we could get a sense of the growth and/or demise of the popularity of these papers?

Ford Risley: Before the war there were about thirty-seven hundred newspapers published in the United States. That's a remarkable number, I think it was about twice the number published in Britain and about one-third of all the newspapers in the entire world. Moreover, the circulation per capita of American newspapers was really far greater than any other country. Now, most of those newspapers were published in the North. The North had the big population centers and it was not unusual for a city like New York or Chicago for there to be eight, ten, twelve newspapers published. Where in a city like Richmond or New Orleans there were only two or three newspapers published.

As to your question about the devastating impact of the war on the Southern press, it was just remarkable. Of course, the great majority of the war was fought in the South. Many Southern towns and cities were captured, once they were, those newspapers disappeared. At the same time the Southern economy was wrecked by the war, so if your newspaper wasn't captured then chances are it was really crippled by the devastating economy, there were shortages of newsprint, of ink, of all the supplies needed to put out a newspaper. Southern editors began facing those shortages really soon after the war began. Southern editors resorted to some really ingenious means of getting their newspapers out. They made their own ink, they printed on any sort of paper they could find, colored paper, there's some newspapers published in Vicksburg that were published on the back of wallpaper. So editors were remarkably resilient, but nonetheless the war took a tremendous toll on the Southern press. I think it's estimated that about more than half of Southern newspapers closed during the war. So the war was devastating to the Southern press.

Antonio Elmaleh: In that light, you also talk about the use of barter. Given the shortages and the technical problems and the financial problems and the logistical problems that the South suffered increasingly as the war turned bad for the South, you talk about this ingenious system of trading, instead of cash, people would barter livestock or flour or anything they could get their hands on with a mutually agreeable value, to buy the papers. Did you see a lot of that in your research?

Ford Risley: Oh yes, virtually every newspaper in the South, certainly small town newspapers, at one time or another, published pleas, first of all for readers to pay their subscriptions, but then if could not afford to pay their subscriptions, editors said we will take really anything in barter. It could be produce, it could be livestock, whatever you've got we'll take to settle up your debt to us. I think it spoke certainly to the shortages that the South saw, and that the newspaper editors suffered those, too. They went hungry, they suffered from food shortages like everyone else. But also, just how devastating the war was to the Southern economy that bartering was commonplace. I'm trying to remember, I think it was the North Carolina Standard said that they would accept everything from two bushels of corn, twenty pounds of bacon, twenty dozen eggs, ten pounds of butter, in exchange for their newspaper subscription.

Antonio Elmaleh: They certainly weren't sending bill collectors to collect, I would think anyway.

Ford Risley: No.

Antonio Elmaleh: I'd like to talk a little bit about Lincoln's astonishing reelection in 1864, made more astonishing by the fact that the man he beat, George McClellan, had been the very, very popular Commander of the Army of the Potomac. McClellan was beloved by his troops, up to a certain point, who was then sacked, I think twice, and then finally decided to run for president. Do you have any comments about what role the press had in turning that around? I think Lincoln even thought he was going to lose, he was kind of preparing both his cabinet and himself for that eventuality, and then Sherman took Atlanta and that turned things around.

Ford Risley: Yes, there was no question that Lincoln was in real danger of not being reelected. The war had not gone well. There was lots of opposition from his own party. Newspapers were split on Lincoln's election. He could count on his loyal supporters but he had plenty of newspapers that were staunchly opposed to him, but there's no question that the press was split on whether it was a good idea for Lincoln to be reelected and he had lots of opposition.

Antonio Elmaleh: Well, that was kind of what I was reminded about in my question earlier in our conversation about the role of the Army. I think certainly McClellan assumed that he would clean-up with his former soldiers and then he lost the Army vote by like 80%, which really just shocked everybody. I think nine states' electoral votes were attributed to the soldier vote.

Ford Risley: Right, it's interesting that the newspapers were widely read by the soldiers themselves. Newspapers were sold in Army camps, particularly in the North, and soldiers were avid readers of the newspapers. There is no question that soldiers played an important role in reelecting Lincoln.

Antonio Elmaleh: I'm struck by the comments you made about how widespread readership was amongst the general population. Do you have any research on the literacy rate that would have contributed to such a wide readership? I know today that some people would say reading is dead because of the visual image of television, etc. Those rates had to be quite high so that people could actually read the, literally read the paper. Do you have any data on that?

Ford Risley: I don't know literacy rates off the top of my head, but they were fairly high for the time. I think what we forget sometimes is just what a big event this was. This was a civil war. This was a war pitting Americans against Americans. Everybody knew somebody fighting, it was likely your husband or your brother or a neighbor, but everybody knew somebody that was fighting in the war, and you wanted to know what was happening to your friends and family. That's one of the reasons that newspaper readership was so high during the war and why editors recognize that this was an event the likes of which we had never seen, and they went to such lengths to cover the war in every way possible. In many ways America became a nation of newspaper readers during the war. I don't think there's any question about that.

Antonio Elmaleh: Again, in that light, do you see any shift in the narrative that both sides pursued in the press articulating the causes of the war and, what the outcome would be if one side or the other won? There had to be some significant shifting of the narrative of the war in the press.

Ford Risley: Oh, you bet, absolutely there was. Again, the war went badly for the North initially, that was reflected not only in the stories but in the editorial commentary that newspapers carried. Many editors were enormously critical of Lincoln and the administration and military leadership, as many were generally concerned that the North was going to lose the war, that the South would be successful. That narrative changed as the North regained the upper hand and began to win. Lincoln became more popular, and was finally reelected. But that narrative was certainly reflected, if you read editorials during the war, not only editors, not only newspapers that supported Lincoln, but those that did not as well. He faced enormous criticism from the Copperhead press, the Democratic newspapers that supported the South. You saw all of that in newspapers of that time.

Antonio Elmaleh: What role do you think emancipation played in the changing of the press' narrative of the reason to fight? We did a show earlier on the international history of the war, and it was very clear from my guests' comments that emancipation radically transformed public opinion towards siding with the Union because nobody had ever fought a war to free slaves.

Ford Risley: Right. Yes, I think that certainly was reflected in the press, many editors wanted Lincoln to move more quickly on the subject of emancipation. The best-known example of that was Horace Greeley and his famous editorial to Lincoln. Once the Emancipation Proclamation was finally signed, then Greeley and others who had been often quite critical of Lincoln, suddenly just turned around and they could not say enough good things about the President and what the war was all about.

Antonio Elmaleh: In turning to the South for a minute, how do you think the loss of so many Southern papers affected morale of both the civilians and the soldiers carrying on the fight, if they just couldn't get any kind of word of what was going on?

Ford Risley: Yes. That's really hard to say, I think it was more difficult for the folks at home who now could not read about what was happening with their loved ones and what the outcome of battles was. What was going to be the end result here? Was the South going to be victorious or not? Readers of newspapers, really for the last year or so of the war, Southern readers were largely in the dark. Southern editors tried to keep up morale as best as possible, and went to great lengths, in some cases almost misrepresenting what was going on in the battlefield, I shouldn't say misrepresenting what was happening on the battlefield but certainly editorially not really giving people the whole picture of what was happening.

To me, I think, in terms of the South, I think the impact was probably more felt by the folks at home who were trying to support their loved ones who were fighting but did not have a good picture of what was happening during the war, especially during the last couple of years.

The Southern newspapers were severely hurt, and the Associated Press was cut off from service in the South during the war. It hurt so much that the South went to great lengths to start its own wire service, which was called the Press Association of the Confederacy. Not the AP, but the PA, which I think was an indication just of how important the wire service, the Associated Press, had been in terms of providing news to newspapers.

Antonio Elmaleh: As a point of information for the listeners, describe what the AP was. I think it's still the same organization to this day, is it not? I don't know if people actually have a sense of how it actually worked and what was involved. Can you shed some light on that?

Ford Risley: Sure, yes. The AP is the Associated Press. It is a cooperative news service. It was made possible by the invention of the telegraph. So for the first time after the telegraph was invented, newspapers could share news and information with one another. This was done by the AP which had it headquarters in New York. It had member newspapers across the country who provided news of what was going on in a place like Philadelphia or Boston or Chicago, but then AP also had its own reporters stationed at news centers. So they provided a lot of the news that a newspaper, say the *Philadelphia Inquirer*, would get from distant locations. Journalists and editors had come to rely on the AP for news of what was happening across the country. Then when the war came along, the AP became even more valuable. So when the telegraphic lines to the South were cut when the war began, suddenly Southern newspapers no longer had that AP service. So they came up with their own way, their own cooperative news service, much like the AP.

Antonio Elmaleh: In that light, given the fact that it was a cooperative pooling of all these different sources, was there any thematic editorial consistency or were people just free to write their personal impression or their understanding of an event? Did the AP try to instill some thematic standards?

Ford Risley: Yes. Now the AP has largely tried to play it down the middle because their member newspapers have different interests and different backgrounds and maybe have a different editorial viewpoint. The AP has always tried to just play it straight to give people the news in the most unvarnished way possible. So, no, there was nothing like that. The AP has never had a real slant in its news, you can't be considered conservative or liberal or Democratic or Republican. That has always been the case with the AP, and it was the same during the war as well because the AP could not afford to alienate, to anger its member newspapers or they wouldn't subscribe to the AP service. I think that's one of the things that's always been most valuable about the Associated Press, the fact that it's news from a very straightforward, unbiased perspective.

Antonio Elmaleh: That would, I would think, lead to the conclusion that if a reporter or a report ran afoul of either Jeff Davis or Abe Lincoln there would be blowback and potentially legal ramifications and the AP was not there to defend its sources like a newspaper editor would. Is that correct?

Ford Risley: Yes, you bet. I've written about the Confederate Press Association and one thing I've found most interesting is that how the Superintendent of the Press Association, in his instructions to reporters, said that stories should be free of opinion and comment. He also wanted to make sure that reporters were not beaten by reporters from other journals. He had real standards that he thought were important for the reporters who worked for the Press Association. In many ways, these were the same standards that the AP had been following for years.

Antonio Elmaleh: I think you and I could both agree that the Civil War brought our country into the modern age in so many ways, economically, politically, socially, militarily, medically, on and on and on. I'd love it if you could discuss the ways in which the growth of the Civil War press impacted us to this very day. You know we're dominated by the discussion around "fake news" etc., propaganda and all this, could you talk a little bit about, feel free to really expand on how the growth of the Civil War press is impacting us as we sit here?

Ford Risley: Yes. Well I think there's no question, as I said, that the American press really came of age during the Civil War. It was already popular before the fighting began, but newspapers and magazines really became essential reading for many Americans. At the same time, journalistic practices became more sophisticated to cover fighting on such a vast scale. Reporting and editing became a profession with its own standards. The editorial page remained popular to voice opinions. We have not talked about editorial cartoons, but they earned a prominent place on the editorial page. And, finally, photography really emerged as an important tool in reporting news events.

I don't think there's any question that the press would become even more essential, influential, certainly controversial throughout the rest of the 19th century and into the 20th century. The number of newspapers continued to grow, the first newspaper chain was launched after the war, ushering in a new era of press ownership. Certainly, in the South newspapers struggled to rebuild from the devastation of the fighting.

At the same time, a growing number of African American newspapers began to emerge after the war, serving this group of Americans who were, perhaps, in greatest need of a strong press and a group that was, frankly, largely ignored by the mainstream press. By the end of the century there were more than one hundred black-owned publications in the United States.

The press increasingly became a big business. Important figures like Joseph Pulitzer and William Randolph Hearst emerged around the turn of the century, these titans of journalism. The journalism during the war really set the press off on something that would just continue to grow and expand and become more important and influential throughout the rest of the nineteenth and certainly into the 20th century.

Antonio Elmaleh: Just makes it a little bit sad that the newspaper growth is certainly shrinking and you know it's a much more difficult craft to be a journalist these days. You mentioned before, and we have to close soon but I wanted to double back on something you just said because we didn't talk about it: political satire and the use of illustrated cartoons to drive an editorial comment. What would an editor consider a political cartoon? Was it the voice of the, the opinion of the paper? Was it just the casual observation of a particular artist? Some of the famous ones, they're famous to this day, are savage.

Ford Risley: Oh, yes.

Antonio Elmaleh: We look at the New Yorker and all these other covers depicting politicians in very unflattering ways. These drawings are just incredibly savage and right to the point. How would an editor treat these cartoons? Was it editorial?

Ford Risley: Yes. I think, and I've never seen any real correspondence or primary source material on this kind of thing, but I it's my understanding that generally the editorial cartoonists were free to express their opinion. They were largely expressing their own opinion, not that of the publication. The editorial cartoons only appeared in magazines, they did not appear, really, in newspapers. They did reflect, to some extent, the views of the publication, but largely they were the views of the cartoonist himself. As you said they could be savage. As a rule, 19th century cartoons were not subtle. Many artists, to demonize the enemy, they used crude caricatures and stereotypes. Racism, frankly, was widespread, not just toward blacks but toward Jews and other ethnic groups. Some cartoonists use humor to make their points, but the majority of cartoons were far more serious. They were different than I think what we would see today, but they were remarkable in many ways, just really pointing out an issue in a way that only a good editorial cartoon can do.

Antonio Elmaleh: Why don't you take a stab at describing some of the most famous ones? I think our listeners would smile if they imagine what these drawings are depicting. It's an interesting point.

Ford Risley: Sure. Yes, well, for example there's a Harper's cartoon that was Jeff Davis Reaping the Harvest. It showed a monstrous looking Davis walking through a field or a swamp at night harvesting skulls. A rattlesnake is coiled at his feet and a buzzard is perched in a tree above him.

Another drawing portrays Davis' inauguration. He was portrayed as a skeleton wearing a crown, seated on bales of cotton on top of a cask of whiskey. These were hardly subtle, didn't take a lot of thought to understand what the cartoonists were doing.

Another popular subject during the war was ridiculing young men who did not enlist in the Union army or who paid substitutes. Harper's cartoon suggested the uniform for the stay-at-home lifeguard. It showed a man in a dress wearing a cooking pot on his head. He's holding a broom as if it's a rifle and wearing, on his side, a duster as if it's a pistol. So, as I said, they were not subtle but they certainly made their points and you couldn't help but probably be moved, angered, amused by what the cartoonists were saying. There's no question that probably the most famous and most popular cartoonist was Thomas Nast. He drew some just absolutely brilliant cartoons for Harper's Weekly.

Antonio Elmaleh: Any come to mind?

Ford Risley: Yes. There was one called Thanksgiving Day, November 26 1863, that showed Columbia kneeling in prayer, thankful prayer at the "Union Altar". In similar smaller scenes surrounding the main image, soldiers, sailors and other groups are giving thanks. He often did these multi panel cartoons that in many ways were quite moving. Lincoln at one point was so grateful for some of the pictures that Nast drew that he called him our best recruiting sergeant.

Perhaps Nast's most powerful illustration was one called Compromise with the South. This is when prospects for Lincoln's reelection really looked bleak. It just showed just what compromising with the South, not reelecting Lincoln, could possibly mean for the future of the Union.

Antonio Elmaleh: You know, Lincoln himself, because of his physical presence, which was unusual to say the least, he had very long arms and big feet, kind of gangly. I don't know how, I've never seen any descriptions of how he moved, but to the political satirists he was depicted as a lumbering baboon. Do you remember any of those cartoons?

Ford Risley: Yes, it's funny you mention that, one of my favorites, and I'm not going to do it justice in trying to describe it, but after Lincoln was reelected there's a cartoon, I can't remember where it was published but the caption was Lincoln a Little Longer. It shows Lincoln literally stretched out. As you say he was tall and gangly, but in the illustration he's made to look even taller and even ganglier. The caption is, as I said, Lincoln a Little Longer, the message was we've got him for four more years.

Antonio Elmaleh: Well, I hate to say this but I think we've run out of time. I'd like to thank you for just a great conversation about the press in the Civil War and remind folks about your upcoming book, *Dear Courier: The Civil War Correspondence of Editor Melvin Dwinell*, which will be published by the University of Tennessee. Do you have any idea when publication is?

Ford Risley: I think it's supposed to be published the summer of 2019. If I could say, just briefly, it's a great series, the University of Tennessee Press series is a great series because it provides original correspondence from soldiers, civilians, North and South during the War. Melvin

Dwinell was an interesting Southern correspondent with his own interesting story. He was a war correspondent, solider correspondent during the war, published some two hundred letters that he sent back to his newspaper in Rome, Georgia. I just found his correspondence very interesting and very insightful.

Antonio Elmaleh: Well, we'll look for it when it comes out.

Ford Risley: All right.

Antonio Elmaleh: Again, thanks for joining us on *Uncovering the Civil War*, Ford. Pleasure.

Ford Risley: Thank you. Thank you so much.

Antonio Elmaleh: I'd also like to thank all of you for listening and invite you to hear another segment of *Uncovering the Civil War*. Until then, stay safe and do good.

UNCOVERING THE PRESS DURING THE CIVIL WAR, PART II

Guest: Dr. David Sachsman

Antonio Elmaleh: Hello everyone. Welcome to another segment of *Uncovering the Civil War*. Today my guest via telephone is Dr. David Sachsman. Dr. Sachsman holds the West Chair of Excellence at the University of Tennessee in Chattanooga. He is the founder and director of the "Symposium on the 19th Century Press, the Civil War, and Free Expression," one of the most prestigious gatherings of scholars for examining and understanding the press in the 19th century.

He is also the editor of seven books that have grown out of the symposium: *The Civil War and the Press*, published in 2000; *Memory and Myth: The Civil War in Fiction and Film from Uncle Tom's Cabin to Cold Mountain*, published in 2007; *Words at War: The Civil War in American Journalism*, published in 2008; *Seeking a Voice: Images of Race and Gender in the 19th Century Press*, in 2009; *Sensationalism: Murder, Mayhem, Mudslinging, Scandals, and Disasters* in 19th-Century Reporting, published in 2013; *A Press Divided: Newspaper Coverage of the Civil*

War, published in 2014; and most recently, *After the War: The Press in a Changing America 1865-1900*. Welcome to the program Dr. Sachsman.

David Sachsman: Thank you very much.

Antonio Elmaleh: I'd like to start off by something that struck me as very interesting. You've written about myths of the Civil War and how they continue to cloud our understanding of it and its significance to our society today. How did movies as the central storytelling medium of the last century influence and advance myths about the war, and did the South win the war of public opinion about the war's causes?

David Sachsman: This has changed over time. The South won the world of public opinion and myth until and through World War II, or at least what white people thought about the war, North and South. After the war and then in the first half of the 20th century you got a Gone with the Wind image of the Civil War.

This Gone with the Wind image was actually based on earlier, much more racist movies. The concept, which is sometimes now called "The Lost Cause" concept, of this brave, wonderful Southern aristocracy fighting for their freedom was the image of the Civil War, I would say, up until the Civil Rights Movement.

With the Civil Rights Movement came a division, North and South again, and that has gone back and forth for the last thirty to forty years. But now again we have again a division between North and South, which is not directly connected to the same causes of the Civil War, but has led to similar separate worldviews existing North and South.

Antonio Elmaleh: In that light, was this a conscious effort on the part of Southern, if you want to call them Southern, opinion-makers to drive this different narrative of the war? In other words, D. W. Griffith, was he approached to do something and then become essentially the poster boy for the Ku Klux Klan with Birth of a Nation, going way back to silent movies, starting to shape that narrative?

David Sachsman: To give you a sense of how widespread it was, Woodrow Wilson was a practicing historian and considered one of the great American historians. He was, I think, president of Princeton before becoming president. The worldview I'm talking about is directly expressed in Woodrow Wilson's writing of history and in the beginning of Birth of a Nation.

Griffith takes the trouble of quoting Woodrow Wilson to set the stage for exactly what happened during the war and after the war and how gallantly the South fought against these forces. This was a worldview that in 1905 was dominant among whites in America.

Antonio Elmaleh: The writ of habeas corpus is codified in the Constitution. Was there anything dangerous in Lincoln suspending that writ given the war that's raging over modern media now?

David Sachsman: I do not believe that there is anything dangerous about this now, but let me say from the beginning that there are no current parallels. The situation at that time was that we had a nation at war.

At that time both governments, the government of the Confederate States and the government of the United States and their administrations, had to decide on an instantaneous basis whether they would enact and enforce the laws of the United States or whether they would go past that and do what they felt was necessary to win the war.

Interestingly, the Confederate administration pretty much held to the constitutional freedoms of the original American Constitution. The Lincoln administration felt it could not hold to some of these basic rights. The most basic right is that if somebody comes and picks you up in the middle of the night and locks you in a jail, that you have a right to see a lawyer.

A lawyer can then go to court and ask that somebody say what you're being charged with and that something be done to start a process of finding out what's going on. The Lincoln administration felt that various civilian elements such as editors, especially in the border states, were doing things that were pro-Confederacy and were hurting the United States war effort, even threatening the safety and stability of these border states. So, a number of people were locked up and held for quite some time, and likewise some newspapers were closed. In response to your question, I don't see anything like that in our current world or in our future, I think. We are not at war. The courts and the Supreme Court would absolutely prevent anything like that from happening.

The last time it happened was after 9/11. Special laws were passed so that if people were in the United States and actively engaged in terrorism they could be locked up without seeing a lawyer. All sorts of special courts were set up and those courts run twenty-four hours a day, twenty-four/seven the whole year. They run to deal with these cases and that's the parallel that is made. But there's nothing other than that going on at this moment, and certainly no concern for the press.

Antonio Elmaleh: Was there a "War Powers Act" at that time, because it seems to me Lincoln was invoking a special power that we now look to the War Powers Act to give to the president in unusual circumstances. Or did that not exist then?

David Sachsman: I don't think it existed nor was it necessary. In other words, the Union did not feel they were at war. They felt these were their states and they were simply retaking control of their own states.

That was the formal position of the United States during the Civil War. There was essentially no recognition of the Confederate government, certainly no recognition of them as a separate nation.

There were many different restrictive laws passed but the Supreme Court was not immediately invoked or involved. These things went on back and forth, certainly in the first half of the Civil War.

Antonio Elmaleh: Do you then feel that abolitionism was truly the first time that, in the press anyway, these views were given real expression and created an alternative narrative or point of view to the prevalent notion that the South propagated? In other words, when do you think the press began to reflect the true divide? Do you have a date or a general period of time when alternative points of view were starting to show up in editorials, in I would assume just mostly Northern papers?

David Sachsman: There is brand new research being conducted at this moment by Don Shaw and Tom Terry. They've done a huge content analysis of newspapers, looking for articles that would reflect that a civil war was coming. As they look at every newspaper and story they can find, they discover very, very little until the 1850s. Then in the 1850s, they begin to find a real reflection of a time of unrest.

Before the 1850s, really before the Mexican-American War, I would say that there was a universal agreement, North and South, that slavery was an institution that was legal and that each state would have the right to deal with it as it wanted to. And the federal law supported slavery, and there was a universal agreement among whites that African Americans were inherently inferior to European white Americans.

Antonio Elmaleh: It was pretty much late in the game, I would imagine, that the whole Nebraska "Bloody Kansas" precursor of the Civil War must have kicked off, and then of course John Brown's raid at Harpers Ferry and his subsequent execution. These things were really lighting rods for galvanizing an anti-Southern, pro-emancipation press viewpoint.

David Sachsman: Exactly. Although it starts earlier than that, it starts with political debate over what shall be done with the land that came from Mexico in terms of whether it would go to slave states or non-slave states. There was the Compromise of 1850 that ended that discussion, but there was real argument in the press all over the country, and threats of secession even at that time over that issue.

The basic issue was whose America was it, whose vision of America was it, and who would be the majority in America? That was the battle between Adams and Jefferson, and Jefferson won. That was a battle that continued to go on.

Antonio Elmaleh: Right. You mention Jefferson and Adams' presidential campaign in 1800. I read that Jefferson actually had his political mouthpieces, for want of a better word, spread the word that Adams had actually died in the middle of the campaign. Of course, how do you verify that when there's no telegraph and it takes weeks for news to arrive? He planted what we would now consider fake news, which leads me to my question: "fake news" and "propaganda machine" are bandied about today with more and more frequency, but can you give examples of fake news in press coverage of the Civil War?

David Sachsman: It's a very good question. The politics of the newspaper in the North played some role in the coverage of the Civil War and the federal government during the war. The war story as told by a pro-Southern pro-Democratic Party Northern newspaper nicknamed "Copperhead" is a different story than you will get from the other groups. There are several other groups, the pro-Republican press, and even the pro-Union Democratic press, pro-Southern press, pro-Union independent press.

In the later book called *A Press Divided* we find many divisions during the war. I would imagine, and I think the research shows it, there's a different understanding of what's going on during the war depending on which of these newspapers you read. The style from the 1830s on or 1840s on, with the coming of the press services, is that each newspaper would receive the basic facts from some place by wire and then would write it to fit their own politics.

I don't think it's to the level of the fake news that we're talking about today. On the other hand, how the war was going was clearly reflected differently in different newspapers, so differently that Mr. Lincoln absolutely believed he would not be reelected because he read the press and he felt that unless something enormous happened in 1864 to his benefit, he had no chance of reelection. And to prove it, he wrote it down and everybody knew it was written down.

Sure enough, he got his deliverance from Sherman and Atlanta and so suddenly now there is a single view of what's going on in the war. After Atlanta no Southern newspaper could say they were winning anymore, and after Atlanta the Copperhead couldn't say the Union was losing anymore. At that point we have an enormous change; at that point Lincoln is reassured of winning his second term in office.

Antonio Elmaleh: It's generally acknowledged now that Lincoln was masterful in handling the press and Jefferson Davis was, to be generous, apathetic towards it. My question really doesn't have to do with is that a correct statement, but more with something that I think is relevant to today: what special quality or qualities do you think a president needs to handle the press in order to advance both his political agenda and influence public opinion about that agenda?

David Sachsman: The most successful president in the United States in terms of handling the press was John F. Kennedy. John F. Kennedy did it by befriending the press on a personal level, by bringing them inside and showing them just what he wanted to show them, by treating them on a first name and by helping them advance their careers. Just about everybody who covered JFK at one point or another was looking at the Kennedy White House with rose-covered glasses.

The most famous of these being Ben Bradlee, who was one of his closest friends, and just about all of these folks knew really what was going on in the White House. For example, they knew about JFK's private life. They would discuss it at the press club. Most of them kept lists of who he was intimate with and who were just speculations. And yet, given the time, such things were not to be discussed. Given their close affinity with Kennedy they all kept their mouths shut, and they kept their mouths shut until Time magazine broke the story ten years later when it turned out that one of Kennedy's girlfriends had been a mafia mole.

Clearly the most successful president was Kennedy, who was really loved by the people covering him. They created Camelot and they believed Camelot.

Antonio Elmaleh: They believed their own press, so to speak.

David Sachsman: That's right.

Antonio Elmaleh: Let me ask you this, because I was surprised by your answer. I honestly thought you were going to say FDR. And the reason I was thinking about FDR is his management of the press and how he managed to get them to do so much heavy lifting for him. He had polio, and all through his career before and up to and then during his administration, that was just not something that was discussed. Obviously, personal intimate matters were totally off the table if you wanted to have any access to him, and his medical challenge was given soft, if any, treatment. I'm sure that he drove that home with the editors, saying, "Look, I don't want people focusing on my disability, that's counterproductive to what I'm trying to project, which is we can do anything no matter what shortcomings we have if we put our minds to it, and the worst thing is fear itself."

Do you have any comment about that, about his handling of the press?

David Sachsman: My guess is that it was never discussed. My guess is that, first of all, FDR worked very hard not to be visibly in front of cameras in a wheelchair so he was up and leaning on things as much as he could be. And the working press favored him, the reporters who were covering it were by then Democrats.

That was not something that would've been thought of as appropriate in that period even though the ownership of the press was completely Republican. I still don't think that they would've crossed those bounds.

Furthermore, I think I'd pick Kennedy first because I don't believe that what we received from coverage of FDR was a myth. I think that the coverage then probably was very strong, although we may gloss over it now. They had debates in the '30s over various plans which the Supreme Court ended up finding unconstitutional, and all sorts of other kinds of issues.

It's further back in history for me, I mean I can tell you that it's clear that the common people thought of him as a savior, but I don't have the same concept of him doing something strategically. What FDR would do that was different is he held press conferences for the reporters who would regularly cover the White House in his office. He was not allowed to be quoted, they were just background, and these paper reporters would come out with information that came from "a source." And so he had that contact with reporters. In reading about FDR, while he had some reporters who were friends, he did not do this thing that Kennedy did that was so extraordinary which was making a friend of virtually every reporter he ran into. Many other politicians since then have figured this out and tried to do the same thing, some successfully and some less successfully, but JFK was the best at it. They really bought into it.

Antonio Elmaleh: Right. In terms of the thing that was so striking, if I could boil it down, was the press created Camelot and they believed their own press, which is an amazing development.

David Sachsman: I believed it, too.

Antonio Elmaleh: Yeah, I think we all did, I think we all bought it. Yeah.

David Sachsman: It was a completely different world for all of us those years.

Antonio Elmaleh: Right, right.

David Sachsman: The world we saw was a world that we saw through the mass media, right?

Antonio Elmaleh: Right, right. In your work, have you found any female journalists of the Civil War, and if you have, how were they treated: equally, unequally, in terms of pay or what stories they were given to report on, or were they really limited to "softer issues" like one guest referred to the inner life of the Army and the cost of the war on civilians, as examples? Did you find any evidence of women going actually into combat as reporters and writing what they saw?

David Sachsman: Almost all of these books include women and the role of women in journalism in the 19th century. *Seeking a Voice: Images of Race and Gender in the 19th Century Press* deals with this directly in terms of who were the reporters, where were they working, and what roles did they play. Women played a significant role in magazines, and less so but still in newspapers starting from I would say the 1830s. You have women editors starting in that period.

No, once it comes to the actual Civil War there were a number of women who were covering it. But the concept that you're asking about: were women reporters embedded with the troops during the Civil War? The answer is I don't have one to give you, but they were writing about the Civil War in their home newspapers and there were several who were quite prominent.

Embedded is a different question. I'm not sure how many reporters were actually embedded with armies at that time. The army didn't like to have them there, many were pushed out either legally or illegally and the war news that we got was often people walking in directly afterwards or being led in by the army. It's an interesting question because as we've discussed, the modern term is the "fog of war." There really was a fog of war existing in each of these battles until the end.

It's at the end that you find out who is really winning and who isn't, and when the press comes in – by this time there's a lot of telegraph service – and so at this time the press can try to cover the story and get it back by telegraph. Incidentally, a lot of the press telegraph was controlled or illegally controlled by the military, and if the Northern army lost the battle it would try to prevent the South from getting the story back literally until a day or two so they could figure out what was really going on.

Yes, the story of the 19th century is a story of women, and even coverage of the war is a story of women.

Antonio Elmaleh: So much of the war is a story of women, which we've tried to uncover in other programs. Editors had a lot of leverage to influence public opinion about the war and the perceptions of how it was proceeding. It is now, I think, commonplace to find examples of the media influencing the financial markets. I remember up until the day of the 2008 economic collapse they were reporting that things looked just fine.

My question really is have you ever found evidence that editors during the war reported a fake news story to result in their own personal financial gain, knowing that if they reported a battle was going particularly poorly or well, that could drive up futures or the market or whatever, have you ever found any instances of that or that's a little too crass?

David Sachsman: In twenty-five symposia, of course twenty-five years with thirty-five or forty papers at each symposium, I've never seen an article that suggests that.

Antonio Elmaleh: Okay, that's pretty authoritative I would say.

David Sachsman: Now if you had asked how often are these editors and publishers wishing they could run for office or wishing that the government in charge would give them one of these government jobs that would make them a lot of money, that's very common. The press through the Civil War and until around 1870 is extraordinarily partisan.

The number of truly independent newspapers anywhere in America is the smallest group. These folks wanted printing jobs, they wanted jobs that would pay them a salary, and that did have a role in what got reported and in how things were handled. But no, other than that the answer would be no.

Antonio Elmaleh: Okay. We all know that people at the beginning of the war both North and South figured it was a ninety-day fight. It was going to be over real quick. One side or the other would win and everybody would go off into the sunset. As the war dragged on and especially as the casualty lists started to be printed, they staggered people into this incredible realization that this was a murderous slugfest that was going to take pretty much everything each side had to give.

Was this the first time in our history that casualty lists were published, and if that's true, who made the call to actually publish, let's say in the Springfield paper, an Illinois regiment lost X number of men? Did the editor decide that they would publish the casualty list or did the government have some unwritten mandate: "We want you to unvarnish the truth here, we want people to know exactly what the cost of this thing is, to mobilize people to keep going." Do you have any comments on this?

David Sachsman: I don't know. It's an interesting question. Folks were used to losing lots of people from illness, they're used to losing babies, they're used to living in a world without effective medicine and the rest, and yet the death toll and the injury toll was extraordinary and was reflected in the press. This is why Lincoln thought he did not have a chance on Earth of being reelected.

Whichever side you were on and however you viewed it, Lincoln felt responsible for the Civil War and everyone in the North and of course everyone in the South was holding him responsible for the Civil War. That meant if he couldn't show that he was going to win it, he couldn't be reelected.

Antonio Elmaleh: Now, as in 1867, impeachment is a daily topic of debate and rhetoric. Can you describe how the press treated the run up to an eventual trial of Andrew Johnson? Is it instructive in understanding the political debates and calculations going on now, or is it just such an unusual occurrence that it's a once in a lifetime situation?

David Sachsman: I would say the impeachment of Johnson is not analogous to the current situation. What might be analogous are the situations involving Mr. Nixon and Mr. Clinton in terms of the possibility of either political wrongdoing or personal wrongdoing. Johnson was a separate case involving extraordinary politics of how harsh one would be with the South. I don't see a correlation there at all with today's times.

On the other hand, if one makes an argument that the Russian situation is a serious situation and that there was conspiracy to keep it quiet, then that would be analogous with the Nixon situation. If one talks about personal peccadilloes, personal behavior that was inappropriate, then a direct parallel would be with Mr. Clinton. If you ask me which one is going to come through this time, I would say there're not going to be enough votes to do anything.

Antonio Elmaleh: Right.

David Sachsman: I think the impeachment issue is wishful thinking among the people who bring it up, and I can tell you down here in Tennessee it doesn't come up at all.

Antonio Elmaleh: In covering Reconstruction, both its concepts and eventual implementation in the South, it seems yet another place where the South or the Southern press or a combination, let's say public opinion-makers, twisted and perverted Reconstruction's meanings and goals in order to continuously win the battle of public opinion over one-hundred-plus years of Jim Crow.

Given that there was no Southern press for some time, how did this narrative of what Reconstruction was truly about and what it was trying to achieve get hijacked, and was the Northern press complicit in that, if at all?

David Sachsman: The complicity is easy and it refers to directly to what I said earlier. Was the North just as racist as the South in terms of African Americans? Not exactly, but it was so close that to make a distinction would be inappropriate. If we go back to that period and we look at Reconstruction, we have a myth that the Northerners all believed that blacks were equal and should have all the rights and abilities as everybody else, that the North thought that it was a good thing that the Southern legislature should become African American and the rest. That's a concept we all believe but it's not found in reality. What's found in reality is that the Republicans who now control everything, and Grant who believed this firmly, believe that the Southern Confederacy would not really be defeated until the Southerners who had fought the war had agreed to certain terms in order to come back as states.

You had this period when there was a real military occupation of the southern half of the United States. This is the period with Johnson and impeachment, and then Grant and Sherman, and they are committed to Reconstruction decisively. But then a deal is struck to determine the 1876 election in which the deal is, "All right, if you let our side win we will end Reconstruction and you can go back to your own ways."

Antonio Elmaleh: We'll pull the US Army out.

David Sachsman: To understand that deal you have to understand the intense and absolute racism existing among whites in this country, not only against African Americans and Native Americans and the Chinese, but against Jewish people and against the Irish and at the start against Germans – although Germans become an almost dominant group. People of German extraction are a very, very large group of the American population.

There's less of that now, but to view this time period as, "We in the North are pro-everyone and the South are anti-everyone," that's not a right view. This essential hatred in the United States for everybody else but us, no one has been able to get rid of. To even argue that today it's reserved for people of one party, I would say is wrong. I mean you can find it at this moment across the board as well.

Antonio Elmaleh: I know that going to school in the South, I encountered a lot of resentment amongst Southerners. Not so much, well, we have different opinions or etc., but the hypocrisy Southerners felt Northerners practice of, what you just described, this smug thing of, "We were right, you guys are all wrong." That myth clouds our understanding of our history just as effectively as any other myth or untruth about the war. It strikes me as ironic that we in the North, we've been living in a bubble ourselves, and it's time that we all recognize that we all share this unfortunate issue around racial inclusion. Finding who is to blame is a no-win, endlessly blind alley.

I'd like to shift over for a second to the telegraph. The telegraph created mass newspaper readership during and after the war. Now the internet is driving down traditional newspaper readership while simultaneously driving it to social media for news. Can you comment on the irony of the technical advance of the telegraph increasing popular participation in the news while social media is actually breaking apart that same audience into smaller and smaller echo chambers reflecting only similar beliefs as well as a growing refusal to entertain opposing points of view? Do you find that ironic or even an accurate statement?

David Sachsman: It turns out that I have two answers. One of my answers is the 19th century history of journalism and the Civil War, but the other has to do with environmental journalism. I'm editing a book now for Rutledge called the *Handbook on Environmental Journalism*. This would be a distinctly international book and so I'm spending my time finding authors from all over the world who can write on this subject.

What I learned from it is that this world that is transforming is transforming in ways that I did not understand before, and it is very different to the understanding we commonly think of as the influence of the internet. For example, I am being told right now that in India and China the dominant news medium is the cellphone.

I asked how people can afford smartphones, because I assumed that meant they were getting what we get from the internet through smartphones. But no, even the cheapest cellphones now have written information delivery capabilities; they can hit a button and get to the news and that's where it is. I don't know where this is going.

The telegraph was revolutionary in that it got news or information to us faster. Now we live in a truly instantaneous age. Whatever happens will show up on my phone and it will interrupt this phone call with a ringing to tell me, like right now, literally: at the moment the alert is from Time magazine. "All of the US is experiencing widespread flu activity right now. Here is why it's so bad this year and what you can do to help prevent it."

That's the news right now, that's where we're getting it, it's coming in these little blurbs and it's hitting one hundred million people instantly. We've never seen anything like that. I don't know how to react to it.

Antonio Elmaleh: Well, yeah, I mean my point was simply that I find it supremely ironic that given the popular belief that technology drives growth, here we have two examples: one, of the telegraph creating essentially a nation of newspaper readers, whereas we have an internet-based technology that's actually fractionalizing and effectively sequestering audiences into more and more, "Well, if I don't agree with you, forget it, I'm tuning you out, I'll just go to my safe news gathering organizations that support my point of view." I just find that very ironic, given the pedestal we put technology on for automatically boosting growth. It's not like that simple.

David Sachsman: Yeah. My response was that model is true, I think, for people like you and me living in the United States, but maybe not true for somebody living in rural India. They may be getting something different and they may not have all of the different avenues we have. The fact that we now have a media with virtually no way to control it, where it is legal to do things on the internet that would be illegal on television or radio because of federal law, has changed things quite decisively.

Antonio Elmaleh: Right. Could you offer any words of caution in noting how a partisan political press drives partisan political paralysis? Is there any way to break this pattern or is it simply baked into the American understanding of the First Amendment and the role of the press that you are always going to have this intense divide and that there's just no way to bridge it, at least through the modern media?

David Sachsman: It's an interesting question and it assumes that we have a very partisan press right now. If we look at newspapers, I would say not so much; if we look at network television, I would say not so much; but as we point to cable stations like Fox, which does approach things in a partisan manner in terms of this...

I don't think the press is playing any role in making Congress as incompetent as it is at this moment. I think the press is staring at it like the rest of us, in blind amazement that it's possible that this week the government might shut down. I think that that possibility is staggering to me, and I don't think there's anybody in the press pushing for that. I think the press in this regard is watching canvas. What we have is a Congress that is sharply divided and sharply divided from more extremes than the rest.

Antonio Elmaleh: I guess I'd like to just be a devil's advocate for a moment and mention the essence of good drama is conflict. Does the press always reflect the partisan division and is it effective in selling newspapers, constantly creating this raging debate?

I know that sounds cynical, but I just offer it up as a possible other way of looking at some of the motives of the media of late. They're getting much of their act together and not I think being rolled as much, but I still felt that there was some complicity there that some people in the press are cynical enough to simply want to play out the drama and the conflicts rather than maybe looking at why the conflicts are there, or more importantly, how to bridge them because there doesn't seem to be a whole lot of talk about that.

David Sachsman: It is certainly true since the very, very beginning of the American press, a major part of the American press and to some degree a very highly valued part of the American press, was its ability and its desire to sensationalize world events. This has been the case all the way through. It was the case in extraordinary terms in the 19th century. Sensationalism was arguably dominant through the entire period, especially the period after the Civil War.

The book on this, called *Sensationalism*, is subtitled *Murder, Mayhem, Mudslinging, Scandals, and Disasters in 19th-Century Reporting.* Certainly, at this moment we are in another one of those times when anything that shows up will be blown up to be sensational. We earlier discussed two times, the time of Franklin Roosevelt and the time of JFK, when personal issues and other things were glossed over when it was felt that that was inappropriate for family reading.

I started in the newspaper business at the *New York Daily News.* In the New York Daily News they would take photographs of crime scenes or accidents and they would airbrush out the things that were particularly gory so that the reader at breakfast and showing it to their kids would not be depressed by the sight of an arm separate from an accident victim. We're back now to the point where we are going to get the arm with the accident victim, we're going to get the train hanging upside-down.

On network television, if you have a particularly horrible picture they're not only going to show it the day it happens, they're going to show it five weeks later or maybe five months later and it goes into their spin of these things. Perfect example of that is the one guy in Hawaii, fearful during this alert about a possible missile coming to Hawaii, who put his daughter in a manhole. Yesterday on ABC News they referred to this in the plural, people putting their children in it.

It's three days later and they keep running these pictures. This poor terrified father happened once, but everybody blows it up as if it's the end of the world. That is the American press at this moment, it was the American press in the 1850s and at the time of the Civil War. And the argument that America is at its most divided now since the Civil

War is a rational argument. The argument that we are at our most sensationalistic now as we were before is also a reasonable argument. I'm paraphrasing Dickens incorrectly, I'm sure, "The best of times and the worst of times."

Antonio Elmaleh: In closing, could you leave our listeners with any last thoughts or facts about the Civil War press and its significance to our political and social health today? I'd love our listeners to come away remembering some salient observations that you may have. Please take your time, because I know it's a bit of a tough question to just answer spontaneously.

David Sachsman: I'd like to end this positively because I've been so negative. During the Civil War the great defenders of personal liberty and personal freedom were both the Southern press and the Northern press. You discussed earlier the fact that the Lincoln administration would lock up editors and the rest. The press uniformly in the North felt that this was inappropriate, including the Republican press. There were literal movements against it.

The word to leave you with is the great value of the American press. The American model of the press is freedom of the press for us, for all of us who see ourselves as journalists, and the rest is central to our belief in terms of what constitutes a democracy. During the Civil War, on both sides this fundamental belief in freedom of the press continued among the journalists and the exact concept is not lost among journalists today.

I would think virtually one hundred percent of American journalists continue to believe almost as a religious tenet in the centrality of freedom of the press and freedom of speech to the American model of democracy. In that regard the press has had enormous value in this country since its earliest times in terms of being the absolute standard-bearer for freedom of the press and freedom of speech in America.

At the end I believe that's true for all of us. I believe that's true for the US Supreme Court, Republican and Democrat, I believe that's true for the many, many people who went to law school and to many

Americans around the nation. At the end, freedom of speech is our central value. It was not lost when the Lincoln administration was trying to diminish it and it is not being lost today.

Antonio Elmaleh: Thank you. That is in fact a very positive way to end our show. I'm afraid our time is up and I'd like to thank you Dr. David Sachsman for a great conversation today. I learned a lot and I would hope that our listeners can take a lot out of this segment as well. But I'd also like to salute you for your significant body of work and for continuing that work to help advance the goal of a deeper and more profound understanding of our press both in the 19th century and today. Again, thank you for joining us, Dr. Sachsman.

David Sachsman: It's been my great pleasure.

FIVE

UNCOVERING THE PRESS DURING THE CIVIL WAR, PART III

Guest: Dr. Debra van Tuyll

Antonio Elmaleh: Welcome, everyone, to another segment of *Uncovering the Civil War*. Today, my guest is Debbie Van Tuyll. She is a professor of communication at Augusta University. She has written five books on the Confederate press and is currently working with Mary Cronin of New Mexico State University on a series of two books that look at the western and mid-western press in the Civil War.

Her interest in the Civil War arose when she realized what she was reading about journalism of the period did not match up with what she was actually reading in the newspapers of the day. When she's not researching the Confederate press, she's also working on the earliest Irish-American press. Her doctorate is from the University of South Carolina. Welcome to the show, Debbie.

Debbie Van Tuyll: Thank you. I appreciate you having me on.

Antonio Elmaleh: It's a great pleasure. I'd like to start off with four words that you use in one of your books: fight, fold, flip, or flee. These are four choices for the Southern press during the Civil War. Could you briefly elaborate on each of those?

Debbie Van Tuyll: Sure. Those words are from the book that looks at the press in the occupied areas of the Confederacy, but that does come down to basically the choices that they all had. Some of them could continue to publish, which is what we were thinking of when we were talking about fighting. Flipping: in the occupied areas, some previously avowedly Confederate newspapers switched over to the Unionist side.

More than half of the newspapers in the Confederacy folded between 1860 and 1865. The fleeing papers were the ones who went on the road and moved to another city, like The *Memphis Appeal* which published for about half the war in Atlanta but still published as The *Memphis Appeal*. They called it The *Moving Appeal* as a result because it actually moved around to four different cities.

Antonio Elmaleh: I mean, it sounds like they would have to be one step ahead of the Union Army, one step ahead of unfavorable opinion. It seemed like it was a pretty precarious occupation, no matter how solidly the government may have been behind it. We can talk about that later in the show.

Debbie Van Tuyll: It really depends on where the newspapers were. If you are familiar with the military side of the Civil War, you've got two theaters of war: you've got the eastern theater which is basically Virginia, and you've got the western theater which is basically Tennessee, a little bit of Alabama, eventually a lot of Mississippi and then down to Louisiana. If you are in Georgia, South Carolina, North Carolina, Florida, the war really doesn't really come to you until 1864, and even then not until the end of 1864.

Newspapers in that area pretty much functioned "normally," and I put that in quotation marks because war times are not normal times at all. That's what I was really looking at: how did the war affect the press in those areas that were more or less functioning normally? I wanted to know how war affects the American press. This is the best laboratory to look at for that, the Confederate press.

There was, in many places, a precarious existence, and it would particularly be precarious in those areas that border on the different theaters. The press in Virginia, the press in Western Tennessee, the press in Eastern Tennessee, were pretty much Unionist so that didn't really change. The press in Mississippi, Louisiana, you'd find more changes there, much more of a precarious existence in those places. If you were in Georgia, North Carolina, South Carolina, or Florida, or even Texas for that matter, you pretty much continued to publish as you always had with a few deprivations.

There were, in the United States, about three hundred and twenty-seven paper mills as the war began. Fewer than thirty were in the South, so you didn't have much paper; in Mississippi, they were reduced to printing on wallpaper, for example. You didn't have an ink manufacturer in the South, so they were reduced to making their own ink. They ran into problems with keeping their newspapers going because of lack of materials for manufacturing. Also, printers were subject to the draft; editors weren't, but printers were, so you lost a lot of your printing staff. All of that had a big impact on the press but it didn't stop them from publishing if you were in the area that was less affected by the actual military efforts.

Now, in the areas where there was military maneuvering going on, you might get run out of town for a while. That happened in Milledgeville, Georgia, when Sherman's troops came through on the March to the Sea. That was the capital of Georgia at the time, and the newspapers in Milledgeville packed up, took their press out into the woods and hid it, and stayed hidden until Sherman's troops went on through Milledgeville. Then they came back and started publishing again. Same thing in Atlanta: when Sherman came through, the newspapers fled; some came back, some went ahead and folded at that point, and some started publishing in other places. There was a really huge range of experience for the press if you talk about the South as a whole.

Antonio Elmaleh: I have a couple of follow-ups. One is more of a historical curiosity: do any of those Southern papers still publish today?

Debbie Van Tuyll: Oh, yeah, here in Augusta, The *Augusta Chronicle* is still in publication.

Antonio Elmaleh: Wow.

Debbie Van Tuyll: It was The *Augusta Chronicle* and *Sentinel* through the Civil War. It's been in existence since 1785, it's had a lot of different names over the years, but right now its name is The *Augusta Chronicle*. The *Richmond Dispatch* is a continuation of The *Richmond Dispatch* from the Civil War period. I name all of these in my book and I can't remember now, but I think there's probably six or eight that are actually still in publication from that time period.

Antonio Elmaleh: That's pretty amazing.

Debbie Van Tuyll: It is pretty amazing, isn't it?

Antonio Elmaleh: Yes, given what they had to get through just to survive the war. Going back to my first question about folding and flipping and fleeing, we know that there were instances of papers flipping editorial viewpoint as the occupation moved through the South. Is there any data that would indicate that the reverse happened, that during the war Northern or Northern Unionist papers flipped to the Confederate point of view? Or was it pretty much as the war got tougher for the South a one-way street, as far as losing that editorial viewpoint?

Debbie Van Tuyll: There were at the beginning of the war a handful of newspapers that were, I won't call them pro-Confederate but they were pro-Southern. By that I mean their position was, "They want to leave the Union, it's a matter of states' rights, let them out of the Union, let's have done with it and get on with our lives." As the war went on I think the positions hardened in the North, just as in some ways they did in the South, and that was, "We're in this to win." And if anything you would see Northern newspapers becoming more devoted to winning the war, more pro-Union, more "put down the rebellion."

Initially they were thinking, or some of them were thinking, "Southern states have a right to do this, this is constitutional," which was a big debate at the time. What it really comes down to is, the more lives that were lost, the more men who were wounded, the more men who were sent home with missing arms, legs and that sort of thing, the harder positions became.

Antonio Elmaleh: Jefferson Davis didn't use the press nearly as effectively in promoting the war's goals and causes as Lincoln did, I think historians would universally agree on that. Yet you write that he was surprisingly more tolerant about press freedom. Is there a disconnect here, and if so, how do you explain it?

Debbie Van Tuyll: I can't explain it, I just look at that and think, what was this man thinking? My husband and I have...

Antonio Elmaleh: Good luck.

Debbie Van Tuyll: I know. Really, my husband and I have morning time conversations over breakfast and we just marvel at what could have been going through Davis' mind. He did an interview during the war with a female reporter and he said in that interview that the press is not to be messed with, the press was to be free under the Constitution. They didn't call it the First Amendment in the Confederate Constitution, but the same words we think of as the First Amendment were in the legislative section of the Confederate Constitution. He really meant that.

I mean there were times in the war when even Robert E. Lee would be writing to whoever was secretary of war at the time, because that changed through time, saying, "Please give us a law, please get Congress to give us a law that will let us get rid of these reporters who are being so pesky covering what we're doing, because they're revealing war secrets that are aiding the Union." The response universally was, "You have power as a general to control who's with your troops. You want to get rid of them, you get rid of them, but the government is not going to violate the rights of the press." That was the consistent response from the Confederate government.

Now the military leaders, of course, had a different perspective, but the civil government, the president and the legislature were clear, "No, we're not going down that road." There was only one time in the war that Jefferson Davis ever considered censoring a newspaper and that was in the summer of 1863 when William Holden, who was editor of the Raleigh Standard in North Carolina, was believed to be leading a peace movement in North Carolina. I don't think he was actually leading it but he certainly was doing his best to be its spokesperson. Jefferson Davis inquired of the North Carolina governor, "Is there any way we can shut him down?" The governor said, "That goes against the Constitution. We're not doing that."

A mob took care of that for a while. The paper was mobbed and shut down for a month. When it started publishing again a month later it had what we would call the First Amendment emblazoned on its masthead and the attitude of, "You may mob me, you may shut me down for a while, but you're not going to shut me up permanently."

Antonio Elmaleh: Do you think that there's any truth to the notion that Jeff Davis might have sensed a propaganda advantage in maintaining this more, let's call it tolerant attitude towards press freedom than Lincoln, and by doing so cemented the argument that this is what the South is fighting for in the court of world opinion? "It's not about slavery, it's about freedom of expression. Here's an example: Lincoln jails reporters and we allow them to write what they want." Or do you think that's reading too much into the record?

Debbie Van Tuyll: No, I think that's exactly right on target. In fact, Davis said in at least a couple of pieces, "We are being true to the Constitution. We here in the South, here in the Confederacy, are living up to not just the letter of the law but the spirit of the law. Lincoln's administration and Lincoln's military shut down three hundred newspapers in the North. We haven't shut down any." Yes, he absolutely used that to his advantage to show that he was trying to do what the Confederate citizens wanted him to do. Now, he had to do that because he was doing some other things that they didn't want him to do.

The Confederacy seceded on the idea of, "We want limited government, we don't want the president to have excessive powers, we want maximum freedom, minimum government." Then the Confederacy adopted a war draft, they adopted a tax in kind, they suspended the writ of habeas corpus. There's a whole long list of state-making activities that they engaged in. Whenever Davis could come up with something, he'd say, "Well see, we aren't doing this, at least." Freedom of the press would've been one of those issues that he could use to his benefit and to the Confederacy's benefit.

Antonio Elmaleh: If it just is a matter of record it didn't really pan out too well, did it, because nobody...

Debbie Van Tuyll: No.

Antonio Elmaleh: We did a show about the international history of the war and it was very clear that the message just did not resonate in Europe, especially with the working classes. They had no interest in slavery or anything. Quite the contrary.

Debbie Van Tuyll: Absolutely.

Antonio Elmaleh: As far as you can tell he didn't exploit that argument too well.

Debbie Van Tuyll: Not as well as he could've. He tried but he didn't do it particularly well. I don't know if you've had a guest ever tell you this, but one of the interesting things that I go back to often is at the beginning of the war, when Davis is first appointed as provisional president of the Confederacy, even his wife said, "He is not the man for this job." She was right. He was not the man. This might upset some of your readers for me to say that, I'll just say as I tell my students: that's the Van Tuylll opinion, you don't have to agree with me. I don't think for a minute that Jefferson Davis was the right person to be president of the Confederacy.

I think about what would've happened if Alexander Stephens, who was the vice president of the Confederacy, had been president. It would've been very different because his perspective was much more conciliatory. He was not what you would call a fire-eater; he was a prewar Unionist, he came from the Whig Party. His perspective was, after a while, "We're losing too many men and if we keep going down this road we're going to get to the point where we can't negotiate a peace that gives us any advantages at all. We're going to be subjugated." That's one of the reasons he started leading a peace movement in Georgia in 1864. I think, gosh, what if he had been president, because he seems to me, anyway, to have better sense about things.

I think what if Robert Toombs had become president. The whole reason he didn't is because he spent his whole time in Montgomery, drunk, which is kind of who Robert Toombs was. I mean he's also one of the richest lawyers in the country. He was at that point making a hundred thousand dollars a year and that's 1860 dollars. He was a fabulously wealthy, very influential, amazing lawyer; if he didn't like alcohol as much as he did he would've made a superb president, I think. That's not what happened and so you have to go with what happened.

Antonio Elmaleh: There's some data to show that Northern papers used women correspondents, sometimes even in combat situations. Have you uncovered any similar data or information on Southern women journalists as well?

Debbie Van Tuyll: I have. There are four that I know of. We don't know their names – we know their pen names, but we don't know their actual names. In the North, correspondents were required to sign their stories with their name or their initials. That goes back to an incident that involved Sherman and a reporter for one of the New York papers. In the South, that requirement didn't exist, especially for women. To reveal who they were when they were writing publicly was considered a social faux pas.

We found four. One of them followed her son into the battlefield in Virginia, but she didn't write for long. Most of her correspondence is from Richmond as she was trying to get to the front where her son was at the battlefield; she did write from the battlefield for about a month. There's at least one who reported for a while. She wrote under the pen name Joan and she wrote for the Charleston Courier.

The others were, I'm trying to think who all they wrote for. You had Virginia, who wrote for a variety of newspapers including the *Mobile Register*, it started out as the *Register* and then merged and became the *Advertiser Register*. There were a couple of others as well; none of them wrote for very long that I've been able to find.

The one who wrote the longest I actually haven't written anything about. I stumbled across her by accident and I haven't had time to write her up yet. Her name was Luna and she was based in Virginia. I think she wrote for more than a year for some of the Richmond newspapers. I suspect she may actually be one of the other women I already have identified and have written about but I haven't been able to do that research yet to prove that, that's something that I'm still waiting to do. There were at least four in the South that we know of.

Antonio Elmaleh: I wanted to double-back to one of our first questions and ask you about the evolution, if any, of the weekly news magazine. *Harper's Weekly* and *Leslie's Illustrated* flourished in the North. Were there any Southern counterparts to those publications?

Debbie Van Tuyll: Sort of. Here in Augusta we had a newspaper called *Southern Field* and *Fireside*. It was very popular prewar, it continued to publish through most of the war, I don't remember exactly when it stopped but it was a family magazine. It covered agriculture for men, it had short stories for women, it even had content for mothers to use to teach their children reading, that sort of thing.

In terms of an illustrated magazine, there was one that existed briefly in Richmond called *Southern Illustrated News*. It began in 1863, I want to say it ran for about a year. Its illustrations weren't as plentiful as the ones in *Harper's* and they weren't as good because there just weren't the engravers in the South like there were in the North.

Prior to the Civil War, if a Southern newspaper or magazine needed an engraving to run in an issue they would buy it from *Harper's*. During the war they were cut off from *Harper's*; they had to find someone in Richmond to learn how to do engraving well enough to give them something for the newspaper.

We did have magazines down here. Those two would have been more general interest. You had a lot of literary magazines in the South as well because there was a big push prior to the Civil War and then during the Civil War to establish a Southern literature that could compete with the literature of the North. Southern writers didn't think they were being taken quite as seriously as people like Hawthorne or Melville. The only one who really was was William Gilmore Simms from South Carolina; once he came out in support of slavery he lost any support that he would've had or any interest that he would've had outside of the South.

Antonio Elmaleh: Let's shift a minute and talk about the African American press in the Civil War. Where and when did it first begin and under what conditions?

Debbie Van Tuyll: In the South?

Antonio Elmaleh: Yes.

Debbie Van Tuyll: The *New Orleans Tribune* began in New Orleans after the occupation of New Orleans in 1862. Nancy Dupont at the University of Mississippi has written extensively about that. It was a Creole newspaper so part of it was in French and part of it was in English. Again, I don't think it lasted particularly long, in part because the war ended and then there were more African American newspapers in New Orleans particularly but throughout Louisiana. It was a pretty good newspaper. I haven't looked at it as closely as Nancy has but from what she says they did a pretty good job of representing the perspective of their audience, which was the Creole audience in Louisiana.

Antonio Elmaleh: Who were their audiences? It must have been a fairly limited audience. Did it reach out to white audiences, or was it strictly confined to upper or middle-class blacks? In other words, who were they actually talking to?

Debbie Van Tuyll: Well, that was certainly true in New Orleans. Because of the Creole population you did have middle-class and very wealthy

African Americans. There were African-American professionals in New Orleans – not all of them could practice their professions, of course.

I know a couple of cases of African Americans who went to, say, France to study medicine, and they couldn't technically be a doctor in New Orleans but they could doctor within the African American community. No one was going to stop them from doing that. They made pretty good money, at least enough for middle-class existence. That's the audience of that newspaper, the middle-class and upper-class African Americans or mixed-race people of New Orleans and the rest of Louisiana, but mostly centered there in New Orleans where the paper was based.

Antonio Elmaleh: There was not much in other areas of the South.

Debbie Van Tuyll: No, that was the only one.

Antonio Elmaleh: The only one?

Debbie Van Tuyll: That was the only one.

Antonio Elmaleh: Okay. As a follow-up, were these papers afforded protection from the Union troops during the occupation or were they left to their own devices, as in much of Reconstruction later?

Debbie Van Tuyll: Well, if you're thinking about the New Orleans Tribune, it's going to publish from a Unionist perspective, or it did anyway. I said that like that was a predetermined situation and it wasn't necessarily, but this one was Unionist, it was publishing stuff that the Union wasn't going to object to because it was publishing pro-Union articles, pro-Union editorials, that sort of thing. There really wasn't much of an opportunity for it to get in trouble because it was doing what the Union occupiers wanted it to do.

Now, for some of the other newspapers, for the white audiences, newspapers like the *New Orleans Times-Picayune*, that one became a shell of itself during the Civil War. Before the war it was one of the top news-papers in the South. It was hefty, it had amazing reporting, it had great editing. It had been very effective in reporting the Mexican-American

War, in fact it pioneered some war reporting methods during the Mexican-American War. It became virtually nothing during the occupation because they couldn't publish information that would upset the Union commanders.

They referred to Benjamin Butler, who was the military governor, I guess you would call him, of New Orleans, as Beast Butler. There were a couple of reasons for that. One was what was referred to as his General Order Number Twenty-Eight. He got tired of the women of New Orleans pouring the contents of their chamber pots out their windows on top of his officers and saying nasty things to his officers in the streets, so he issued an order saying any woman who did any of those things would be treated as if she were a lady of the streets and arrested. That earned him the nickname Beast Butler.

He took the same hard line towards newspapers. If the newspaper published anything that was pro-Southern, then that newspaper was shut down. Now, that's not to say that there weren't newspapers that would publish news from the South, they did publish news from the South, but it wasn't anything that was going to be controversial. They would even publish some war news, but it would be more like this battle happened, there were these troops involved, but the papers never took a side. It was very objective, "This happened and that's all we're going to say about it," because that was really all they could say about it safely.

Antonio Elmaleh: Just to close the loop on old Beast Butler, I think it's interesting to note that given the vitriol and the violent reaction, people were calling it the most grievous miscalculation of justice known to civilized man. The Southern press went bonkers.

Debbie Van Tuyll: They did.

Antonio Elmaleh: Flipping it around, it seems as if it worked.

Debbie Van Tuyll: It did.

Antonio Elmaleh: There were no more instances of chamber pot dumping on passing by Union officers.

Debbie Van Tuyll: That's right.

Antonio Elmaleh: I guess he figured out a way to make it work for his needs, that's for sure.

Debbie Van Tuyll: He was a pretty smart fellow.

Antonio Elmaleh: He was.

Debbie Van Tuyll: Maybe not a nice man, but pretty smart.

Antonio Elmaleh: Not a great general either. Given the South's poor transportation and communication systems during the war, and especially as it got turned worse for the South, how did papers get circulated, if at all, beyond their immediate vicinities?

Debbie Van Tuyll: There were a couple of different ways. One was rail. You're right, we didn't have the same level of rail system in the South that existed in the North. What would happen is they would go as far as the railroads could go and then they would be taken on wagons to other places in the South. The other thing that the South did the North did, too, and it helped circulation not of the physical newspaper but of the content of the newspaper: they used what they called an exchange system. I could mail one copy of my newspaper to any other newspaper in the South for free, then that newspaper was free to take anything out of my newspaper they wanted to use and use it in theirs. The exchange system helped get information circulated through the South. That's the system that existed throughout the country before the war.

Between rail, wagons, and then the mail system – John Reagan, who was this postmaster general of the Confederacy, he actually did a pretty good job or as good a job as could be done with the mail system in the South. Now, of course you're going to have disruptions in areas where there's fighting over the Union occupation, mail was slow and it wasn't always reliable, but it actually worked better than you would anticipate in the South.

Antonio Elmaleh: Well, the poor postal service just doesn't get any respect. It's been here since Ben Franklin. We assume that a letter gets dropped in a box and it arrives, we absolutely assume and yet it's under this attack. I'm just impressed that given all the shortcomings and the shortages that the South experienced over the course of the war that the postal system remained an effective, reasonably effective way to distribute information.

Debbie Van Tuyll: In areas where there wasn't any fighting, it was much more effective than in areas where there was fighting, of course.

Antonio Elmaleh: In an earlier show, we touched on the use of barter in Northern papers to pay for subscriptions. Given the South's persistent shortages of most goods, mostly from the Union blockade but also increased military occupation, and factoring in the shaky fluctuation of Confederate currency especially as the war turned worse, was barter used in any great frequency? Or did papers simply become subsidized by their publishers and gave up on being paid for?

Debbie Van Tuyll: A little of both. Barter was very widely used. There was one editor who wrote, I think in Sandersville, Georgia, he would trade newspaper subscriptions for anything a man could eat, wear, or burn, meaning firewood; if it was food, if it was clothing, if it was firewood, and you brought something in, then you could get a paper. I've read instances of people bringing in chickens and trading those for newspapers, bringing in strawberries or peaches and trading them for newspapers. Yes, bartering was a huge way to pay for newspapers.

They also stopped using what they call the credit system in the South, where you would order the newspaper and then pay for it later. They learned pretty quickly that that wasn't going to work. That was when the bartering really started, I would suspect, when people realized they didn't have the money. Inflation in the Confederacy reached one thousand percent at one point. Money was worth virtually nothing, chickens you could at least fry them up and eat. That was something with some tangible value.

Antonio Elmaleh: What strikes me is the priority given to newspapers. You have a scarce list of things that you can afford, and you're trading things that you could eat for the newspaper. I mean, correct me if I'm wrong, but it sounds to me like people consider the paper to be vital.

Debbie Van Tuyll: I think that's absolutely true. Now this is a Northern person, but Oliver Wendell Holmes, who was a Supreme Court Justice, wrote a little bit later but I think it still applies then, that newspapers were one of the absolutely essentials of life. I think that was true particularly during the war period because of the mail disruptions that would occur between battlefield and home.

With the illiteracy rates, you might send your husband, your son, your brother, off to war and not hear anything through letters. You would rely on lists of casualties in the newspapers to tell you something, or a story about your family member's unit that might be in the newspaper. If it was a local unit then often there was someone in that unit who would write back to the newspaper and function as a correspondent. You might get your news that way.

There was a definite increase in demand for newspapers during the Civil War. The Augusta Chronicle, for example, reported it was getting orders of seventy-five new subscriptions a week, which was just a tremendous increase. The newspapers that continued to print did see increases in circulation. They also saw increases in prices for their raw materials, it's not like they were making any money.

I think what impresses me the most is that these editors were willing to continue publishing when they were having to spend their personal fortunes to see that they continued to publish. They believed in the public service motivation of the press that I don't think exists so much anymore. Again, that's Van Tuyll opinion, you don't have to agree.

Antonio Elmaleh: The news from the fronts pointed to an increasing likelihood of Southern defeat. In your research, did you see any evidence of papers painting a continually rosy picture? Did the government clamp down on things like publishing casualty lists like the Germans and the Japanese did in World War II? If you were living in those two countries, you just assumed that victory came yesterday. Did you see any evidence of editorial manipulation of the actual outcomes of military news to just keep the morale up, or did editors just generally try to stay as close to the facts as they could? Or is there no way to generalize on it?

Debbie Van Tuyll: What I would say is you saw a range of things. You had a lot of editors who would put a rosy spin on battlefront news. I'm thinking particularly of The Fayetteville Observer. It was a weekly but it was a very important weekly in North Carolina and its editor would say, "Even though we lost this battle, we're winning the war." Well, but you reported we lost the battles, how can we still be winning the war?

Antonio Elmaleh: Sounds like LBJ.

Debbie Van Tuyll: Exactly. You also had a peace movement in the South. Those editors were reporting, "Look, guys, we keep losing battles, we keep losing men, we've got to negotiate peace now before we get so broken down that we have no negotiating room." This was the same message that Alexander Stephens was sending out, in fact he had a whole network of newspapers here in Georgia that supported him and they were allowed to report that. Toward the end of 1864, early 1855, I think a military police officer actually did go see the editor of The Augusta Chronicle. He said, "Come on guys, you've got to stop printing this." The editor's response was to throw the military police officer out and he said, "I'm going to publish what I want, you arrest me if you want to, that's the only way you're going to stop me from publishing." Nobody came to arrest him so he kept publishing.

You had a range. I would say most editors would have gone more toward, "We've got to keep public morale up in order to keep support for the war going, let's paint this looking a little bit better than it really does." Which is one of the reasons I particularly have respect for those editors like Nathan Morris who was the editor of The Augusta Chronicle, or William Holden who was editor of The Weekly Standard in Raleigh, who I feel were telling the people the truth and had a clear view of where this war was going and what was going to happen if this outfit didn't negotiate a peace earlier than they did.

Antonio Elmaleh: I'm pretty convinced Lincoln and Seward felt that publishing casualty lists in papers was a powerful, albeit dark way to stiffen backbone. It didn't always work, and in fact in the first two years of the war it almost killed the entire war effort especially as the causalities grew and the battles stretched on. Did Southern papers publish accurate casualty lists as well, or was the fact that they knew going in that that numerical superiority in men in the Union would ultimately force the issue if the Union decided to keep fighting?

Debbie Van Tuyll: The best I can tell you is as far as I know the lists that were published were accurate. I know the reporters in the field themselves felt very much that one of their chief duties was to get ahold of those casualty lists and get them back to their newspapers as soon as possible. I know more about what the reporters did, and that was they tried to be as accurate and as complete as they could.

Now, I've never seen any evidence, probably because the editors wouldn't talk about it, of editing done once the lists got back to newspapers. I just can't answer that, I don't know. I would suspect that there might've been times that editors decided, "You know what, we can't publish this," and they would put something aside. I know the correspondents did their level best to get every piece of information they could about casualties. There may have been a disconnect between what the reporters were doing and what the editors were doing; I can't speak to that because I haven't seen any evidence.

Antonio Elmaleh: In other words, you think that there was a certain amount of rose-colored glasses going on?

Debbie Van Tuyll: No doubt.

Antonio Elmaleh: In the evolution of American journalism, what does the Confederate press experience show you about its importance, its place, in the evolution of the American press in general?

Debbie Van Tuyll: I think, and this may sound a little schmaltzy, the second part of it: one, it shows us war is not good for journalism, which we probably could've already known for sure, but it's good to actually get the data to back up our assumptions. With more than half of newspapers going out of business during the war, that tells you the conditions were such that they were not conducive to support the newspaper industry. War and the press don't mix. It's just not a good thing for a press to be in a country that's at war in a domestic war.

I think the other thing it shows is that the public service model of journalism that we associate more with Adolph Ochs and The *New York Times* in the 20th century actually existed long before that. If you read some of the newspapers at the period, when editors are saying why they're continuing to publish it's almost always because they don't know what else to do but publish. They know that their community needs news, they are the ones who have the facilities to give them even a little bit of news – I mean some newspapers are reduced down to the size of half of a sheet of paper by the time the war was nearing the end because paper was so scarce, but they still put out at least a half sheet so that the public would have some news.

I think about the newspaper in Columbia, South Carolina, for example, after Sherman's men went through Columbia and they really did a number on Columbia. As soon as the newspaper staff could get a printing press put back together again they were publishing a half sheet of paper because they knew the public needed to know certain information, and they risked their lives staying in Columbia when Sherman's men came through so they could continue to publish. I think that sacrifice speaks to the best nature of journalism.

I'm sure that's true of the Northern press as well, but my area of expertise is the Southern press. I think if we look at that and we were to use the work Civil War era journalists did as a role model for today, we might have a better press than we have today. That's a little schmaltzy, I know, standing up for the public's right to know. And the press being a watchdog on government doesn't ring particularly true to some people today. But I'm, for one, convinced that's the reason the press should exist in a democracy. And the Confederate press did that to the best of its ability under the circumstances it was publishing in.

Antonio Elmaleh: You talk about how war is not good for the press but yet so many areas of American life were transformed radically, one might say completely, by the war: all sorts of institutions, military and commercial, industrial, social, etc.. Would you agree the war improved the quality of journalism in spite of the draconian conditions? Did the war improve not just Northern but Southern journalism?

Debbie Van Tuyll: I absolutely do agree. In 1863 the South created a really high-quality wire service and the superintendent of that wire service was a man by the name of John Thrasher. John Thrasher created a code of ethics for his reporters, one of which required objective reporting. He created a news network, he created a new definition of what constitutes news, he created rules of engagement with commanding officers. What can you ask, what should you ask, when should you ask it? All of that sort of thing.

I think the work that Thrasher did in terms of professionalizing the Confederate press stuck, even after the war. The effect on journalism, on what few newspapers were left, was to make them much more aware that how they present the news will have an impact on how it's perceived. You had personal journalism and very political journalism in the South prior to the war; you still have that to a fairly large degree after the war but it's starting to change, you're starting to see that professionalism that begins in the war take hold, take root, and start to reach fruition as you get to the end of the 19th and into the early 20th century. Yes, absolutely, it had a definite professionalizing impact on the press.

Antonio Elmaleh: I wanted to double-back to my question about weekly news magazines and ask you if political satire in the form of cartoons was as popular and as prevalent in the Southern press as it became in the Northern press. Everything was fair game for vitriol and ridicule and sheer debasement of everything sacred and important. Did you see any evidence of that, or was it limited by the fact that there were no outlets to begin with?

Debbie Van Tuyll: Well, because there weren't outlets for getting the engravings done, you didn't see the visual satires like you would see in the

Northern illustrated press. You did get written satires. You also sometimes got a very definite statement of, "Y'know, if we're going to have to put up with this despot Jefferson Davis we might as well be under Lincoln." Which just shocks you when you read that the first time. I think what we forget is the South was not a monolith. Southerners were not monolithic in their thinking, they enjoyed a good satire just as well as anyone else. The satire in the South would've been of Jefferson Davis just as well as it might've been of Abraham Lincoln. Some of the general's team were occasionally the subjects of satire, Braxton Bragg comes to mind, for one.

Antonio Elmaleh: Well deserved.

Debbie Van Tuyll: Well deserved, well deserved, don't get me started on Braxton Bragg, that's what my husband and I talk about at breakfast.

Antonio Elmaleh: We could have a little discussion about him, there's no shortage of people to single out for incompetence in this ...

Debbie Van Tuyll: That's right.

Antonio Elmaleh: You mentioned the monolithic South, which is something very top of mind for me, this branding of the two sides as either this or that and deliberately not either, incapable or unwilling to acknowledge the subtleties, the differences, all the things that make us human in our teaching of this history. Do you find a resistance to that even in the work you're doing with the press, that attitude of, "Well, they were all secessionists or they were all typical Southern whatever…"?

Debbie Van Tuyll: I do, and you'll be probably not surprised to hear that where I get that the most. I do a lot of public speaking with groups like the Sons of Confederate Veterans; they really don't want to hear that. I was at one recently and when I started talking about the Peace Movement and the Southerners who would say, "If we've got to have a tyrant as our leader we might as well have Abraham Lincoln, why are we fighting this war if we've got someone like Jefferson Davis in office?" I just got looks from them. I said, "Okay, this is not going to go over well, I'm going to have to change the subject here."

By the same token, I've been to other groups where they're nodding with me. I was in an area where you would anticipate that you would be getting that monolithic South perspective, but they were educated enough about what happened to say, "You're right, not everybody thought the same." It's amazing to me that people who have such interest in the Civil War have never picked up on the fact that not everyone in the war on either side thought the same.

Antonio Elmaleh: I'm not even sure this is a question, I'm going to put it out anyway because it might just be a matter of a little more discussion. When you look at the way the war changed so many different things in this society, and when we look at the journalism piece of it, how do you separate out the nature of the arguments for secession or supporting slavery from the persuasiveness of the actual journalist? In other words, propaganda. People spoke with incredible admiration of Leni Riefenstahl and the quality of her work, forgetting about the message, "Oh, let's just disregard the fact that she's promoting Nazism and let's just look at how she did it." Do you find it difficult to hold that line between the morality of the causes these papers might've been arguing about versus the art of the argument or the quality of the reporting? Does that make sense to you?

Debbie Van Tuyll: It does. There's a word that historians use called "presentism." I don't know if you've heard that or not.

Antonio Elmaleh: No, I haven't.

Debbie Van Tuyll: When we use that, we're saying you cannot use 20th century, 21st century perspectives to judge people who lived in an earlier timeline. In the South there was slavery and there was a lot of newspaper support for the institution of slavery. In fact, there were those who wrote even at that time that the Southern press was benighted and behind the times because nothing in a slave society can be good. And therefore, simply because the journalism of the South is journalism of a slave society, it can't be good journalism. That was Hinton Helper's perspective in his book *The Impending Crisis.*

I can't accept that. I can accept that journalism is different in a slave society. In fact, one of the pieces that I've written delves into that. It looked at the effect of slavery on journalism. The effect of slavery on journalism was to create a much more libertarian society than what you might have in other places. In other words, people were much more devoted to free speech, free press, than they might've been in other parts of the country because they saw daily what happens to someone who lost their freedom, and that made them all that much more jealous of guarding their own freedom, even freedom of speech and freedom of press. I think the thing we have to keep in mind is that slavery was an evil system, there's no question about that, nobody should be owned by anyone, that's beyond question. But that's not how people at the time saw it. They saw it a different way.

Antonio Elmaleh: It was actually legal then.

Debbie Van Tuyll: It was. They thought it was ordained by the Bible. I mean, they had ministers telling them it was okay. They had sermons, they had devotion books telling them slavery is something that is ordained by God. They believed that. That's going to create a particular society. You have to recreate as a historian what that society was, not what you might want it to be, not what you might think it should be based on your beliefs today, but what it was. My sense is you cannot bring a presentist attitude to historical studies and do a good job as a historian. You've got to take the people at the time as they were and say, "Well, I may not look at this the way you look at it, but this is the way you look at it and this is how it affected this world at the time that you lived."

That's what I try to do, is look at slavery and to say, "Fine, okay, I may not think slavery is a good thing." I have an African American son-in-law; clearly I have some pretty strong feelings about how African Americans ought to be treated. I love my son-in-law and I don't think of him as being anything different to my daughter in his value or worth to the world. People at that time would've been absolutely appalled if I had said such a thing. That's fine, they can be appalled, I understand that. I understand where we stand today. But I am going to write it up as they were. I'm not going to impose my views on them, I have to understand their views and interpret those views for today's readers. I don't know if that makes sense, but that's the way I look at that.

Antonio Elmaleh: Absolutely. That reminds me of the time I spent studying cultural anthropology in college, albeit for the twelve minutes I was in college. That's another story. The first thing they say is, "You've just got to take off all assumptions and park them at my door. When you go into this other culture you've got to have as close to a blank slate mind as you can possibly summon. Absorb everything as if you're seeing everything for the first time in order to have some ability to analyze what you're seeing." I mean, your answer makes complete sense to me even though the message may be very different than the messenger in terms of how history treats both of them.

Debbie Van Tuyll: Absolutely.

Antonio Elmaleh: The other thing I wanted to ask – and it's a bit far afield, but I'll just ask it – I'm fascinated with how the narrative of the war shifted over time from secession to abolition and freedom of the slaves. Then Reconstruction, to legally and technically implement those laws and social changes. Then that was watered down and essentially eradicated. Then we had a hundred plus years of Jim Crow. If this is a too far afield of your expertise I understand, but do you have any sense of how the Southern press would have or dealt with this narrative of Reconstruction once the war is over and the South has lost? Suddenly you have African American legislators, you have farmers owning the land that once they worked as slaves. And the white majority just couldn't bear it and started to take the law into their own hands. Do you have any sense of how the Southern press may have played into the shifting of that narrative over time?

Debbie Van Tuyll: This still wasn't monolithic because you certainly had those newspapers that said, "It's imperative we keep the black man in his place. We can't believe we've got black legislators, we can't believe we've got black congressmen, we've got to stop this. We've got to make this a white man's world again." Then you had other newspapers whose perspective was, "Our region was decimated by this war. All that political stuff, let's just put that aside and let's focus on rebuilding and gaining some prosperity so that our people can feed their children."

You have again a range of responses to that. You even had some who were leaning more towards reconciliation, which is what Reconstruction was supposed to do, not calling for an integrated society but a live and let live society. It would've been more of a separate but equal, but that would've been the far end of the reconciliatory approach in that period. I mean, you get into the late 1890s and you have the first separate but equal lawsuit for education here in Augusta, the Ware High School case. There was an African American high school, and the African American community sued for the same support for it that the white high schools had. The Supreme Court essentially said, they didn't use these terms, but they basically said, "Well, if this is a public high school and it's a public high school of Richmond County, which is where Augusta is, then there should be similar funding, similar resources available and that sort of thing." Now, it didn't happen that way. It's like Jackson and the decision saying you can't remove the Indians, "Well, I have the army and you don't, try and stop me" thing.

There were certainly those attitudes at the time, of reconciliation, that were basically live and let live. Then there have always been the, I guess you'd call fire-eaters, that's what we called them in the lead up to the war, those who are hell-bent for leather saying, "We've got to keep this black man in his place." I think that's one of the things that makes the South so interesting is there's nothing about it that is or ever has been monolithic. It's just a very interesting place with all kinds of interesting characters, different points of view. Somehow or another it still continues to function, even now. I mean, who do you think we are?

Antonio Elmaleh: I don't think I'll touch that!

Debbie Van Tuyll: I know, I know. I think the last presidential election speaks to that. I'm getting too much into the present time now.

Antonio Elmaleh: That's another show, anyway. Do you have any publications or upcoming books that you'd like to tell our listeners before we close it up?

Debbie Van Tuyll: I think if they're interested in the overall history of the Confederate press they might want to look at my book. The publisher entitled it *The Confederate Press in The Crucible of the American Civil War.*

Antonio Elmaleh: Did that fit on the cover?

Debbie Van Tuyll: That's what it says on the cover. What I wanted to call it was *The Third Stripe.* The reason for that is the Confederate national flag, not the battle flag with the stars and bars, but the one with the three stripes and then a blue seal with the stars in it: The first stripe stood for the country, the Confederacy. It was red. The white stripe stood for the church. The last red stripe stood for the press. There's never been a national flag anywhere that recognizes the press as so important that it should be recognized as one of the chief institutions in a country. That's why I wanted to call it *The Third Stripe,* but I couldn't convince the publisher of that.

Then, if they want to know about the correspondents themselves, there's a book that Pat McNeely, Henry Schulte, and I did called *Knights of the Quill.* It is chapter-length biographies of all of the Confederate correspondents that we could identify. I've got chapters in it on the women reporters that you mentioned earlier, not by name because we couldn't find names, but I looked at their correspondence and surmised a biography based on what they were reporting.

I think these would be the two that would be of the most general interest. The third one I'll mention, which is probably more than you want, there's one that I did with Nancy Dupont and Joe Hayden, *Journalism in the Fallen Confederacy,* that looks at newspapers in the occupied areas. That's a companion to *The Confederate Press in the Crucible of the American Civil War.* You've got the free Confederate press and then you've got the occupied Confederate press. Readers will get a sense of the range of experiences if they look at those two.

Antonio Elmaleh: If you could leave our listeners with one overriding thought about Southern journalism during the Civil War, what would it be? What is its legacy?

Debbie Van Tuyll: They should be absolutely impressed that there was even a single newspaper published in the South much less, I think, by the end of the war there were two hundred or so still publishing. That was a feat beyond imagining, given the situation that they were in with the lack of manufacturing, the lack of raw materials, the lack of correspondents to put in the field. You had hundreds of correspondents in Northern newspapers; Southern newspapers didn't have the money to do that. They had to rely on soldier correspondents and a handful of professional correspondents.

I think their overarching achievement was to continue to publish, continuing to get news of some form into the hands of at least some of the citizens. You have just an amazing effort —it's like what you've seen on TV, some people see their kids about to be hit by a car and there's this superhuman surge of strength that lets them stop the car before it gets to their kid. In a sense I think that's what we're seeing in the Confederate press: it's a superhuman effort to get news out. There's a devotion to the public and a devotion to news and a devotion to the profession. I think that's the legacy, along with what's going on in the North. It's where journalism starts professionalizing.

Some people might argue today that, well, we certainly lost that idea, but we at least had it for a while if you take that perspective. If you look back into the 20th century you're going to see the legacy in investigative reporting and advocacy reporting.

A fellow that the Charleston Courier referred to as "The Prince of War Correspondents" was the only war correspondent for Georgia. His name was Peter Alexander. In 1862, after Antietam, he was looking at the Confederate Army and he saw men without shoes, men without blankets, men without tents who were about to go into a Maryland winter. Maryland gets cold in the winter. He wrote a story saying, "The Confederate government can't equip our men. The Confederate people are going to have to do it." That story ran all across the South and raised thousands of dollars, got women knitting socks, just created an entire black market war industry off the books, so to speak, to supply the men in Virginia with what they needed for that winter.

That advocacy reporting is reporting at its best, I think, where you identify a social evil and then help find a solution for it. I think that is really the legacy: the professionalism, the advocacy, telling the truth and letting the pieces fall where they may.

Antonio Elmaleh: Thank you for that. Well, I'm sorry to say we've run out of time.

Debbie Van Tuyll: It was a pleasure talking to you.

Antonio Elmaleh: I want to thank you Professor Debbie Van Tuyll, for giving us a unique and fresh perspective on uncovering the experience of the Southern press in the Civil War. Thank you so much.

Debbie Van Tuyll: Thank you, I enjoyed it.

Antonio Elmaleh: To my listeners, thank you for spending this time with me covering the Civil War. Until next time, stay safe and do good.

SIX

UNCOVERING PORNOGRAPHY DURING THE CIVIL WAR, PARTS I & II

Guest: Dr. Judith Giesberg

PART I

Antonio Elmaleh: Greetings everyone and welcome to another segment of *Uncovering the Civil War*. My guest today is Professor Judith Giesberg. Judy Giesberg is a professor of history at Villanova University and is the author of five books, her latest being *Sex and the Civil War: Soldiers, Pornography, and the Making of Modern Morality*, published in 2017. Currently she is curating an exhibit on Frederick Douglass and W.E.B. Du Bois for the Philadelphia Library, and she is beginning work on her next project, a study of the 1870 census. Welcome, Judy.

Judith Giesberg: Thank you for having me, Antonio.

Antonio Elmaleh: My pleasure. I'm very excited about today's podcast because as I was doing my research for our discussion today and reading Judy's book, I realized that, like me, many of our listeners might not have any idea of the role pornography played in our Civil

War. Today we will be discussing topics such as how our federal government attempted to assert governmental authority over private sexual relations, how pornography caused a crisis in gender identity, the popularity of pornography before, during, and after the Civil War, how pornography impacted troops on the battlefield and helped forge strong bonds between them, and how authors of pornographic material went to great lengths to sidestep censorship. We will discuss other topics as well.

I'd like to begin by setting the context for our discussion, so please bear with me a minute. In January 1865 the federal government passed Senate Resolution 390 mandating changes in the postal laws and regulations. Understanding this legislation illustrates the nation's attempt to assert its governmental authority over private sexual relations, especially through the lens of the distribution and active appreciation of so-called obscene, pornographic materials, into the camp life of the United States Army during the Civil War.

In your book you make the case that the Civil War caused a crisis in gender identity, shaking the whole idea of what it meant to be a man and a woman and notions of virility and womanhood, and at the same time it had the effect of fortifying preexisting power relationships between the sexes and helped sustain them in the practice of maintaining gender hierarchy.

How did I do?

Judith Giesberg: That was fantastic.

Antonio Elmaleh: Okay, off to the races we go then. In 1748 Fanny Hill and the Memoirs of a Country Gentleman was first published; it is still in print today, two hundred and seventy years later. In 1842 the first listing of the word pornography was inserted into the Oxford English Dictionary. Could you briefly trace other events that illustrated the growing popularity of pornography prior to the Civil War?

Judith Giesberg: Sure. Those are two good touchpoints for us to start with, and then there are back and forth conversations between the United States, Great Britain, and France in the period in the 1840s and early 1850s about matters of erotic materials being traded or imported back forth between these countries.

The legislation mentioned at the start of the show that was passed by Congress in 1865 is one of a series of laws that were passed at this time. The first couple were passed in the early 1840s and 1850s. They had to do with the importation of the materials here in the United States and they were snuck into a customs law in the United States in 1842, sort of tucked in there. In Great Britain and France, there are similar measures underway at the same time.

The differences between the ways these measures are put into place in these three countries are also very interesting, but for starters it's important to understand what's happening in the antebellum period were all three countries are really trying to get a sense of where this stuff is coming from, how they might prevent it from reaching a mass audience, and what were the best ways to root it out at its source.

Of course, it's probably no surprise that when the United States tries to prohibit erotic materials from being imported into the country, this is where we begin to refer to items as French postcards or French playing cards or French condoms; they are associated with a foreign import. But when United States tries to prohibit the stuff from coming into the country, what in fact happens is they set the foundation for the flourishing of a domestic manufacturing community of people who manufacture the stuff domestically.

In the last few years before the Civil War begins, there is this back and forth between Great Britain, France, and United States as American lawmakers attempt to prohibit importation, and then there are lots of entrepreneurs who see this as an opportunity and really jump on it and begin to produce the stuff domestically. Mostly the stuff is the same. There aren't any copyright laws protecting these erotic materials; books like *Fanny Hill* are not protected by any copyright. So, there are lots of book manufacturers in New York City, for instance, who simply start to produce the same thing under different labels here domestically to avoid the customs prohibitions against the importation of the stuff.

Antonio Elmaleh: Well, let's advance it to the Civil War and the implications of our setting the scene. Let's explore your statement that American pornography was increasingly associated with soldiery. How did anti-pornography legislation seek to preserve and protect the concept of manhood and virility as well as the ability of soldiers to fight with strength and courage?

Judith Giesberg: One of the first ways I'd answer that question, I think, has a lot to do with the timing. There was this back and forth going on and there was this new federal interest, though short-lived and not really effective in understanding this as a problem, that preceded the war. And then of course the war begins at the precise moment when there's a birth of domestic manufacturing, a group of domestic manufacturers who were eager to find new ways of distributing this stuff, and when the war comes there's a high concentration of young men in army camps throughout the country.

And because of expedited delivery of mail made possible by railroads and other technological and organizational innovations, it's easy to get to these men wherever they happen to be concentrated in large numbers. The material is out there and the manufacturers and distributors of the stuff take advantage of the opportunities opened by the war. And then there are army whistleblowers, people who complain about the stuff. There are editorials written in the newspaper expressing concern about what kinds of morals these men develop or what kinds of immoralities they find in army camp. Those kinds of concerns are raised from the very beginning of the war.

I think the last little piece that we should keep in mind when we think about how this stuff became associated with soldiers has to do with the unique demographics of the US Army. The US Army soldiers, in comparison to the Confederate Army, are statistically-speaking slightly younger than their counterparts in the Confederate Army. They're less likely to be married than their Confederate counterparts. In song sheets, popular songs and poems and things like that, these men are often referred to as "sons." Certainly the way Congressmen talk about them when they're considering this legislation is that they're thinking of them as younger men.

What are the kinds of influences these younger men are coming into contact within the army, and significantly, certainly by 1865, what sorts of men are these boys becoming and what sort of men are they going to welcome back after the war? I think this worry heightens the connections between the stuff and the US Army. The truth of the matter is the stuff was quite accessible in the army. It wasn't an exaggeration at all to say that pornography was a problem that had affected the US Army; the stuff was widely available in camp.

Antonio Elmaleh: But also, let's remember that the way the US Army and to a great extent the Confederate Army was actually organized was around counties, regiments formed by people from the same town, from the same county, almost hermetically sealed from the outside world. These soldiers, these boys if you will, are leaving home and traveling hundreds of miles and, in the case of when they go on campaign, fighting people with strange accents that they can barely recognize what they're saying. The net effect is you've got essentially totally innocent young men being exposed to life for the very first time in their lives.

I just want to make the point that the way young men came to these camps had to be an incredible culture shock for them.

Judith Giesberg: I like to think of camps as these moving cities. There are so many men gathered together from so many different places. Of course, as you say, these regiments were often locally raised and you served in a company of men who you knew very well, but once you became a part of the Army you were mixed in with others. Certainly, as the war progressed, the local nature of this organization broke down and you came in contact with men from many different places in the country, as you said, people with whom you didn't share common prewar experiences, that you might not be able to understand. You didn't share their opinions, their politics, yet you served in the same army with them.

Interestingly, what I found in the court martial records is that these erotic materials actually helped to sometimes become a common language between men from different regiments and certainly from different classes, different regions of the country. They quickly shared bawdy songs and playing cards. Things like that helped to integrate or to overcome some of these differences among the men. As long as the men who circulated the materials or who shared the materials followed the informal rules among men in camp, exchanging materials could help to overcome some of those differences that you described that men had to face when they got into army camp.

It had to be an eye-opening experience. We know, of course, depending on what parts of the country the young men were recruited from and wound up in the army, they had fewer defenses against diseases and other sorts of things that you should be prepared for when you come in contact with large numbers of people. I think the same thing might be said for access to these erotic materials. Men who lived in rural areas didn't have access previously to the stuff that was being published so widely and circulated so well out of places like New York. Once they got in the Army, they could have access to it much easier than they could have before.

Antonio Elmaleh: I think what I hear you saying is it had an unintended effect of also forging bonds between officers and enlisted men as well. The impulse to eliminate pornography was commonly explained by the people leading that charge was that it undermined a soldier's morale and spirit to fight; they maintained it would lead to the Union losing the war. Paradoxically, no one questioned how the war's violence and savagery would also impact the soldier. It leads to a disconnect between the government and the Army. Can you elaborate on that?

Judith Giesberg: Yes. Some of this is related to this notion in the ascendancy in the second half of the war, certainly after 1863, that the Union Army is fighting on the side of good. We talk often about the symbolic significances of the twin victories in July of 1863 and how many people on the Union side saw those victories as a sign that the Union Army had the endorsement of God, that they were moral. This is, of course, all tied to emancipation.; people saw that as a sign that the Union's war aims were moral. Certainly by 1865 the Union government could see itself from that perspective as well, that it was really morally righteous, that this campaign and the state that emerged from it was morally invigorated. And then it was also charged with thinking about what this new morally energized state would look like.

That translated into a conversation about the men and what was happening to them in the war. Their concerns were not about what they had seen on the battlefields, and that's because these Congressmen – some of them had seen the destruction in the battlefield but many of them were once removed from it and were really legislating for men who were currently in the fight – for them, they believed that this anti-pornography legislation that they passed early in '65 was part and parcel of their reimagining this new morally invigorated state.

As much as we think of this war as different from many of our other American wars, there certainly was a disconnect between what people in Northern home front at least believed what was going on and what soldiers were seeing. Soldiers were careful about not always revealing all the darkness and everything that they were experiencing in the war, so there was a disconnect between what civilians thought about the destructiveness and the violence of this war and what soldiers were actually experiencing. So, it's not a terrible surprise that Congressmen thought an important thing to consider in the last year of the war was the porn and not the violence.

Of course, soldiers when they first come back from the war are quiet. They don't actually tell their stories right away either. It takes some time after the war for soldiers to really put down on paper what they experienced. And only at that time are we really going to begin to get a fuller picture of just what this violence meant to that generation and how much it affected them.

Antonio Elmaleh: And I think it's also good to remind listeners that the notion of PTS syndrome, it didn't exist medically or socially. There was no psychological counseling. Soldiers showing severe impacts of the war had either what they called "nostalgia" or "soldier's heart." In

World War I it was shell shock, in World War II it was combat fatigue. But there were no platforms encouraging soldiers to speak about the violence and the savagery they experienced. No wonder there wasn't much talk about its impact on these poor innocents over the course of the conflict.

Judith Giesberg: Right.

Antonio Elmaleh: You assert the governmental censorship efforts had the unintended effect of forging bonds between officers and enlisted men in the Army. Why?

Judith Giesberg: As you read the court martial records, there are clearly ways in which these military men are talking to one another and the way that erotic materials are described or mentioned that is very different from the way lawmakers talk about it. Really, what I found in the court martial records is there was widespread sharing of these materials. Court martial records suggest that officers would share it with enlisted men, that enlisted men would share it with one another. There was an expectation as you described it earlier, a democratizing effect that occurs because the exchange of this stuff creates its own rules.

Enlisted men believed, and we see this in the court martial records, they should have access to the stuff. They should be able to monitor and watch each other and what they were reading and who they were spending time with. There was this whole culture of seeing and being seen that, in these court martial records, was more important than what men were reading or what kinds of cards they were playing with. As long as people followed those rules military men were fine; if they broke those rules or if they turned out to not be good soldiers then they found themselves in trouble within the military.

So if you're getting court martialed in the military and they're talking about the porn, that's not the reason you're in trouble. You're in trouble because you broke those informal rules, you didn't adhere to the rules that said your enlisted men should be able to weigh in on what you were doing in your private time, that they should be able to watch you; those rules you didn't want to break. You didn't want to be a bad soldier either, as an enlisted man or an officer. If they were a bad soldier and broke other rules, didn't respect the enlisted men in the ranks or did other things that violated these informal codes of military relations, then they got into trouble.

But they didn't get in trouble because they read Fanny Hill and they didn't get into trouble because they showed pictures of naked women or stereographs or those kinds of things. But if they didn't respect the demands or the expectations of enlisted men to also be able to access this stuff and to be able to determine with whom they shared it, then they could get in trouble.

Antonio Elmaleh: You make a point which, I think, is quite fascinating. Well, two points. Bonds were not simply forged between enlisted men, but this anti-porn government effort actually had the effect of creating a fraternity amongst officers. I suspect one reason is they recognized human nature. The young men are cooped up in these horrific camp conditions over the course of the winter, they're not campaigning so there's no adrenaline going, and the distribution and consumption of pornographic materials was actually a great release of steam, so to speak, and that it was a morale sustainer for troops who otherwise would just be incredibly inefficient in the face of all this indolence.

I think they also recognized it made their job of commanding soldiers in some ways easier. I think they recognized, hey, you know what, government? Get off our backs, we're the ones fighting, we're the ones with our feet on the ground on this, we know that this works so leave it alone and best just don't get involved in it.

The other thing that I wanted to mention that you bring up in your book is when a soldier failed in soldiery, very often it wasn't because they were a coward or they got scared and ran, which is normal. It was instead ascribed to the corruption of their soul, of their inner life by pornography. So, it was an easy way to hang all kinds of other shortcomings that had nothing to do with their moral characters.

It's a catchall to avoid having to get too involved in, all right, why did this soldier really not perform his duty? It wasn't simply because he was reading smut, there are other reasons. Is that correct? Am I repeating your assertion in the book correctly?

Judith Giesberg: I guess one way I think about porn is that it's a kind of currency that could be exchanged between men and that could be used to signal one's membership in this culture of the army camp. Now, as far as weighing in on whether or not porn made bad soldiers, really only Congressmen were the ones that thought that way, and whistleblowers, people like Anthony Comstock, who's kind of the elephant in the room throughout this whole book. He's the elephant in the room because he, in the end, was an aspirational good soldier, one who was never really was tested, and one who felt alienated. And then he became the biggest crusader against the exchange of pornography and the mailing of pornography.

He was ultimately a failed soldier or he was one who never really got to prove himself as a soldier, but he was an outsider. So, there was certainly that misinterpretation from outsiders that this stuff was bad for men; that was the outsider's perspective.

From the inside, there were officers who worried and complained and tried to get the stuff out of their camps, but when push came to shove what was important was for the men, as you said, to be trained adequately, to have some sort of entertainment when they were not actively campaigning. And as long as discipline wasn't negatively affected and there weren't problems with civilian populations, which of course there could be as well, then pornography doesn't get soldiers in a whole lot of trouble within the army.

But from the outside, that was the fear of Congressmen and in particular those who were concerned about what kinds of men were being made in this war.

Antonio Elmaleh: You're not seeing a whole lot of eyewitness accounts saying, "Hey, don't bug me, I'm reading my smut."

Judith Giesberg: No. They do talk about how they're careful about what they have on them when they go into battle, what did they not want to be caught with, what materials they do not want sent home with their personal effects should they die in that battle. So they're conscious of it, but they're not writing home about it, the stuff isn't winding up in their personal collections. One of the biggest challenges to doing a project like this is that pornography is not collected among soldiers' personal letters, so you can't find it in the usual places you go to study the Civil War, you're not going to find it in their collections of letters. They're not going to stick it into the pages of their diaries. They try to be really careful, they're not going to put a naughty book in their haversack when they're actively campaigning. They want to keep a safe distance from the stuff if they should ever wind up having to face difficult questions from family members. So that makes it kind of tricky to work on this stuff.

Antonio Elmaleh: Yeah, also they run the risk of somebody else stealing their material out of their haversack, as you say.

Judith Giesberg: That is true. One of the court martials I mention in the book talks about *Fanny Hill*. Either there were five or six copies of it circulating around camp or one copy kept getting taken from one soldier and winding up in the tent of another soldier because it was pretty widely circulated.

Antonio Elmaleh: It's also noteworthy that the postal legislation that we've cited at the beginning of the show deleted a mandate that all pornography seized by the censors had to be destroyed. One free speech advocate asked about what would happen to all that confiscated but intact material. It's a pretty good question when you think about it because ...

Judith Giesberg: It is, yeah.

Antonio Elmaleh: ... They must have confiscated a mountain of material. So my question is, what do you think are some of the implications of the deletion of language that would have ensured the destruction of the materials but leave it in circulation among the postal employees or the federal censors or wherever, but certainly not with the soldiers?

Judith Giesberg: Right. The legislation that's passed early in 1865, there are several Congressmen involved in that debate who see this whole conversation as politically motivated, that obscene materials or obscenity as the term that they're using to describe the pornography, could be misused to apply to critics of the Lincoln administration. What's to stop somebody from using an anti-obscenity measure to confiscate, let's say, newspapers associated with the Democratic party or newspapers that expressed the opinions of the Copperheads?

Once this legislation is passed, some of the critics ask where does this end. They were some of the first critics that raised that concern from the beginning: we're potentially giving these postmasters great authority to define what it is to be obscene.

Later 20th century court cases will struggle with that as well: what makes something pornographic? A case in the 20th century considers that and the Justices in the end say something like, "Well, you'll know it when you see it." In the end, kicking the can down the road, nobody is clear about what makes something obscene or what makes something pornographic.

That conversation is there in 1865 when they pass this first measure. Then the measures that are passed in 1872 and 1873 also would think of this stuff as potentially contagious. Just the handling of it or the collecting of it is, in and of itself, a dangerous and potentially disruptive act. What do we then do with it, do we destroy it? Well, certainly those people who see these anti-obscenity laws as an attack on free speech were opposed to giving postmasters the authority to destroy the stuff, that was anathema, this was not what the state was fighting for, this is the opposite of what the state was fighting for.

It was uncomfortably compared to the censorship that had gone on in the South. In the 1830s, abolitionists had blanketed the South with abolitionist material because they knew postmasters in the South were collecting it and trying to burn it as fast as they could. There were these images in Northern newspapers of postmasters in Southern cities burning any newspapers or any literature that came from the North that might be considered contagious, that might have abolitionist ideas. So for

Northern Congressmen, Union Congressmen, US Congressmen, to talk about empowering postmasters with this flew in the face of their ideals.

The Republican party first established itself with this slogan, "Free soil, free speech, free men." The free speech part was about opposing censorship associated with the corrupt South. For the postmasters to be emboldened with this power was very concerning, and in the 1870s, when the federal Comstock law and then the state laws were being passed, those questions came up again. Comstock came to the Capitol Building when he was supporting the 1872 measure, apparently with bags of porn, and just spread it out all over the tables in the Capitol Building so the Congressmen would know what he was talking about. But even so, people were wondering about the potential contagion of it. Comstock was pretty proud of all of the stuff that he had confiscated.

There were instances of people saying the stuff is so dangerous that they should burn it. There was somebody who wrote Lincoln and sent Lincoln a pornographic circular and claimed in his autobiography that he burned a pile of erotic stuff right there on the White House lawn. Nobody else reported that, I certainly can't find any mention of it in the newspaper or anybody who was in the Lincoln administration talking about this stuff. But those were open questions about who has the authority to do that kind of stuff. In the end, they wrote that out of the legislation because the implications were really bad.

Antonio Elmaleh: Forgive me for another cynical interpretation of this banishment or deletion of the language, and we'll talk about the parallels with Prohibition later, but it also strikes me that, to the question this free speech advocate asked, well, what happened to all this material? Well, it seems to me that it's a golden opportunity for the bureaucrats and the law enforcement folks to jump in and start taking advantage of this material and selling it themselves. There's a market value every bit as powerful for pornography within the civilian population as it is in the camps in the Army.

So why on Earth would they not, as in Prohibition later, why would it not also have this incredibly corrupting influence on the very people meant to so-called safeguard morality, because, guess what, they erected this beautiful smokescreen of this patriotic this and preserving the moral character of our soldiers, but if I've got twenty-five pounds of interesting and salacious photographs, you think if I walked over to Nassau Street in New York I might be able to sell them for five bucks? Nobody's going to question that. I just like to bring that up because it strikes me that there's an opportunity to see a parallel in terms of the implication I'm drawing and what truly does happen in terms of Prohibition later. As I said, we will get to that later in the show.

Judith Giesberg: Sure. It always strikes me as so convenient, we see reverberations of that today as well, Congressmen who stand so morally righteous on some issues and then it turns out that they themselves are guilty of the very things that they have been most critical of or legislation they've passed to prohibit behaviors that they themselves indulge in. So, there's certainly a modern ring to that. When pornography enters the lexicon and becomes this thing people talk about, they always refer to it as something that somebody else has, "I don't have any of this stuff, what I have is art, what that guy down the street or what my neighbor has, he has porn, I have art."

Antonio Elmaleh: Right. I want to shift the tone a little bit because we've been talking about pretty serious stuff. Let's see if we can get some comic relief here. Authors went to great lengths to title their works in order to clearly suggest the character of their work to soldiers, obviously for marketing purposes while simultaneously avoiding the censors. Would you tell us some of your favorite titles of these books?

Judith Giesberg: Oh, thanks for this question, this is one of my favorite questions to answer. My all-time favorite title of one of the works that was described in a circular that was confiscated in camp at Tennessee is *Storming the Enemy's Breastworks.*

Antonio Elmaleh: That is mine, too.

Judith Giesberg: It's just my all-time favorite, it's something that certainly one of my teenage sons could have come up with himself had I ever challenged one of them to do it, it's just fantastic. I like the double entendre nature of *Storming the Enemy's Breastworks*, it's just so perfect for men in the war to giggle at that and to see the irony of a title like that, and of course ...

Antonio Elmaleh: It's very creative too, it's very creative.

Judith Giesberg: It's so good. It describes an image that was supposed to be about a Union soldier making a pass or maybe in the modern lingo hooking up with a Southern belle. At first she resists him, but then of course how can you resist an enemy, such a formidable enemy as the Union Army was in that equation. So that's one of my favorite ones. And then there's *A Bedroom Bombardment*, another one that might have had a nice ring to it in the third year of the war; you could see where that might be appealing. I found some of these images since I've published the book, art dealers have gotten in contact with me and said, "Hey, I have these images," and they've sent them. So I know what they look like now, which is pretty exciting.

They're all pretty tame, as you can imagine. *Bedroom Bombardment*, I think, is a group of semi-dressed girls. They're having a 19th century equivalent of a pillow fight. So, it's a pretty tame and discreet image, but the title certainly must have made some soldiers chuckle. And then there is *Recession Slaves*, which were enslaved women in the kingdom of Turkey, in harems. That was something people were wringing their hands about, trying to solve problems like women enslaved in harems, but I think they also just enjoyed telling those stories and imagining what these women looked like. I think these titles are fun and funny, they give us a sense of people's sexual imaginations at the time, they humanize 19th century people in a way that I think we need to keep in mind. You get to see their sense of humor, you get to see how creative they could be, you can imagine even if you couldn't buy any of the prints that were being advertised. Just saying the titles out loud could get your imagination going, could make you think about what that image might be.

I have a really fantastic foldout that I discovered in the archives that I couldn't put in the book, and I don't really describe it because I just don't know how to do it. But if you remember the last page of *Mad Magazine*, there was always one image and when you folded it there was another image that was hidden in the first image. There's a fantastic one that tells John Brown's story. The first page is John Brown's face and then you open it up and it talks about how he was conceived. As you fold it out it becomes longer and it says, "This is how John Brown was hung," and it's John Brown's penis. It's hysterical.

Antonio Elmaleh: How he was hung.

Judith Giesberg: Yep.

Antonio Elmaleh: Tell our listeners what breastworks actually means in military terms.

Judith Giesberg: Breastworks were one of a number of different entrenchments or defensive walls. By the end of the war, both sides were really quite adept at creating these defensive walls in ways to keep or frustrate the enemy's advancement. So, breastworks were a version of these defensive walls that became more and more common as the war wore on.

Antonio Elmaleh: We've talked a lot about pornography aimed at men. Was there any simultaneous effort to provide pornography for women, or was that totally off the table?

Judith Giesberg: I didn't find anything that was convincingly produced for female consumption. There was a short-run newspaper published in New York in which people would write in and talk about sexual questions or sexual fantasies. Sometimes there were female correspondents who wrote in to that column, but it's very hard for me to find out whether it was really written by women because they seemed to be more about male sexual fantasies than they were about women describing their sexual fantasies.

Even something like Fanny Hill, there were moments where someone might have interpreted it as being something intended for a female audience, when women are in control of the sexual situation or moments when women are having sex with women. But in the end those are always filtered through a male voice and portrayed through a male gaze. So I never found anything that would convincingly have been produced for a female readership, but that's not to say that women didn't get access to this stuff and potentially enjoy it.

Antonio Elmaleh: Well, we're out of time for today's podcast. But Professor Giesberg has graciously agreed to return to continue this fascinating discussion about sex and pornography during the Civil War. Please join us for part two of our discussion on our next podcast, *Uncovering the Civil War*. Until then, be safe and do good.

PART II

Antonio Elmaleh: Welcome to another segment of *Uncovering the Civil War*. Today we will pick up on our discussion with Professor Judy Giesberg of Villanova University about sex and pornography in the Civil War. Welcome, Judy.

Judith Giesberg: Thank you for having me, Antonio.

Antonio Elmaleh: My pleasure. Can you comment, Judy, on the advent of the camera and the camera technology in advancing the promotion, the distribution and appreciation of pornographic materials in army camp life?

Judith Giesberg: The new technology that's available during this time is really quite important to the story. The access to photographic technology; the wide accessibility to things like carte de visite, which your readers, of course, know are those small card-sized images affixed to a hard back that you could tuck away in your pocket and easily exchange; stereograph technology that created these twinned images that when you look at them through something like a viewfinder the images looked like they were three-dimensional and you were inside the image.

All of those technologies really become widely available and easily accessible in a period of five or six years right around the time of the

Civil War. And when you study some of the earliest images produced on all of these new technologies, it's not a surprise that some of the first images were exotic landscapes such as Jerusalem or Niagara Falls, but then the next thing the photographic technologies are used to produce are pictures of naked women.

So the wider accessibility to photographic technology, how these images could be cheaply and easily reproduced, play a very important role in the expansion of porn or what I like to think of as this period's triumph of pornography, and the images, the new advancements, come thick and fast.

One of the advancements I talk about in the book are the Stanhopes. These are miniaturized, beaded images that you could install in the head of your cane or the handle of your pistol, and when you held them up you could enjoy them very discreetly. So, each renewed Comstock Law added more and more different photographic technologies to the list. They started just with erotic books and other materials, and then they added playing cards, they added stereographs, they had to add these miniaturized images. The lawmakers had a hard time keeping up with all these new photographic technologies, so it's very much part of the story.

Antonio Elmaleh: It reminds of something you wrote about in the book, which is the portrayal of dead bodies through the camera had a profoundly different effect on the person looking at them than drawings in Harper's Weekly because the illustrations wouldn't go near the same level of graphic detail. So Mathew Brady and Alexander Gardner and all the early photographers were breaking new ground because they understood the power of a recorded image to create an effect that no drawing, no writer's or illustrator's imagination could possibly conceive of. And I think that it's quite a powerful step forward, just in terms of heightening the appreciation and the awareness of just how brutal and savage the fighting was, because these photographs don't pull punches.

Judith Giesberg: No, they're shocking, right?

Antonio Elmaleh: Yeah.

Judith Giesberg: They're very shocking.

Antonio Elmaleh: Absolutely. Even by today's standards, they are.

Judith Giesberg: Oh, absolutely. Just to sort of add one last thing to the pictures: what was also shocking in these first images of nude women is actually seeing nude women and not seeing classical portrayals of nude women's bodies. And real women's bodies don't look like the classical drawings, so those were also quite shocking, to see a woman who has pubic hair as opposed to classical drawings of women who seem to be sort of suspended in a pre-pubescent state. Those images could be quite shocking, so you could imagine the multiple waves of shock of seeing real things for the first time and trying to process those images and what they meant.

Antonio Elmaleh: What do you think was behind the government legislating private morality: new political alliances, graft, repressed sexual feelings? I mean, there's any number of ways in which you can look at the subtext of this effort. Any of the things that I mentioned, do any of those resonate for you?

Judith Giesberg: So, I don't know about graft…in order to be able to argue that, I'd have to dig into what anybody who was involved in this legislation might have had to personally gain from it, at least on Congress's side. Certainly, the private organizations that are most invested in this legislation and really do the most to enforce it are the reformers who are members of New York's chapter of the Young Men's Christian Association or the YMCA, and their anti-porn wing. And, of course, the YMCA had a mobile chapter during the Civil War that we know of as the United States Christian Commission.

So the sort of cluster of elite New York financiers and other elite New Yorkers, they have a lot to gain from positioning themselves as moral authorities, policing the sexual behaviors before the war comes around. They are concerned about erotica, they're trying to protect young, middle class boys who are now coming into New York to work in white collar jobs. They really see this as a way to retain their class status which they feel is being stripped from them. They believe the elite is no longer as influential as it used to be – now you have these urban democratic machines who can control things in the city and who have marginalized this New York elite – and these men see porn as one of many different attempts to regulate the sexual behavior and to control the terms under which the working class and other young men who are coming into the city live their lives. It's really about class, and certainly that's operating to some extent with Comstock, though I do think with Comstock – for your listeners, Anthony Comstock becomes the tsar of the anti-pornography campaigns that emerge after the war – and for him, it is about class. For him it's also about sexuality and his own sort of uncomfortable sense of who he is as a man that drives his interest in being the first Postmaster General to oversee the administration of these post-war laws.

So certainly, questions about his manhood and masculinity drive his interest in it. And probably to some extent those men who are funding the effort through the YMCA and who lobby Congress very successfully to pass amped-up measures in 1870, the federal Comstock Law, they're invested in their class aspirations and that's wrapped up with who they are as men or who they believed they used to be as men and now they're losing it. So there's certainly that. That's all part of it for these private individuals.

Antonio Elmaleh: It seems to me also we should mention that Anthony Comstock falsified his war record. You don't need a more telling indication of some kind of conflicted self-image than maintaining that you're a combat veteran because you have a scar on your cheek, and I think he got it from some domestic accident in camp and pretty much spent the war consigned to guard duty. That doesn't really fly if you're trying to defend the moral character of soldiers and defend their willingness to fight if you're actually trying to pretend that you're something you're not, as far as your war experience. And I think a lot of it comes from being overshadowed by his brother who was killed at Gettysburg after fighting at Antietam and Fredericksburg, two of the worst battles of the whole war, and the example his brother gave that he must have felt he could never live up to.

Judith Giesberg: I think you're right. Yeah, I don't think Anthony ever got over being the lesser of those two sons, and he certainly felt it when he joined his brother's regiment after his brother died. He never fit in, he sort of prided himself and he believed he was going to live up to his brother's standard but was never given the opportunity to do so, and then spent the rest of his life trying to find an equivalent to that by writing and sponsoring these biographies, you know, this biography of himself or endorsing this biography that tried to create an alternative veteran status for him. Yet the war that he was really fighting was against people who were selling porn and people who were providing information about birth control and abortions. But yeah, you're right ...

Antonio Elmaleh: He was also fighting a war within himself, clearly, I would say.

Judith Giesberg: I think so, too. I don't think he ever really figured out what kind of man he was. He knew what kind of man he felt had ostracized him and who he never really felt he belonged among. But I don't think he ever really figured out what kind of man he was. He thought he was always trying to rescue boys from themselves but I think the one who most needed to be rescued was Anthony Comstock.

Antonio Elmaleh: It's clear to me that the Civil War legislation parallels the later laws about prohibition and abstinence from drinking. Do you think there's anything to my assertion about this?

Judith Giesberg: Oh, sure, yeah. So the Women's Christian Temperance Union begins in the post-war era and it is interested in the anti-pornography campaign that Comstock has begun. They are actually very interested in lots of things, not only temperance, but they're also interested in rescuing women from prostitution and other sorts of things.

Comstock talks a lot about trying to save children from this erotic material. He doesn't do anything about that other than write a book about how bad it is for young men to read this stuff, he really spends most of his time rounding up people who are selling the stuff and bringing them to jail.

But the Women's Christian Temperance Union actually does spend time thinking about children, and also about women in a way that Comstock doesn't ever really think about women as being affected by this stuff. And of course the Women's Christian Temperance Union becomes very powerful and amasses a huge following. Many, many people, women, sign up to become members of the Women's Christian Temperance Union, lots of local chapters, and they are really building the foundation for the prohibition laws that will pass. They are really spreading that word and really doing the footwork for that campaign.

Antonio Elmaleh: Prohibition was designed to legislate private social activity: drinking. Daniel Okrent, who wrote Last Call: The Rise and Fall of Prohibition, said these laws had the unintended effect of creating a nation of lawbreakers. Because everybody said "I'm going to take a drink, I don't care what you say." And so they're saying "Yeah, we want a drink!" and guess what? Al Capone's saying, "I got the booze."

So you've got this kind of devil's bargain with the legislators unwittingly opening the door for lawlessness and a corruption that swept the country that they could never have imagined.

Judith Giesberg: Yeah, that's a good parallel.

Antonio Elmaleh: Well I'd also like to mention, and please comment, the incredible irony of abolitionists also taking the side of anti-pornography. I find it ironic that they were perfectly willing to fight for the freedom of slaves but when it came to the freedom of speech they were about as restricted and restrictive and unforgiving as Anthony Comstock. Do you see that parallel?

Judith Giesberg: The one thing that people will want to keep in mind when they're thinking about these early measures is that they really didn't elicit any conversation at all; there really wasn't any. The measures that were passed in the 1840s were subtly snuck into custom laws. There wasn't a public forum about it, nobody voted for them, candidates didn't endorse it. And the 1872 measure was the same. There really wasn't any public conversation about it all. So, it's really hard to tell where people fall on the side of this.

Once the law was in place, organizations like these temperance unions were arguably more conservative than some of the abolitionist movements before the war, although there was some overlap sometimes with these organizations. The temperance crusaders did not think that women should have the right to vote, for instance, whereas antebellum abolitionists often endorsed both and believed that both things could happen simultaneously, that you could have abolition and you could enfranchise women. So, it's a little . . . those are important nuances to remember.

I'd also say abolitionists before the war believed that slavery was immoral and they also liked to criticize the slaveholders as being enslaved, as they say, to their passions, that they didn't have control of their own passions. And, of course, abolitionists, like most middle class people in the antebellum period, believed that you should control your passions, you should control your emotions. To be middle class, you had to control all of that stuff, right? You didn't drink water that was too cold or too hot, you drank sort of lukewarm water and you didn't drink spirits or any of those things that you thought would agitate you and would cause you to lose control of any of those passions. So they prided themselves in controlling those passions and they saw slaveholders as not being in control of those passions. Yet, ironically, abolitionist literature liked to walk a tightrope. They oftentimes included explicitly erotic passages in their literature as they sought to condemn slaveholders.

Antonio Elmaleh: I have this image of a pastor. He's got two books, one under each arm. One is the *Book of Job* and one is the book of temptations, except the book of temptations is *Storming the Enemy Breastworks*. And suddenly he makes a mistake and picks the wrong book to start his sermon.

In your book, you make a fascinating comment. You said the Thirteenth Amendment abolishing slavery also triggered an intense debate about marriage between slaves. So the question is, would an emancipated slave woman be as free as an emancipated male slave?

Judith Giesberg: So there's a really interesting debate that goes on in Congress about marriage, and it's begun because by the end of the war in 1865 some one hundred and eighty thousand black men will have served in the US Army during the Civil War. Most of those one hundred and eighty thousand black men who serve in the US Army of course are enslaved, and many of them have families that remain enslaved in the Confederacy and their status is an open question.

Congress talked about that from the beginning. These men are fighting and their wives and children remain enslaved. So what are we going to do about that? How can we do something when the Emancipation Proclamation really only works when the troops are on the ground and are actively seeking to free enslaved people? The Thirteenth Amendment would complete the process. But while they're waiting for it, what can Congress do to guarantee to enslaved women whose husbands have gone off to fight, who are now more vulnerable in the slave South, what can we do to help them? How can we, and importantly, what can we do so that more enslaved people will sign up for the US Army, right? Would you sign up as an enslaved man if you knew you were leaving your wife and children home to be victimized by the master who now has even more reason to treat them roughly and to abuse them?

So this conversation is happening in Congress about freeing enslaved wives of enslaved men who are fighting, and then they begin to talk about what does that mean, because marriage among slaves has been prohibited. So what does it mean to be married, what does it mean to be a married slave family? And they begin to have that conversation about marriage at the same time as they're beginning to consider this measure that I talk about in the book. These things are all part of the same conversation in Congress about imagining what the post-war state is going to look like, imagining what the responsibility is of the state, the federal government, to define things like marriage. Is that a federal thing? Well, no, usually it's the states that define what marriage is. But the federal government at that moment is considering this measure that's going to free the enslaved wives and children of soldiers, and in the process they're actually coming up with a federal definition of marriage.

We're kind of in the same moment now, when we talk about what authority does the federal government have to dictate the terms under which gay marriage is accepted in the states. We're still at that same moment. And, of course, the federal government has limited authority to do that.

But through these Comstock measures, the Comstock measure that's passed, you can see the expression of some of those concerns about regulating morality. They can't do it necessarily through legislating what it means to be married or the terms under which people can get divorced, as all of that stuff is controlled at the state level. But they passed this Comstock Law saying that any obscene materials that are mailed through the federal mail can be prosecuted as a federal crime, and in the process they make many kinds of interactions or expressions illegal. Anybody who talks about birth control or who writes about birth control can now be arrested and thrown in federal prison because they broke the Comstock laws. Anybody who offers birth control services or who provides abortions are now susceptible for being charged under the Comstock Laws and arrested.

Antonio Elmaleh: You ask in your book and I think it's a fascinating query: where would white men continue to assert their masculinity once the sovereignty and integrity of white males no longer relied on slavery? Can you elaborate on that?

Judith Giesberg: Sure. This is where that crisis that we talked about at the beginning, I think, is important to remember: people were concerned that hierarchies had been upended in the war. The end of slavery was certainly a moral right but the result meant there were going to be adjustments between the races that were important. Was the end of slavery now going to mean that black men were going to have the same political rights as white men? Did that mean that white men had lost something if black men had gained something? Similarly, as black men had equal rights to marry and to have families, in the sort of imaginings that all of this was zero-sum game this news could be received as a loss: that if somebody's gaining then somebody must be losing. And that was certainly the case with the end of an economically and socially important significant institution like slavery.

But also there were concerns, among people living in the North in particular, about how women had asserted themselves in the war and how potentially the proper balance between men and women had been upended during the war. That's part of, I think, every war when men come back and they're suffering from psychological problems like PTSD but also physical injuries and ailments, that can feed the sense of crisis if men are coming back but not fully as men. Does that mean that women somehow have stepped into their place?

All of those things, I think, lend themselves to feeding the sense that there's potentially a crisis, a crisis of manhood that the war has put into place—

Antonio Elmaleh: I think also, if I may interject...

Judith Giesberg: Yeah.

Antonio Elmaleh: ...That as far as the notion of woman is concerned and the upending of traditional assumptions about what the role of the woman is, the fact is that the war drains most communities of men. So who's left to...it's not enough to be able to take care of the children, you're going to have to put food on the table, you have to go out and possibly make a living, you have to do all these things that traditionally women were, simply, not allowed to do.

And suddenly, by force of circumstance, they have to do it. So this necessary readjustment of the role of a woman at home when the men are either away fighting, come home basket cases and unable to function, or psychically complete invalids, had to have caused an upending, especially of women. We talked to female reenactors and the statement came loud and clear: "Well, if they're freeing slaves, what about us, we're slaves too." So you know, where do they get off freeing slaves but not women? And I think that that's a fair point.

Judith Giesberg: Right, yeah. There's certainly a lot of people writing about their fears, about what the war has wrought all these manly women. And the anti-suffrage cartoons that emerge in the post-war era really expressed that so clearly, you know, these pictures of these women smoking cigarettes and waiting at the voting booths while their husbands are home holding babies. The first ten years after the war, that's the way the threat of suffrage is portrayed. It really expressed the kind of fears that the war has wrought.

I've talked about this in one of my previous books. There were moments when it really did seem like the war had absolutely forgotten the differences between women and men. I talk about that in a study that I did about explosions at federal arsenals where young women were working, this one arsenal outside of Pittsburgh, in Allegheny, Pennsylvania where young girls were torn apart by this explosion. People talked about it like walking through a war zone. It happened at the same time as Antietam and people in Pittsburgh and elsewhere thought, "Holy cow, this is the war come home to roost, these are young girls whose bodies are being torn apart by shrapnel."

And that stuff really stuck, and people saw that as an indication of something very threatening and potentially permanent. A lot of ink is shed about how we can bring things back to where they were before, before the war disrupted them. And the Comstock law is one solution. I mean, the big irony here is that the law initially began as a way to control man's sexuality, but it's no surprise to your listeners that this law did not effectively eradicate porn, right? I mean the fact that we can get porn anywhere is a pretty good indication of how badly this law failed. But what it did do really well was it controlled women's access to information about birth control. It really did. And it outlawed abortion.

Antonio Elmaleh: Yeah, I want to come right to that, that's the nature of my next question. You point out that anti-abortion laws increased dramatically after the war. Can you give us some insight as to why?

Judith Giesberg: These anti-abortion measures were written into local, into state-level Comstock laws. So when the federal government passed the Comstock laws, states followed with their own Comstock measures or their own anti-obscenity measures. And these anti-obscenity measures usually shared some of the wording of the federal measure which was based really on the 1865 law I start the book off with.

These state-level measures prohibited the mailing of erotica, prohibited the exchange of erotica. They had conversations at the state level and added to the list of obscene materials that were prohibited. They added any publication that talked about birth control or talked about abortion or that gave information about birth control and abortion. And these riders were the result of lobbying on the part of medical doctors, many of whom had served in the army, and in the army there was a push to professionalize the medical field, close ranks, and to control access to who could become doctors.

The American Medical Association was born in this moment and that was all about sort of controlling and defining who was a doctor. And the people who were involved with that became keenly interested in the Comstock measures because they could write into these measures riders that prohibited or made it illegal for those who didn't have a medical degree to practice medicine, such as homeopathic doctors or midwives or others who were prohibited from going to medical school but who were very important providers of medical care. In particular for women who wanted information about birth control, these were the kinds of people that they would frequent, and with these Comstock measures they put these irregular medical practitioners out of work or in jail. So now they had to keep under wraps what they did. They had to be very careful. At any time they could be arrested under these local obscenity measures because they were giving information about birth control or abortion. And those measures were put into place at the state level by doctors who were seeking to professionalize medicine.

Antonio Elmaleh: And wipe out so-called abortionists, as well as homeopaths and any kind of competition to their practice.

Judith Giesberg: Yep.

Antonio Elmaleh: Right. At the end of your book you trace the relationship between war and sexuality. And we could probably devote an entire program to that relationship, but would you mind elaborating on where you were going with that?

Judith Giesberg: So for me, the big questions that this book posed for me and that I wasn't really able to fully answer in the book, is that if we look at beginning of this time period, the United States, Great Britain, France are all on the same page, or at least have not diverged dramatically, with their concerns about what erotica is and what it does to people.

But when we look back today, we have very divergent histories. The United States does with Great Britain, and certainly the United States does with France, and it's not entirely clear to me how we got there. But I do think that the timing of the Civil War is an important part of the answer to that question, and the way that the post-war state emerged from the war feeling very emboldened and empowered to dictate morality. It's a uniquely American thing that occurred because, as I suggested, the anti-pornography campaigns in both Great Britain and France were very, very different than the Americans.

And I think today we still have the reputation of…I don't think we've ever gotten over that. I think in the eyes of France and Great Britain we probably still seem like we are obsessed with the stuff and we can't seem to get over it. So I do think there's something unique about our history with pornography and with the government sense that they can regulate and control very personal things like marriage and sex and morals. And there's something about that time period when this precedent was set, but I am still researching this.

I think it's very interesting how we, as Americans, retain a deep, deep interest in the United States Civil War, that we think of the war as a uniquely American experience, but we don't often think about things like sex and sexuality during the Civil War. And I do think there's something really important that occurred at this time among these people that I don't think we've quite gotten over yet.

Antonio Elmaleh: I think I might like to refine my word "war" to "violence." You know, the relationship between violence, specifically combat-related, and sexuality. Does that make the point clearer to listeners that you thought there might be a relationship between the two? A linkage, in fact.

Judith Giesberg: This is where I really go out on the ledge because I'm a historian, I'm not a sociologist or an anthropologist or a psychologist or...

Antonio Elmaleh: And it's not conjecture.

Judith Giesberg: Any of those things, I really need my sources to lead me there. There are many things we don't know about the way people experience violence and how they get over it and how they survive it. I think there's a way in which it brings those people who experience it together and alienates those who don't have a similar experience. We know among Civil War soldiers, a certain percentage of them were, statistically speaking, homosexual. We don't know anything about their experiences during the war and how being in these kinds of intimate spaces with other men, how they negotiated those feelings and how those feelings were aggravated by everybody's feelings for one another, and, for others, were aggravated by being around the kinds of violence and having to deal with the violence every day.

There's an interesting way in which these Congressmen, as they were thinking about regulating men's sexuality, believed there was some connection between sex and violence. They were trying to put their finger on it. And Comstock certainly was one of them. He believed that when people saw erotic materials they were moved to violence. Which was very interesting because, of course, he emerges from the war in which some would argue that sex allowed men to escape the violence, right? And to feel human again, to touch and to be touched is an intensely human thing that allows one to get over things like horrible acts of violence, either witnessing or perpetrating them.

Antonio Elmaleh: To connect with a life force, after witnessing and experiencing so much death.

Judith Giesberg: Exactly. And I don't think that they had that whole thing figured out. But instead of trying to regulate the violence or to think about the violence and to open questions about PTSD for example, "how do you get over that kind of violence?", they thought that you could regulate sex, that it was easier to regulate sex than it was to ask questions about what the violence did.

Antonio Elmaleh: It strikes me that this is a parent's eternal nightmare. How do you control pornographic material on the internet? The access is ridiculously easy, but more importantly, in the discussion that's going on right now about video games, specifically violent games that accentuate women as love slaves and the violence they're entitled to. I mean, we're still in it, I think there's a really clear through line to what they were struggling with back in the day. So it just goes to show you that all roads eventually lead back to the Civil War.

Judith Giesberg: I agree.

Antonio Elmaleh: In my opinion. So if you could leave our listeners with one final observation to take from our discussion, what would it be?

Judith Giesberg: I would go back to the questions I was just raising for you, which is, what is it about America's experience of the war that cements American morality? What is it about this war in particular that makes the American experience, or American self-image, as being a moral actor in the world? What is that connection? And then, a second part of that question, what are the effects of that, what does it mean? How did we see ourselves as morally right? If the outcome of this war is morally right then what are the effects of that? Those are the questions I would leave your listeners with.

Antonio Elmaleh: I think we're out of time, and before we go I'd like you tell our listeners about your new book and when you anticipate its publication.

Judith Giesberg: I'd love to. I'm working on a project, it'll be an article for sure, hopefully a book, on the administration of the 1870 census.

Which is, once again in my mind, a very timely thing to think about. The 1870 census, for anybody who's involved in genealogy or who's hopped onto Ancestry.com to study their family's history, was the first census taken after the war. It's the census we use to try to figure out how many people actually died in this war and how many people survived it. It was the first census too, that counted former slaves as individuals and named them.

It was a wildly important census and, like every census before and after, it became very much wrapped up in politics because it was being administered during Reconstruction when the post-war South was occupied by federal troops and the Three-Fifths Compromise, which had always given the Southern slaveholding states an inordinate influence in Congress, was eradicated. So there were many questions about the way the census was going to be pulled off, and when the results came in, what that was going to mean. Were the Southern states now going to have less power in the House of Representatives or were they going to use the census to enforce the freshly passed 15th Amendment, which as your listeners of course know enfranchised black men.

So the census is happening at a very fraught political time in the nation's history when Reconstruction is under way. Civil rights are now being enshrined in these post-war amendments, and in the middle of all of that they're trying to get an accurate count of how many Americans there are in 1870. It's a very interesting moment in American history which sheds light on some of the questions we're asking today about the administration of the 2020 Census.

Antonio Elmaleh: That's what I was going to go with.

Judith Giesberg: Is everybody going to get counted, right? And...

Antonio Elmaleh: And gerrymandering, that's exactly where gerrymandering can really play an incredibly destructive role in allocating political power.

Judith Giesberg: That's right, and the census could really help to dismantle gerrymandering, right? Or it could also be used to enforce new anti-immigration measures. So there's all sort of potential ways the 2020 census is going to be played out, and they're very reminiscent of the way the 1870 census was administered. I'm really excited about this project.

Antonio Elmaleh: I think it's eminently fascinating and also incredibly timely. So I want to wish you the best of luck and keep us posted on how and when it comes out and we'll certainly do something on our website or just announce to people that it's out so that you can have the benefit of wider readership.

Judith Giesberg: That would be great, thank you.

Antonio Elmaleh: I'd like to thank you, Professor Judy Giesberg, for making this an informative, fascinating, and provocative discussion. I really would. I think it's just been awesome, and to all our listeners a special thank you for taking the time to tune in to another segment of *Uncovering the Civil War*. Please come back again. Until then, be safe and do good.

SEVEN

UNCOVERING A LONG TRAIL OF TEARS

Guest: Dr. Clarissa Confer

Antonio Elmaleh: Welcome, everyone, to another segment of *Uncovering the Civil War*. Today, my guest via telephone is Dr. Clarissa Confer. Dr. Confer is Professor of American History at California University of Pennsylvania. She has published extensively in the area of Native American history, particularly the experience of residents of Indian Territory in the Civil War. Her works include The Cherokee Nation in the Civil War, published by the University of Oklahoma Press.

Welcome, Dr. Confer.

Clarissa Confer: Thank you for inviting me.

Antonio Elmaleh: My pleasure. Let's begin with, if we could, with setting the context for our discussion. What was the Cherokee Nation? The name "Nation" implies a capital and a constitution and a formal system of government, was that true?

Clarissa Confer: Yes, they're all those things. Nation is a term we tend to use more now in American Indian history rather than "tribe". Tribe has certain connotations that might not be accurate. Cherokee

Nation was very much what we would regard as a nation by the time of the Civil War. They had made a conscious choice to form that type of centralized structure, not what we call the Five Civilized Tribes with five southeastern Nations in Indian territory did to that same extent, but the Cherokees are very much a model of nationhood. It was a reaction to the pressures of Euro-American settlement and demands.

A lot of ways it met what you would think of as a nation: they certainly had a constitution, they passed a constitution, one of the early ones, 1827, and it looks a lot like our Constitution; they created branches of government; they had a Cherokee Lighthorse, which we would think of as the police force; they had Cherokee Supreme Court; they did have a capital.

Antonio Elmaleh: I saw your book includes the Cherokee Constitution. Was that difficult to find?

Clarissa Confer: You can google the 1827 Constitution and it'll come up and you can easily read the text. Remember, no Native groups had a written language when Europeans arrived, so Cherokee is one of the very few written languages among Native peoples, and it was a 19th century creation by the Cherokees themselves. When you look at the cover of the book you see there's some Cherokee on there: Cherokee is a syllabary and it's a very different-looking language but they were very bilingual. All or most of their documents were written both in languages, in Cherokee and in English; their newspaper, for example, was published in two languages, which is one of the things that helped them to become literate so quickly, because you could read an article in Cherokee on one side and then the English translation would be on the other side.

Antonio Elmaleh: I wanted to just clarify for our listeners what the territories encompassed. My understanding, it was Arkansas, Oklahoma, I don't know how far west they spread, maybe into Texas. What the general geographical boundaries of this Nation, and was there an actual capital?

Clarissa Confer: When the Cherokees were removed into the west their territory was entirely what you would think of as Oklahoma, and it's sort of an "L-shape" in the northeast corner of Oklahoma, so that's what the government called Indian Territory, the official name was Indian Territory. And all five Nations were, it's a little more complicated than that, but all five Nations who were removed were designated certain regions of Indian Territory, all primarily east. So Cherokee were designated the northeast, it looks a little bit like an "L", and their capital is called Tahlequah and if you go to Tahlequah today you can see quite a few things written in Cherokee, the street signs and things like that. That's where their Supreme Court was, that's where their government offices were.

Antonio Elmaleh: Wow. Tell us a little bit about Andrew Jackson and the Trail of Tears and why it marked so profoundly the experience of the Cherokee.

Clarissa Confer: Well we could talk all night about Andrew Jackson. Jackson oversaw the official removal of the Five Civilized Tribes with the Indian Removal Access Pass in 1830. It was very much with Jackson's support, and the Nations fought against removal in various ways. The Cherokee are the ones who took it to the Supreme Court and had some very strong historical cases of the Supreme Court, but Jackson defied the Supreme Court and pitted his executive power against judicial power and won. And then he used the military to forcibly remove the Cherokees to Indian Territory.

Antonio Elmaleh: From Georgia primarily, wasn't it?

Clarissa Confer: Yes, Georgia is what started all this, so the Cherokees moved from there. The Chickasaws, Creeks, Choctaws, and Seminoles were all removed from their remaining land, and Seminoles of course are a whole different story because they were in Florida and ended up in actual combat in the Seminole War. But the Cherokees lived from northwestern Georgia on the creeks to eastern Alabama, the Choctaw and Chickasaw were from Mississippi. It was the last major removal and stripping of Native peoples of their sovereign lands east of the Mississippi.

That happened in the late 1830s, so in the 1840s the Cherokees are trying to reconstitute their lives and everything that they've left behind and lost. And then the Civil War comes just twenty years later. A key part of the Civil War story is the removal was so close in time to the crisis of the war. The two greatest crises the Cherokees ever faced and they occurred within two decades of each other.

Antonio Elmaleh: This takes me to a question that I was going to ask later in the show but it seems like a logical connection here. The Supreme Court actually issued several landmark decisions supporting Cherokee rights and autonomy. Why do you think the Supreme Court was so ineffective in influencing Cherokee/federal government relations and yet had such a profound effect, practically driving the nation to war with the Dred Scott decision and the Fugitive Slave Act? How do you account for this strange lack of any teeth to decisions in this area, and yet it was incredibly influential in driving the nation into war?

Clarissa Confer: I suppose I would debate the role of the Supreme Court before the Civil War a little bit, but let's leave that aside.

Antonio Elmaleh: Okay, you could do that, too.

Clarissa Confer: Yes. Jackson was pitting the executive branch against the judicial branch, and I think it's important for everybody to remember that the judicial branch had quite a different status in the 19th century than it does today. The Supreme Court is much more arbiter of every controversy that we can think of now. And Jackson, if there's one thing you teach about Jackson it's that he strengthened the executive office. Whether you think it's a good thing or a bad thing, in so many ways, the Nullification Crisis, Bank War, and Cherokee Removal are three prime examples of Jackson taking power in the executive at the expense of other branches. In this case, it's at the expense of the judicial branch.

As much as John Marshall carved out a space for the Cherokees in his decisions, he did call them "domestic dependent nations." And what does that mean? There is no place in our system, really, for such a thing, and most Americans were not comfortable with that concept of having a nation within a nation. They saw another sovereign power. There wouldn't have been a lot of political support for that position necessarily. And, as Jackson said, Marshall made his decision, let him enforce it. The Supreme Court has no enforcement power, they have to rely on the respect of the other branches to honor their decisions. And the other branches ...

Antonio Elmaleh: And the Army.

Clarissa Confer: Yeah, Jackson, he's the Commander in Chief and Congress had passed the Removal Act, so both branches were not going to honor the Supreme Court decision. And the Cherokees, they had a choice. My students always ask me, "Why didn't they fight?" Well, it's the late 1830s, they had been pressured by the US for decades, a century, kept hearing, "Oh, you're savages, you're savages, you're not civilized people, you can't live nearby, near us." So they spent the last forty years proving to the US that they were quote "civilized people" and civilized people use the court system. I don't think it ever occurred to them that winning in court wasn't going to change anything. There was so much pressure for removal, land hunger is such a dividing force in American history that the odds were against them.

Antonio Elmaleh: Was mixed heritage as common among Cherokees as it was between white slavers and black slaves?

Clarissa Confer: Very common. John Ross, the Cherokee Chief, is only one-eighth Cherokee. Cherokee is actually his second language. The Cherokees were very intermarried by this period, they had been living close to white society for a very long time.

Antonio Elmaleh: You write that mixed blood Cherokees were really the predominant slave owners in their Nation. Can you tell us why that was?

Clarissa Confer: I'll leave that question aside for a minute why mixed race had the dominant position. But why did they own slaves? Because they literally had taken the word of the whites, "You need to be just like us, you need to be, quote, civilized." What does civilized mean? It means nuclear family, Christianity, capitalism. So many of those values meant moving away from their matrilineal heritage. They looked at their white neighbors and what were their white neighbors doing? They were engaging in a market economy with slave labor. So, the Cherokees said, "Yeah, we can do that." And they bought into the system, bought into the agricultural market economy with slave labor and slowly, gradually became larger and larger slave owners.

It's also really interesting to trace their change in attitude towards slavery. They become more and more restrictive on slavery and slave rights, just as their white neighbors did. After the Turner Rebellion, the South really cracked down on the slave system and it became much more constricted; and we see that mirrored in the Cherokee Nation, as well, through their legislation.

Antonio Elmaleh: In reading your book, you write about the economic pressure that Cherokees faced to increase the agricultural output of the lands that they lived in. Was cotton a driver in that pressure?

Clarissa Confer: Yeah, sure. About 1830s, cotton is king. We can see this transformation of the South, what we call the New West of the South, in Alabama, Mississippi, but Western Georgia as well. And, if that's a pressure, that's where the financial gain is, and so the Cherokees and the Choctaws would grow quite a bit of cotton as well. That's what there was, that's what the market would offer to them, there weren't a lot of other options.

Antonio Elmaleh: So, when they're talking about agricultural output, they're really talking about cotton?

Clarissa Confer: Those engaged in the market economy are. I mean there were plenty of Cherokee farmers, particularly once they moved to Indian Territory, who were growing staple crops on family farms. But those who were rising to the positions of wealth and leadership would have engaged in a cotton economy.

Antonio Elmaleh: I think that the average person's understanding of history doesn't associate Cherokees or Native Americans with owning black slaves. Did the Cherokees, especially the ones who were not slave owners, rationalize their participation in slave owning when that very experience must have reminded them somewhat of their own experience with whites?

Clarissa Confer: That's a hard question. It's not something that they wrote about or left us a lot of documentation on. We don't have the types of defenses of slavery that come out of the white culture. And this is also a difficult question: what were Native concepts of race? Native concepts of race seem to have developed in tandem with their exposure to Euro-Americans, they seemed to have internalized ideas of race that were probably not there before that exposure.

There's quite a bit of controversy and angst over slavery in the years before the Civil War, but that appears to me to be more part of the political situation and the political spectrum from pro-slavery to abolition, much of which comes to them from outside, rather than internal debates. I'm not aware of a lot of evidence of massive internal debates or justifications of race-based slavery among the Cherokee. And there is also not a lot of, what you might assume would be a natural empathy perhaps, between seeing yourself as a victim of whites and seeing African Americans as victims so that there'd be some sort of bond. Now, that might have developed in some places but it's not for sure. You can't say, "Okay, clearly Native peoples are going to see a kinship or some sort of similar situation for African Americans." The Creeks and Seminoles have a very different relationship with African Americans than the Cherokees do, so it's very individualistic.

Antonio Elmaleh: The history of the Cherokee Nation experience is defined by a struggle for an ultimate loss of their own autonomy. How did the Civil War hasten the loss of that autonomy?

Clarissa Confer: It's directly related to the loss of the status of nationhood, so that when Oklahoma becomes a state in the beginning of the 20th century, that statehood is predicated on the end of the Native

Nations. Oklahoma currently has more Native people, more different Native groups, than any other state, I think, but they don't exist as Nations.

The Civil War hastened it in so many ways. It divided the Five Civilized Nations, Cherokees included; it divided them bitterly and made them less unified and therefore weaker in meeting any challenges to their autonomy. They were treated by the US Government after the war as losers. The Indian Territory became something that the rest of the country knew about. A lot of veterans from both sides had seen the grasslands, for example, in Indian Territory. The railroads could not wait to get into Indian Territory and put their lines through. Indian Territory sort of became discovered.

When the Native Americans were sent there, no one could imagine wanting it. That's why they put them there. Remember how we developed this country; we leapfrogged. We went to the Mississippi and then we jumped over to California and then we left the middle for last. Oklahoma was where people were going to put Native peoples because where else? They were pushed from the east into Oklahoma but then Cheyenne and Apache and other groups were pushed from the west into Indian Territory. Then when oil was discovered in the 20th century, that changed the calculus quite a bit. But the Civil War absolutely hastened the dissolution of the Nations.

Antonio Elmaleh: It's overriding economics that probably drove the spike in.

Clarissa Confer: Yes.

Antonio Elmaleh: Let's shift to the war itself a little bit more, and let me start off by making a comment. It seems that there are many similarities between the Confederate and Cherokee experiences. Food shortages, refugees, enemy occupation, guerrilla raids, forced relocation being among them. Do you think that, in turn, rivalries within the Cherokee Nation break down on questions of North/South allegiance or, more distinctly, were there internal Cherokee divisions which war brought out, accelerated them?

Clarissa Confer: The war definitely accelerated the divisions. That's why removal is such a critical part of this story. It happened in all the Nations but if you look particularly at the Cherokee, the Stand Watie/ John Ross division mirrors removal. And it's ironic, of course, because John Ross was a slave owner and Stand Watie was not, and John Ross is Union and Stand Watie is Confederate. And I always felt it wouldn't have mattered which side the one picked, the other would take the opposite just because they were political rivals.

So the Indian Territory does experience a lot of the same things, particularly a border region like Missouri. The well-documented horrors of guerrilla warfare and chaos in Missouri well described the experience in Indian Territory. It's almost like a colonial war in many ways, the same way France and England fought their rivalries. Their rivalries fought out here on American soil with American participants like the French and Indian War. First the Union, then the Confederates, supplied the weapons and the motivation and the organization for an internal civil war among the Cherokee.

Antonio Elmaleh: Again, reading your book, time and again the Cherokee battles fought during the Civil War seem to pit primarily only Cherokee against Cherokee, and not against either Northern or Southern regular troops. I think Pea Ridge in Arkansas might be an exception to that. Is it possible that the civil war within the Cherokees was really a sideshow that had more to do with internal struggles for dominance within the Cherokee Nation and not much to do with preserving the Union or defending slavery and secession?

Clarissa Confer: Yes, that's true, I think it very much played out the internal divisions. Not that they didn't believe in some of the causes of either the Confederacy or the Union, but they layer that with the defense of their culture, how the Cherokee Nation should progress and go forward. And the battles are mostly Cherokee against Cherokee for two reasons: one is because the Union and the Confederacy never bothered to send troops into Indian Territory in any great numbers; and because the treaties, by Native choice, required them only to fight in their own territory. They had no interest in, like you said, the much broader national cause of preservation of the Union. They had no interest in going to Louisiana or Virginia; they were only fighting for the Cherokee Nation.

They tried neutrality; it didn't work. They were very much caught up in and part of the larger United States, no matter whether they wanted to be or not. And by 1860 that just wasn't a choice.

Antonio Elmaleh: I keep thinking of putting myself in the shoes of a Cherokee who is asked to put on a blue uniform and fight for the North, when you spent years killing Blue Coats. I mean, what kind of major hoops they must have had to go through to reconcile this notion of taking up arms in support of the very people who are trying to move them off their lands and steal whatever they had.

Clarissa Confer: Right, that's definitely a hard choice, and that's one of the reasons ...

Antonio Elmaleh: That's a hard one.

Clarissa Confer: Picking North or South was difficult. The federal government, the Union, removed them officially. But the people who moved in and took their land were Southerners.

Antonio Elmaleh: I guess I can imagine the commanders are trying to motivate these warriors to put on uniforms when they really, emotionally and otherwise, have no allegiance or identification with either.

Clarissa Confer: Really, all the Nations, and the Seminoles more strongly than any of them, are following their tribal leaders. If John Ross said, "This is what's best for us, this is how we're going to protect our sovereignty," then they turned out because John Ross asked them or told them to. The Seminoles, who don't have as organized and centralized an institution of nationhood, follow their band leaders. And that's true across all five Nations: it's much more personal. Local or national or tribal identity really informs people's choices in Indian Territory.

Antonio Elmaleh: It's remarkable that the Civil War, given how much it affected so much of the country, from the Cherokee point of view was not predominant in their thinking and in their actions. It must have been quite confusing, to say the least.

Clarissa Confer: They couldn't live in a bubble. There's no way that they could live in a vacuum, and the tensions that were tearing the country apart in the 1850s came to Indian Territory and came to their Nations. Anti-slavery and pro-slavery forces were both there. The best thing, realistically, would have been to be able to spend a couple more decades getting their lives back together after removal, without having to go through the crisis of Civil War. And John Ross said that. He said, "We need to stay neutral, we need to not get involved."

Antonio Elmaleh: Let the white people knock each other off and leave us alone.

Clarissa Confer: Yeah, you guys go and ...

Antonio Elmaleh: You guys work it out, we're going to go about our business. Kind of cynical but it's a survival tactic, for sure.

Can you talk a little bit about the irony of missionaries, and preaching on both sides of the fence on abolition? And the subsequent Cherokee banishment of abolitionists in the Indian Territory?

Clarissa Confer: Well, missionaries, that's been a two-edged sword for Native peoples since they've been around. Some of the missionaries came to Indian Territory, removed with the Cherokees. And in "Worcester vs. Georgia," of course, Worcester was a missionary. Some of them had been very dedicated to staying with the people they preached to. But there are several denominations represented in Indian Territory. And most missionaries try to steer clear of politics, but not all. There were some strongly abolitionist missionaries and there were some strongly pro-slavery missionaries. And to layer confusion and complexity, some of the national boards that sent the missionaries had certain policies that, pro-slavery or anti-slavery, were going to be almost impossible to carry out on the ground. And the missionaries on the ground knew that, but the dictates of their national bodies told them to behave in other ways.

In general, missionaries get kicked out of the Native Nations all the time for meddling, for overstepping their bounds, or not providing what the Natives want from them. And then again, this goes back to the mixed blood: the mixed blood elite, who tended to be the slave owners, also tended to be the leading Methodists, for example, and they made it very clear that their livelihood and their choices were not going to be questioned by white missionaries in church on Sunday. So, yeah, some areas made those missionaries leave.

Antonio Elmaleh: And again, I find it ironic that they would banish people who were advocating the very thing that the Cherokees would prize, which is autonomy, freedom. But I guess the ideology, as it is with so many things in history, is window dressing for more pressing economic forces and motivations. Do you think that's true?

Clarissa Confer: Right. The principle of freedom for the Cherokees is the freedom to make our own choice: if we want to all paint our houses purple, we get to. That's what sovereignty and autonomy really are. You don't get to like our choices but you need to let us make them, if we're really a sovereign nation. That's the bottom line on every issue.

Antonio Elmaleh: Yeah. Let's turn for a moment to Reconstruction. You wrote, and this really struck me quite forcefully: "Southern and Cherokee Reconstruction had many similarities: forced relocation, refugees, disrupted or nonexistent civil services, revenge. One important distinction is that no Southern state was ever forced to give up its land, while the Cherokee Nation had to." Can you explain that?

Clarissa Confer: In many ways, Reconstruction is just another land grab.

Antonio Elmaleh: There you go.

Clarissa Confer: In 1866, when the Cherokee Nation had to deal with the federal government, the federal government declared they had all been Confederates. And it's true, they had signed treaties with the

Confederacy. But three of those Nations walked away from those treaties and raised troops and fought with the Union for the last two-thirds of the war. That was conveniently forgotten. And Jackson had done the same thing after the Battle of Horseshoe Bend; he stripped the Creeks of twenty-three million acres of land, even those who fought with him. It's a longstanding tradition. But the Cherokees were so divided, they sent two delegations to Washington asking for different things.

More Cherokees were loyal to the Union, a larger percentage, than loyal to the Confederacy, but all that got washed away. And what, of course, they demanded in the Reconstruction treaties was land, and the federal government denied just that. The Cherokee Nation was reduced to somewhat of a shadow of its former self, but more specifically, some of the Creeks lost a lot of land. The Chickasaws and Seminoles lost a lot of land, as well. And then many other Native Nations were put into Oklahoma on what was formerly the five southeastern Nations' land. It became a dumping ground for everybody they could think of: Potawatomi, Shawnee, Kickapoo. That's how Jim Thorpe's family got there, the Iowa Osage. It goes on and on.

Antonio Elmaleh: But still, you look at this, you see no instance ever of a radical Republican notion or attempt to take parts of Georgia away. The land grab you're talking about, which is economically driven, it just doesn't show up in the Reconstruction of the South.

Clarissa Confer: Right.

Antonio Elmaleh: And here's a region that certainly brought upon a lot of death, a lot of destruction, a lot of potential for revenge, and yet that didn't play out. But with the Native Americans it was rampant. I mean there has to be a racist influence there, because it just defies... it's not consistent, let's just put it that way.

Clarissa Confer: Right. Native people have always been a different category, they've always been treated in different ways. When Andrew Johnson revoked Sherman's orders, which is where the forty acres and a mule story comes from, he gives into white Southern planters who demand their land back. And as we know there is no redistribution of land of those who lost in the Confederacy, only in Indian Territory. But that's part of the larger picture of dispossessed peoples that is the history of America. It fits in the larger picture nicely; it just doesn't fit in the rest of the Civil War story.

Antonio Elmaleh: Well, you just hit on one of those things. You could call it a land grab if you want, but there certainly was an attempt to redistribute land. The whole thrust of forty acres and a mule was to empower and give former slaves the ability to start building a life for themselves by being able to feed their families. That's completely stripped away in the Reconstruction debates and ultimate collapse of the whole effort.

Clarissa Confer: Yeah, that wasn't actual government policy. I mean, the forty acres and a mule never really ...

Antonio Elmaleh: No, no, no, I understand.

Clarissa Confer: It's what could have been and it shows where we could have gone, but it also shows the racial solidarity of this country that did not happen.

Antonio Elmaleh: There it is, rearing its ugly head again. How is the Cherokee Nation faring today?

Clarissa Confer: The current Cherokee Nation is very active. They have a website, they have a Twitter feed as a matter of fact. If you just go to Cherokee.org you will find quite a bit about them. They have a healthcare system, a government, they keep an active program of Cherokee language learning so the next generations will continue to value their culture and their language.

Antonio Elmaleh: I know that traditional history teaching has been woefully inadequate in understanding Reconstruction, which, to me, is the most critical piece of the war. I mean, if you really want to understand race relations in this country and you don't start with what Reconstruction was, you're really missing the boat.

Do you think that the Cherokees now, in terms of their educational thrusts with their children, are able to bring a truth and a kind of a clarity to this tragic history? I'm looking at it against how woeful mainstream US education has fallen down on this most critical chapter in our history.

Clarissa Confer: I think that removal probably still resonates with the Cherokee people a lot more than the Civil War and Reconstruction. Removal is so unique to their culture. There's almost no family among the Cherokee who didn't lose somebody on the Trail of Tears, who wasn't touched by it in some way. I think that's much more of a touchstone for most Cherokee people than the Civil War and Reconstruction, so I think that that's more of an educational focus than the period that we're interested in.

Antonio Elmaleh: I'd like to call this episode "Uncovering the Long Trail of Tears: The Cherokee Nation's Experience Through the Civil War," because it didn't stop with that relocation, it just kept going.

I'd like to double back to what I meant to ask you at the beginning and didn't, which is how did you first get involved in this subject? What prompted you, what was the motivator, what sparked you to dive into this and make this your area of scholarship?

Clarissa Confer: I knew you were going to ask me that, everybody does.

Antonio Elmaleh: Well, I saved it for last.

Clarissa Confer: I should come up with a good answer. I've always been interested in Native history, and I was originally a colonial historian. And when I went to Penn State, the 19th century program was so strong and I was so impressed by Gary Gallagher and the other professors that I could work with, that I really wanted to see if I could find a way to meld my interests. I was fascinated by the Civil War but I have minor degrees in Anthropology and I didn't want to give up the Native aspect to it.

There were maybe one or two books on Native participation in the Civil War, and so I saw an opportunity for that. And then once you start, you get stuck down the rabbit hole, and then you do more on it. You have to research something you enjoy, and I really enjoyed uncovering the story and bringing what I think is a poorly known aspect of the war to light.

Antonio Elmaleh: I went to Duke University for all of about 12 minutes, but while I was there I remember the book by an anthropologist named Weston La Barre, and he wrote a book that had to do with sleep and dreams in Native American culture. Have you ever delved into that? I know this is a bit far afield from the Civil War.

Clarissa Confer: Not really, but there's a pretty famous well-known source called Myths of the Cherokees, where James Mooney in the 19th century went around and tried to collect as many of what we in mainstream America would probably call myths, stories and creation beliefs and the stories Cherokee kids are brought up on. And that's an important source, as well as anthropology books by Hudson on the Southeastern Indians, to try to get an understanding of traditional culture.

One of the things I argue in the book is that Native soldiers aren't going to behave in the same way, necessarily, that white soldiers are going to behave because they don't grow up with the same traditions. They don't grow up hearing about how George Washington stuck it out at Valley Forge, they grow up with stories of Tecumseh. They grow up with their own traditions, which teaches them a different model of behavior, a different model of bravery, a different model of honor. I think that that's where I would use stories, not so much about sleep but stories of traditions and oral traditions, and cultural aspects.

Antonio Elmaleh: I'm going to do a show later on sleep and dreams in the Civil War, and what strikes me in doing research on it is there is a recurring theme in these dreams: it's typically the soldier worrying about the faithfulness of his wife. He's so homesick, but he's so terrified that while he's gone she'll take up with someone else or when he gets home she won't be there. It's a constant theme. I wonder whether in looking at Native American dream life you could find something along the lines of being displaced, or acculturation or being uprooted or uplifted out of their natural environment into an alien land. Because, I think we all are scared of that, quite frankly.

Clarissa Confer: I always think if I'd be in battle I would be worried about getting shot, but the home front is incredibly important.

Antonio Elmaleh: Right.

Clarissa Confer: You cannot talk about any war if you only look at the military, the home front is a huge part of it. And we do have letters in the Cherokee Nation. For example, Stand Watie and his wife write back and forth, and she's writing to him about all these family concerns, and he's like, "How are the boys?" and she's worried that they'll become too violent because they're growing up in the middle of this war. Yeah, those are the type of things that apparently you spend a lot more time thinking about than if you're going to get shot.

Antonio Elmaleh: Well, the dreams typically are not, "Oh, I suspect you of being unfaithful." It's always, "I dreamed that I couldn't find you." They couched this deeper fear in the context of more of a mystical situation, they don't want to nail it right on the head with these letter, because it shows that they're mistrusting their own spouse. The dream and the letter writing is about masking that. "I dreamed you weren't on the shore waving to me coming home," something like that. Kind of oblique but it makes the point.

Clarissa Confer: One of the reasons for desertions is because men got letters from home saying, "Honey, I won't be here when you get back." And we know the power of that connection, the worry of the home front. That's one of the big arguments for why the Confederacy fell. It was the loss of will from the Confederate home front, particularly Confederate women.

Antonio Elmaleh: Thank General Sherman for that, among others. If you could leave our listeners with one overriding thought or image of the Cherokee Nation's experience in the war, what would that be?

Clarissa Confer: That they participated. And the resilience of the Cherokee as a people. The fact there still are Cherokee, they are still united as a people, living in the 21st century. They don't seem any different than any of your neighbors but that unique identity and heritage of being a Cherokee is so important. And the Civil War was another major crisis but it wasn't the only one, and it wasn't one that destroyed them. They come out of the Civil War battered in many ways but still intent on being Cherokee people. I mean, that's always my takeaway for my students. The Native people still survive, we still survive.

Antonio Elmaleh: They're still there.

Clarissa Confer: Yeah, and not as a diorama in a museum, but living, breathing, progressing people, for whom every day is a challenge on how to balance being Cherokee and being American, and being a woman and being a mother or being a businessman. There's so many levels. Everybody has levels to their identity, but a tribal identity and a Cherokee kin network identity is a whole other layer.

Antonio Elmaleh: Do you have any population figures between now and the so-called height of Cherokee existence? When you look at these population figures, what do they look like?

Clarissa Confer: Well, there are more Cherokees today than there were when I studied them, certainly. But Cherokees don't all live in Indian Territory. The majority of Native-registered people do not live on reservations. I think there's over a quarter of a million Cherokee people today, it's exponentially higher, but Native people in general are still only about one percent of the US population. The US population has grown exponentially, too.

Antonio Elmaleh: But I remember a figure of something like twenty thousand around the Trail of Tears. Is that off by a lot or is that pretty close?

Clarissa Confer: Yeah, the Cherokee figure they lost about a quarter of their population on the Trail of Tears. You would be forgiven for thinking that perhaps the Cherokee people stopped existing, but they are, in fact, vibrant still.

Antonio Elmaleh: That's fantastic. Do you have any parting thoughts? Or is there something I might have left out of our discussion? I'm sure there is, but ...

Clarissa Confer: We've talked about everything!

Antonio Elmaleh: Are there lingering thoughts that you wanted to bring up for our listeners?

Clarissa Confer: There's also many other Native peoples who were impacted by the Civil War, participated in the Civil War. Ely Parker, who was a Seneca, was often seen in pictures with Grant. He was Grant's personal secretary.

Antonio Elmaleh: Quanah Parker, was it?

Clarissa Confer: Ely Parker.

Antonio Elmaleh: Oh, I thought it was Quanah.

Clarissa Confer: Quanah Parker, yeah, he's Comanche, but Ely Parker was Grant's personal secretary. If you ever look at the picture of the signing of Appomattox, that famous painting, there's a Native-looking man in the picture. That's Ely Parker. There's so much diversity to Civil War history. When I first started this project, my dissertation, my advisor was Gary Gallagher, and ...

Antonio Elmaleh: Oh, wow.

Clarissa Confer: He's like, "You're going to write on what?" But he, by the end of reading my dissertation many, many, many times, he came to be very interested, I think, in that other aspect. There's so many aspects of the Civil War and it's a story that goes beyond just the armies people study. There are so many stories out there, there's nobody in the country that wasn't touched by the cataclysmic event. Those are so many ways to be interested in the Civil War that I think everybody should look into it, read more.

Antonio Elmaleh: I think we've run out of time. I want to thank you, Dr. Confer, for a terrific conversation today. You've helped us uncover a greater understanding of the Cherokee Nation, as well as how the Civil War affected everyone in this country. Thank you, again.

Clarissa Confer: Thanks so much. I enjoyed the conversation.

Antonio Elmaleh: And thank you to all our listeners for taking the time to listen to our show. And, I invite you to come back again for another segment of *Uncovering the Civil War*. Until then, stay safe and do good.

EIGHT

UNCOVERING LINCOLN'S WAR WITH THE SUPREME COURT

Guest: Dr. Jonathan W. White

Antonio Elmaleh: Hello, everyone. Welcome to another segment of *Uncovering the Civil War*. Today, my guest is Professor Jonathan White. He is an associate professor of American Studies at Christopher Newport University, and the author or editor of eight books, including *Midnight in America: Darkness, Sleep, and Dreams During the Civil War*, published by the University of North Carolina Press, and *Abraham Lincoln and Treason During the Civil War: The Trials of John Merryman*, part of the series *New Dimensions of the American Civil War*. He's also the author of numerous articles on the war. Welcome, Professor White.

Jonathan White: Thank you so much for having me.

Antonio Elmaleh: Well, it's a large topic we've taken on, which is essentially the relationship of Lincoln and the Supreme Court, and, by extension, Lincoln's relationship with the judiciary all through the war. I thought we might start out with laying some groundwork and I'd like to ask you if you could please describe the Judiciary Act of 1789, and its impact on events seventy-five years later.

Jonathan White: Yes, that's a great question. So, the Judiciary Act of 1789 established the federal court system, and it was a different kind of court system than we have today. It had two trial-level courts, which were known as district courts and circuit courts. These were federal courts that were staffed by Presidentially-appointed judges. The district courts were staffed by what were called District Judges; and then the circuit courts would have two judges presiding over them, they would have a U.S. District Judge, and then they would also have a Supreme Court Justice. And the justices did something in the early Republic and Civil War era that was called "riding circuit," and it meant that they would literally, at the very beginning, get on a horse and ride around a certain area, sitting in these circuit courts or these trial courts all over the country. Then the Supreme Court Justices of course would also sit on the Supreme Court of the United States, which meant in the national capital.

So, if you had a lower-level federal case, it would usually be tried in a district court. If it was a more important case, say, a capital crime, something for which you could be executed, that would be tried in a circuit court, and you would have again, a District Judge and Supreme Court Justice presiding over your case. There were a few ways to get to the U.S. Supreme Court, there were not a whole lot of ways to appeal a criminal case but you could get to the U.S. Supreme Court, and then you would have the court reviewing a case that actually one of the Justices had already sat in, as a circuit justice. And the reason the Judiciary Act is so important is because it did limit the ways that cases could get up to the Supreme Court.

Lincoln was able to use the Judiciary Act of 1789 in a way that he could choose not to appeal certain cases that he lost in lower courts or in state supreme courts, and basically preclude the supreme court from ever hearing certain kinds of cases.

Antonio Elmaleh: How were the judges assigned districts?

Jonathan White: So, a district judge would be appointed to a district by the President himself, so you might be appointed to the Southern District of New York or the Eastern District of Pennsylvania, and you could be appointed there if a vacancy arose, if a judge resigned or died while holding the office.

But the circuits were appointed by the judiciary itself. The Supreme Court would determine where the Supreme Court Justices would ride circuit, so they assigned where they would sit and where they would ride circuit. And the circuits would change over time, as more states were added to the union or as more districts were created, the circuits would change. But generally, the justices would ride within a particular area, which might include New England or the mid-Atlantic states, or the upper South, or different parts of the Deep South.

Antonio Elmaleh: Did this selection process follow any kind of political roadmap? In other words, what further criteria would there be for these Supreme Court Justices be assigned specific districts?

Jonathan White: Well there were some things in cases where Justices would be assigned to districts, usually a Justice would be assigned to a district from the area from which he came. So, during the Civil War Samuel Nelson was a Supreme Court Justice from New York and he presided in the circuit that included New York and the states around it. The Chief Justice would tend to preside over the circuit that surrounded the national capital. Roger Brook Tawney, who was the Chief Justice from 1835 until he died in 1864, presided over the circuit that included Maryland and Virginia, and then when he died and Salmon Chase was appointed by Lincoln in 1864, Chase took over those circuit duties.

Antonio Elmaleh: I think as we'll learn later on, where Tawney hailed from became quite important and we'll get into that later. Perhaps the most significant case the Supreme Court decided, happened even before the Civil War started. Would you tell our listeners about the Dred Scott decision of 1857 and its impact on the tensions that led to war?

Jonathan White: Sure. So, Dred Scott was a slave from Missouri, and he had an owner who was an Army doctor, and whenever I talk to my students about this case I always ask them "Are any of you Army brats, any of you raised in military families?" And I usually have a few, and they have an experience of having moved around a lot. Soldiers today move around a lot, and it was no different back then.

Dred Scott's owner/master was an Army doctor who moved around a lot and took his slaves with him. He moved up to Illinois and then up to what's now Minnesota. Dred Scott went with him to these different places, and then when Dred Scott was taken back to Missouri he sued for his freedom. His argument was that, "I was taken into free territory and therefore I became a free man."

Prior to the 1840s, the Missouri Supreme Court was controlled by Whigs, and they had actually ruled in favor of slaves. And when slaves sued and said, "I became free by going into free territory," the court agreed and would set them free. So, Dred Scott sued, thinking that he would be able to win his freedom. But the composition of the court changed and now there were more Democrats on the court, who tended to be more pro-slavery, and so they ruled against Dred Scott in the Missouri Supreme Court.

At that point he was owned by a new master; his master had died and he was owned by someone from New York. So Dred Scott decided to try again; this time instead of the state court systems, he thought "I'll try in the federal courts" under a concept known as diversity jurisdiction, which essentially says if you have a case that involves parties from different states you can try it in a federal court. So Dred Scott tried again, and he sued in the federal courts this time, and made it all the way up to the Supreme Court, where Roger Tawney decided that he would hand down a decision that would forever determine the role of slavery or the place of slavery in the United States. He handed down the landmark decision in 1857, and this was the second time in American history that the U.S. Supreme Court struck down a federal law.

The first time, of course, is, "Marbury v. Madison." It doesn't happen again for another fifty-four years until Dred Scott. And in the Dred Scott decision, Roger Tawney determined that African Americans were not citizens and therefore did not have a right to sue in the federal courts. He said that black people had no rights that the white man was bound to respect.

Now Tawney could have ended the case there. He could have said, "Dred Scott doesn't have the right to sue, therefore he loses, and the case is over." But there was a major issue going on in America in the 1850s and that was the question of whether or not slavery could expand into the territories. Southerners believed that slavery should be allowed to expand into the territories; Northerners, especially Northern Whigs and then Republicans, believed that Congress had a right to legislate regarding slavery in the territories, and if Congress wanted to, it could prohibit slavery from expanding into the territories.

Roger Tawney thought it could be good for the Supreme Court to step in and lay down a major pronouncement on this issue. So, Roger Tawney held in the Dred Scott case that Congress had no right to legislate regarding slavery in the territories, and he said that Southerners had a fundamental, constitutional right to own slaves and to take them into federal territories. And in the process, Tawney held that a law dating all the way back to 1820 was unconstitutional. That law was the Missouri Compromise.

The Missouri Compromise had essentially drawn a line through the Louisiana Purchase, saying North of this line slavery is prohibited except for in the state of Missouri. South of this line slavery is permitted. And what was interesting about Tawney deciding to do this was that the Missouri Compromise had actually already been repealed in 1854. So, three years after the law was repealed, Tawney was saying that law was unconstitutional. It gives you a sense of just how stringently Tawney wanted to be able to put the Supreme Court on one side of this issue and say "Congress cannot legislate regarding slavery in the territories."

One other thing I would point out about the Dred Scott case is that it was looking like the Supreme Court was going to divide along sectional lines. There were six Southerners on the court, and three Northerners. It was looking like the three Northerners were going to dissent, and the six Southerners were going to come down in the majority.

And the President-elect, a guy named James Buchanan, was a big D.C. insider, and he met with one of the Justices, a man named Robert Greer who was from Pennsylvania, Buchanan's own state. He essentially convinced Robert Greer to change his vote and decide with the Southerners so it wouldn't be six-to-three, South against North, but it would be seven-to-two, with one Northerner siding with the Southerners on the Court. Buchanan knew what was going to happen, and when he was inaugurated President in March 1857, as part of his inaugural address he said, "You know, it's understood that the Supreme Court is going to hand down a decision dealing with slavery in the territories, and we should abide by it, whatever it may be."

And of course, a day or two later the Supreme Court hands down its decision and it looks like there's a conspiracy afoot. The executive, the President, is working with the judiciary behind the scenes, and working with members of Congress behind the scenes, in order to make slavery a national institution. And this really set off a lot of Northerners. People like Lincoln went out, giving speeches against the Dred Scott decision; and it really motivated Northern Republicans to want to fight against what Southerners were doing in the federal government to make slavery a more national institution.

Antonio Elmaleh: That's pretty amazing, isn't it? I read in one of your books or in one of your articles that there's some evidence that Tawney actually gave Buchanan a heads-up about the decision before the inauguration, so that Buchanan would look good by saying he was abiding by the decision, knowing full well that he supported the decision that was already made. Can you comment on that, is there any truth to that?

Jonathan White: I think that's right, Buchanan certainly knew what the outcome of the case was going to be, so he would have had to have gotten it from someone on the court.

Antonio Elmaleh: I'm wondering then, as far as the impact of this decision, what were some of the impacts on the Supreme Court, either in this process, we just talked briefly about the confidentiality issue and a Justice leaking or giving advance notice of a decision for what has to be construed as political gain or process? Can you comment on what some of the impacts of this decision were on the operation of the court?

Jonathan White: Yes. I think that for many in the North, it caused a crisis of confidence in the Court. People like Lincoln looked at this and they doubted that the Court was really acting in a non-biased way. Lincoln argued that the case had been made with really bad history. So, for instance, Tawney tried to make what we would today call something like an originalist case. He argued that African Americans were not part of the people in 1787 when the Constitution was drafted and later ratified, and therefore they could not be considered part of the people in the Constitution. What Lincoln did was he showed that the Court made its decisions based on what Lincoln called "assumed historical facts" that are not really true. Lincoln laid out a point-by-point argument showing how African Americans actually were part of the people, and that the Court was ignoring the history that it professed to know so well, or to lay out so well, in its opinion.

We have to understand that the people in the 19th century also had a different view of the Court, in the sense that today we expect the Court's decisions to be final, so if the Court pronounces on a hot button issue in our contemporary society we kind of expect that's the end of the line, that there's no other place to go, the Court has announced and that decision is binding on all others. Lincoln and a lot of other 19th century Americans didn't necessarily view the Court that way. So for Lincoln, he said, "Okay, the Supreme Court has decided this case and it applies to Dred Scott and his family, but it doesn't necessarily apply to other African Americans who try to gain their freedom or who try to bring cases into the court system." For Lincoln, he thought this case is only binding on the litigants involved and we can try to bring other cases, and we can try to win elections so that we can put other judges on the Supreme Court who might decide it differently.

Prior to 1925 the Court had very little say in terms of what appeals it heard. Today the Court gets hundreds of appeals every year and it selects, I think, about eighty. So, in that day, Lincoln really believed and had a plausible case to make that other cases would come up and if the Republicans worked hard enough they could hopefully bring about a different outcome in a future case.

Antonio Elmaleh: In that light, do you think that had the decision gone differently, Lincoln's attitude might also have been different? In other words, it wouldn't have drawn this line between an individual slave and slavery as a larger issue if the court had ruled in favor of upholding slave rights?

Jonathan White: Well certainly if the Court had gone the other way, Lincoln wouldn't have had any grievance with the Court's decision. It's an interesting question because a lot of times when you look at these court cases, especially in the 19th century, it almost seems like it just depends on whose ox is being gored. For instance, in the early Republic around 1829, Andrew Jackson, as President, had ignored the Supreme Court. So, the Supreme Court ruled in favor of Cherokee Indians in Georgia, and Jackson is believed to have said, "John Marshall has made his decision, now let him enforce it." Historians kind of question whether Andrew Jackson would have had such a quip. Whether he would have been so quick-minded to come up with that, but at any rate Andrew Jackson ignored the Supreme Court.

Then, in 1832 Congress passed a law re-authorizing the Second National Bank of the United States. People expected Andrew Jackson to sign the law, they thought politically he would be forced to do it, and one of the arguments they made was that in 1819 the Supreme Court held that the Bank was constitutional. But Andrew Jackson vetoed it, and in his veto message he made an argument that the Bank was unconstitutional and he wasn't bound to abide by the decision of the Supreme Court.

This is all really helpful background for thinking about Lincoln and the Dred Scott decision because Lincoln would point to Andrew Jackson's Bank veto and say "Just because the Supreme Court has said something doesn't mean it's binding on the other branches of the government." And then Lincoln's chief political rival in Illinois, a man named Stephen Douglas, who was a U.S. Senator, had been very supportive of Andrew Jackson in the 1830s in his decision of sort of ignoring the Supreme Court. But then Stephen Douglas in the 1850s points to Lincoln and says, "How could you say you would ignore the Supreme Court? You can't do that. The Supreme Court's decision is binding."

I think there's a real political level to the constitutional debates that were going on in the 1850s, where when one side was happy with the court's decision they would say to the other side, "Well, you have to abide by it." And if one side was unhappy they'd say, "Well, we don't have to abide by it, we can fight it in other ways."

Antonio Elmaleh: And then if the circumstance is merited, they could each switch their notions, if it fit the political bill, so to speak.

Jonathan White: Right, that's right. One of my favorite instances, in 1814 and 1815, again involving Andrew Jackson, Jackson was in charge of the American Army at New Orleans. He dug in the Army there, got ready for a British attack, this was at the very end of the War of 1812, in fact already after peace has been established, but people in New Orleans don't know that yet. So, Jackson is preparing for an attack from the British, and in order to prepare the area and to try to stifle espionage he declares martial law and he seizes a lot of property. He wins a tremendous victory over the British but he refuses to lift martial law until after he receives official word that peace has been declared and that the war is over.

Now, people in New Orleans get really upset about this because they're living under martial law and they don't think the threat survives anymore. They begin criticizing Jackson, and when one man published an op-ed in the newspapers criticizing Jackson, Jackson had the guy arrested. And when the guy had a lawyer who then petitioned for a writ of habeas corpus to be released from prison, Jackson arrested the federal judge who granted the writ and Jackson held the federal judge in prison for some time. When word of peace arrived, Jackson released the judge. The judge then promptly held Jackson in contempt of court and fined him a thousand dollars, which Jackson paid.

This moment rankled Jackson and he never forgot it for the rest of his life. By the 1840s Jackson was able to convince Congress to reimburse him not only the thousand dollar fine but I think six percent interest, which was a lot of money back then, especially if you think about over a thirty year period. But what's fascinating is, if you look at the debate in Congress, the Democrats of the 1840s say, "Andrew Jackson did the right thing and he should be reimbursed." And the Whigs in Congress say, "Jackson was a tyrant, he shouldn't be reimbursed."

Well a lot of those guys who were in Congress in the 1840s were still involved in politics when the Civil War began, and now that the shoe is on the other foot, their views changed. The Democrats who had supported Jackson then, when they saw Lincoln violating civil liberties, said Lincoln is a tyrant. And now the Whigs who are now the Republicans in the 1860s, say Lincoln is doing the right thing. It's almost, if their guy was doing it, it was okay; but if their opponent was doing something, it was not okay.

One of the people who had supported Jackson in the 1830s and 40s was none other than Roger Tawney, who was his Attorney General and then appointed to the Supreme Court by Jackson. But then thirty years later, when Lincoln does things that are similar to Jackson, Tawney takes a completely different view of things.

Antonio Elmaleh: Kind of like a free-for-all.

Jonathan White: Yes, very much so.

Antonio Elmaleh: Could we double back for a second on the question of circuit judges and Supreme Court Justices, and could you tell our listeners what was the most famous use of the statute as it related to the Civil War and the Supreme Court? It turns out not to have actually been the Supreme Court case at all, yet history leads us to believe it was.

Jonathan White: At the beginning of the Civil War, Lincoln was really concerned about the safety of Washington, D.C. He was concerned because you had a national capital that was surrounded on one side by the state of Virginia, which seceded from the Union in April 1861, and on the other side was surrounded by Maryland, which was a slave state with a lot of pro-secession sympathizers in it. Lincoln was concerned because he needed troops to be able to get to Washington, D.C. to defend the national capital, and, from there, to go off and fight in the South if need be. So, he suspended the writ of habeas corpus in able to arrest people who were seen as disloyal or somehow hurting the Union war efforts or helping the Confederate war efforts.

One of the first people to be arrested was a Baltimore County farmer named John Merryman. Now Merryman had a farm just north of Baltimore city, so just south of the Mason-Dixon line, which is the line basically dividing the slave states from the free states. Soldiers had been coming down from Pennsylvania and Massachusetts, and they all had to go through Baltimore in order to get to Washington, D.C. Well, when these first soldiers made their way to Baltimore it led to violence in the city and rioting. This caused a lot of upheaval in the city and a lot of concern among Maryland leaders, that every time soldiers pass through the city there's going to be more violence and bloodshed.

So, on April 18th and again on April 23rd 1861, the leaders of Maryland ordered local militia officers to ride around the city of Baltimore and the city of Annapolis and burn all the railroad bridges surrounding these cities. Their idea was, "If we can stop soldiers from coming and passing through our cities, then we can prevent further rioting and bloodshed."

Well one of the militia officers in charge of burning railroad bridges north of Baltimore was this Baltimore County farmer named John Merryman. Lincoln, after issuing this order that suspended the writ of habeas corpus, permitted people like John Merryman to be arrested for treason for what they had done during this really climactic moment in April of 1861 with the rioting and burning of the bridges.

So, in late-May of 1861, John Merryman's asleep in his home in Baltimore County, and his home is actually now a country club just north of Baltimore, but he's asleep in his home and about 2 AM, Union soldiers show up at his home. And they arrest him and take him to Fort McHenry. Fort McHenry, of course, is very famous because of the location where the Star-Spangled Banner was written during the War of 1812. Now Merryman was held in Fort McHenry for about six weeks, from May 25th until mid-July. He was held officially without charges. He didn't officially know why he was being detained there, although I'm sure he must have had a hunch of why he had been arrested. And while he was in prison he was given access to lawyers, so he contacted his lawyers and they decided to appeal or petition for a writ of habeas corpus.

So, they travel down to Washington, D.C., where Roger Tawney was living, and they explained what was going on, and they submitted a petition for a writ of habeas corpus. Tawney rushed to Baltimore, eager to hear a case like this. As far as Tawney was concerned Lincoln did not have the right or the authority to suspend the writ of habeas corpus because Tawney believed that that was a legislative power, because the suspension clause is in Article I of the Constitution.

So, Tawney rushes to Baltimore, and he convenes a session of the circuit court, which in those days, the circuit court and the district court, they didn't have their own buildings, so they actually met in the Masonic Hall in Baltimore. He convenes this session of the court and he grants the writ of habeas corpus for John Merryman. He orders his Federal Marshal to go to Fort McHenry and give the writ to the commanding general at Fort McHenry.

What a writ of habeas corpus essentially did was it commanded the person who had arrested someone to bring their body into court and to explain why you were detaining this person. Tawney was essentially saying to the Union general, "Bring in John Merryman's body, explain why you're detaining him. If I think you're detaining him for a good reason, a lawful reason, then he should be sent back to prison and charged with a crime in a civil court. But if I think he's not being held for a legitimate reason, then I'll order him to be released."

Well the Federal Marshal went to the fort and was not granted admittance and came back and had to explain to the judge that he wasn't able to serve the writ. The next day a soldier was sent into court by the general, and the soldier explained that the writ had been suspended and therefore they would not be bringing Merryman's body into court. This really set Tawney off, because as far as he was concerned, the President was exercising a power that he did not have the authority to do. Tawney issued a verbal opinion and then later a written opinion, arguing that Lincoln was violating the Constitution by suspending the writ of habeas corpus, and he had a copy of the opinion sent to Lincoln. Tawney also knew that he was powerless to enforce this opinion and so there was really nothing he could do.

Lincoln presumably got a copy of the opinion that Tawney sent, although no one has been able to find that actual copy of it. But if he didn't actually get the copy, he would have read about it in the newspapers, and Lincoln's response was simply to ignore Chief Justice Tawney's opinion. From Lincoln's perspective, he had an order to fight, he had a Union to save, he had a Constitution to uphold, and he needed to do what he could do to preserve the Union.

This connects back to Lincoln and Dred Scott. From Lincoln's perspective, he, as President, could interpret the Constitution to mean what he believed it meant. He didn't have to listen to what the Chief Justice of the United States said the Constitution meant. Just in the same way that Andrew Jackson had said, "I, as President, can interpret the Constitution for myself. I don't have to listen to what the Supreme Court says."

This was a really incredible case, a really incredible moment at the beginning of the Civil War, because here you had the highest judicial officer in the land butting heads with the highest executive officer of the land; the Chief Justice against the President. But ultimately the President had a huge military force at his disposal, and the Chief Justice did not. So, throughout the war Lincoln would ignore writs of habeas corpus in most cases, and allow his military officers to do what they needed to do to raise an Army, use the Army to fight and win the war.

Antonio Elmaleh: Tawney, from what I read, did not act as a Supreme Court Justice in that "Ex Parte Merryman" case, he acted as a circuit court judge. Can you explain to our listeners why he chose that and what kind of game was he really playing? Because it was obviously slightly disingenuous.

Jonathan White: Yes. It's actually in some ways almost the opposite of that. It's been a really controversial matter among historians and lawyers and political scientists. Was Tawney sitting as a circuit justice or was he sitting as a Supreme Court Justice at chambers, meaning in his own office, essentially? A lot of historians argue that he was sitting as a Supreme Court Justice; I think, as you've said, that he was sitting as a circuit justice.

When Merryman's lawyers brought the petition to Tawney they petitioned him as the U.S. Supreme Court Chief Justice and a circuit justice. And what Tawney did was he actually crossed out the part that addressed him as a circuit justice so that it was as though they were only addressing him as a Supreme Court Justice. In a sense, Tawney wanted it to seem as though he was presiding over this case in his highest official capacity, as a Chief Justice of the United States, but I think that Tawney was playing games there when he did that.

The records of the court itself, I think, bear this out. For instance, Tawney did not use the clerk of the Supreme Court to handle the case papers, he used the clerk of the circuit court in Baltimore to handle the case papers. So, it's the clerk of the circuit court who sends the case to Lincoln, not the clerk of the Supreme Court. The records in the case are actually still held by the federal court in Baltimore. They were never transferred over to the U.S. Supreme Court, so they're not in the National Archives in Washington, D.C., they're still held by the lower level federal court in Baltimore.

And then the other thing I found as I was doing research, I wrote a whole book on the Merryman case, is that I found Tawney's manuscript version of the Ex Parte Merryman decision, where you can see how Tawney was playing with the words to try to figure out, "How can I make this appear to be a Supreme Court decision?" even though he was hearing it in Baltimore in a U.S. circuit court. When he first wrote the opinion, he said that the general in Fort McHenry had to produce the prisoner before the court, he said, "In order that I may examine the case." So he talked about the court, then he crossed out "the court" and wrote in "judicial tribunal" so that it now read, "produce the prisoner before the judicial tribunal, in order that I may examine the case." Whether he used the court or judicial tribunal, it was clearly a circuit court, it was not just a judge or a justice in chambers.

And then he thought, "Well, that doesn't work." So, he crossed those words out again and then rewrote it to say that he was requiring the general to "produce the prisoner before a Justice of the Supreme Court in order that he may examine the case." He changed it from first person to third person, and changed it from "court" to "Justice of the Supreme Court."

I know this is really arcane but you can see what he was trying to do was figure out, "How can I pitch it so that I am sitting here in my highest position of my highest authority, so that it appears like I'm really stating the law of the land from the highest court in the land?" It wasn't semantics, I think it was almost a game on his part.

Antonio Elmaleh: Well, it's quite a fascinating game between two expert gamesmen. I'm just wondering though, since the quote "Southern Bloc" was so firmly established at that point, why didn't he just simply go and convene the Supreme Court and not bother with this kind of linguistic tap dance?

Jonathan White: At that point there wouldn't have been a way to necessarily appeal that right to the Supreme Court. In a case from 1807 called "Ex Parte Bollman and Swartwout," which was a case involving treason and Aaron Burr, John Marshall had held that the Supreme Court could only issue writs of habeas corpus as part of its appellate jurisdiction, meaning that a case had to be settled at the lower level before it could be appealed at the Supreme Court. There wouldn't have been a way for Tawney to just bring this to the U.S. Supreme Court, it would have had to have been appealed there first. He didn't really have authority to just bring it by his own volition to the court.

Antonio Elmaleh: And I think there's also the factor of time. How long would it have taken to get the Court to convene and go through all the hoops and ladders that were necessary to bring a case before them? And you make that point very clearly later on.

I have another, it's a minor question, but it struck me as kind of peculiar: I came across the phrase "the supreme court of the district court in Washington, D.C." Can you tell our listeners what that was and, if it doesn't exist anymore, what happened to it?

Jonathan White: Sure. At the beginning of the Civil War there was a federal court in Washington. Most of the judges, I think all of the judges on it, there were three or four were Democrats, were Democratic appointees. At the beginning of the Civil War they started to do things that were very frustrating to the Lincoln administration. The thing that they did the most of, was issue writs of habeas corpus for minors who were in the Army.

So, here's how it would basically work. In the 19th century there were no official government identification photo ID sort of things. If a young boy wanted to enlist, he could go enlist and generally he needed his parents' consent, but a lot of boys figured out they could enlist without their parents' consent by lying about their age. And what boys would often do, this was a Victorian era, they were concerned about honor and honesty, what boys would do sometimes is they would take a piece of paper and they would write the number eighteen on it and they would stick it under their shoe, and when they went to the enlistment officer, the officer would say, "How old are you?" And the boy would say, "I'm over eighteen." And that way he wasn't officially lying because he was standing over the number eighteen. So they had these minors getting into the Army this way, but when their parents found out, their parents would then go to a federal judge and say, "I want you to issue a writ of habeas corpus ordering the military to release my son from the Army because he's a minor and I didn't consent to it."

So, the federal court in Washington, D.C. was doing a lot of this, in particular a judge named William Merrick. The Lincoln administration got really frustrated with Merrick and his court, because here you have an Army that's mobilizing and trying to get ready to go fight the Confederates, and you've got this federal judge in the nation's capital ordering generals to come into court to deal with sixteen-year-old, seventeen-year-old boys who had enlisted in the Army.

So, in the fall of 1861 Secretary of State William Seward had Judge Merrick placed under house arrest at his home in Georgetown, so that he couldn't keep doing this sort of thing.

Congress decided to get involved, and in 186, Congress passed a law that abolished this federal circuit court in Washington, D.C., and then created a brand new one that they called the Supreme Court of the District of Columbia. It's this really interesting moment where Congress thought, "We've got this court with these judges who we think are disloyal. The Constitution gives us the authority to create new courts, or to abolish old ones, so we're just going to abolish this old court in D.C., and then we'll create a new one." So that's exactly what they did. In the process, they were able to get rid of these judges with life tenure, who were thorns in Lincoln's side. And when they created a new court it created four vacancies and Lincoln was able to appoint four Republicans to sit on this new court in place of the disloyal Democrats who had been on the old court.

That court remained in D.C. for decades as the Supreme Court of the District of Columbia. I think it was only in the 1930s that it changed its name to the U.S. District Court for the District of Columbia, and now it's the same federal court that still exists in Washington, D.C., but it has this really interesting footnote, which is unlike, well you could think about it this way: the 9th Circuit often goes against Republican policies today, it's seen as one of the more liberal or progressive courts today. Imagine if President Trump and the Republicans in Congress decided, "Well, we don't like the way this court is acting, the decisions it's making, so we're just going to abolish the 9th Circuit out in California and Oregon and Washington, and create a new one." And then that would give Trump the opportunity to appoint however many new judges, that's essentially what Lincoln did with Congress in 1863.

I think today if that happened there would be a huge outcry. You can't just abolish a court because you don't like the decisions it's making, but Lincoln was able to pull it off for some reason in 1863.

Antonio Elmaleh: Well, I think one reason is he had the Army behind him, and I think we'll talk about that as to what extent the Army and the military played a significant role in allowing Lincoln to essentially get away with what has to be in some ways an illegal act. As he just said, "This is a time of war and I'm doing what I have to do." In one of your articles, you go to great lengths to describe why the Supreme Court was strangely insignificant during the Civil War, yet it played such a huge role in setting the stage for it.

Jonathan White: Yes, I think there's a couple reasons and it is a really interesting problem because there were so many Constitutional issues during the Civil War: things like the suspension of habeas corpus and people being arrested without charges, things like Lincoln's Emancipation Proclamation, which was really controversial and many believed unconstitutional. With Emancipation in particular, Lincoln in 1861 when he was inaugurated President, said, "I have no power to free the slaves. As President I can't just do whatever I want, I have to abide by the Constitution." And Lincoln believed that the Constitution protected slavery where it existed in the South. Two years later Lincoln comes out and says, "Guess what? I can free the slaves." So, this was a really controversial thing, and a lot of people believed it was illegal.

If you look at the way the Lincoln administration acted, it acted in ways that were very careful legally to try to prevent cases from ever getting up to the Supreme Court. With Emancipation, for example, a lot of people today criticize the Emancipation Proclamation, "Why is it so dull and dry? Why is it so legalistic? It's this great document where Lincoln essentially frees millions of people, why didn't he write it in the Gettysburg Address?" I think the reason is that Lincoln knew that this could be challenged in court, and if it was challenged in court it could get up to the Supreme Court, and for most of the war Roger Tawney was presiding over the Supreme Court.

So, Lincoln wanted to write the Emancipation Proclamation in a way that could hold up in court, so it's very dull, dry, legalistic language. It's very limited in its scope. The Emancipation Proclamation didn't free any slaves in the loyal border states like Missouri or Maryland or Delaware or Kentucky, it only freed slaves in areas of rebellion. And the idea was that emancipation is a military measure, it's something that's necessary to win the war, so we can free the slaves of the rebels in order of the help the Union win the war and hurt the Confederacy in their war effort.

By narrowing the scope of the Emancipation Proclamation, Lincoln hoped that he would keep it from being struck down in court, and Lincoln went to great lengths to that end. There's this one fascinating case where a Kentucky slave owner named George Robertson had slaves who fled to Union lines, and Robertson was really angry because the Union Army was harboring these slaves. So, Robertson actually sued the Union military officer who was preventing the slaves from being returned to this Kentucky slave owner. Lincoln actually corresponded with the slave owner and said, "Hey, I'll pay you $500 for your slaves. I'll buy them." And some people have looked at this and said, "That's a little shady. Lincoln wanted to purchase slaves?" But what Lincoln was trying to do was figure out, "How can I keep this slave owner from beginning a suit in the court system, because I don't want that suit to eventually get to the U.S. Supreme Court to actually have the Emancipation Proclamation struck down." So, Lincoln worked really diligently to prevent cases from being brought into the courts and then ultimately elevated to the U.S. Supreme Court.

Related to that, when there were cases that were brought in the state court system, if Lincoln lost at the state supreme court level he just chose to let it go. He and his administration realized it was better to lose in a state supreme court and just stop the appellate system right there than it was to appeal it to the U.S. Supreme Court and run the risk of having the Supreme Court strike down a federal law or a federal action.

The one that's my favorite example along these lines is a case from Pennsylvania called "Kneedler v. Lane." In 1863 Congress passed a legislation known as the Enrollment Act, this made it lawful to draft men into the Army, I think ages eighteen or twenty up to forty-five. The draft law was really controversial because people looked at it and said, "You can't force people into the Army, this is unconstitutional." Well, several cases were brought into the state court system in Pennsylvania, and the state supreme court, in the fall of 1863, ruled that the federal draft was unconstitutional.

At this point, under the Judiciary Act of 1789 Lincoln could have appealed this case, Kneedler v. Lane, up to the U.S. Supreme Court, in the hopes that the Supreme Court would have said, "No, the draft is constitutional." But there was no way of knowing how the Court would come down, and Lincoln didn't want to take that chance. So, Lincoln chose not to appeal Kneedler v. Lane up to the U.S. Supreme Court because he didn't want to risk the court interjecting and saying, "No."

Now what was fascinating about Kneedler v. Lane is that the case was decided in September of 1863, so the court, by a three-two margin, the Supreme Court of Pennsylvania says, "Conscription is unconstitutional." There were three Democrats and two Republicans. In October of 1863 there was an election in Pennsylvania and one of those Democrats lost a seat on the state supreme court, so now instead of a three-two Democratic majority there was a three-two Republican majority. So, in November or December of '63 this Pennsylvania Supreme Court reheard the case and then in January they handed down an exact opposite decision, now saying that conscription was constitutional.

Lincoln played his hand very shrewdly in this case, in fact when the Supreme Court of Pennsylvania first heard the case in September of '63 the Lincoln administration didn't even bother sending lawyers because they knew that they weren't going to be able to convince the Democrats to uphold conscription. When the case was re-argued two months later though, or three months later, they did send lawyers and they were able to argue that conscription was constitutional and then they won. Under the Judiciary Act of 1789 the losers in that case could not, in January of 1864, they could not appeal the decision to the U.S. Supreme Court because the state court had upheld federal conscription, and the way the law was written at that time you couldn't appeal the case if the law was upheld. So, Lincoln very shrewdly was able to protect a very controversial conscription law by using the courts system to his advantage.

Antonio Elmaleh: It's amazing to watch as we talk about this, the game of chess that's going on between Lincoln and the judiciary. He's fighting not just the military war but a legal war and all while trying to keep the country together. I want to just follow up on our last point and ask you to describe the "Prize Cases," which I think is a pretty important case.

Jonathan White: Sure. So, at the beginning of the war Lincoln issued a proclamation that declared a blockade around the Confederate ports. This was a really controversial decision on Lincoln's part. You get the sense a lot of these decisions are really controversial. It was controversial because under international law you were not allowed to blockade your own ports. So, Lincoln was essentially recognizing the Confederacy as an enemy belligerent nation outside of the Union when he decided to blockade their ports. Now the reason for the blockade is pretty obvious, Lincoln wants to strangle the Confederacy, he wants to stop them from being engaged with commerce, and he wants to stop conditions of war to be sent into the Confederacy from other nations. So, the blockade was a very logical thing, but when it was instituted people said, "If you're doing this, you're recognizing the Confederacy as an enemy nation."

Lincoln always denied recognizing the Confederacy as an enemy nation, from his perspective the war was a rebellion, these were disloyal people within the Union who were fighting a massive insurrection. So, cases ended up coming into the federal courts involving people who were running the blockade and people who were acting as Confederate privateers. A series of these cases ended up making their way to the U.S. Supreme Court in March of 1863, and they were bundled together as the Prize Cases.

These cases had the potential to really undermine Lincoln's war effort, because if the Supreme Court held that Lincoln was acting unconstitutionally by blockading the Confederacy, it could hamstring Lincoln's war effort. It could even say to foreign nations, "Look, the Confederacy is a legitimate nation, you can recognize them as a legitimate nation." So, Lincoln was very concerned about how the Prize Cases would be handed down.

Ultimately the court came up with a solution, where they essentially had a legal fiction, saying that you could treat the Southern states as a belligerent nation through things like the blockade, without recognizing them as a belligerent nation. Essentially recognizing that there is a real state of war, without granting the Confederacy those belligerent rights.

This case came down to the wire, it was a five to four decision. Interestingly, the decision was written by Robert Greer, that Northern Pennsylvania Democrat who had switched over in Dred Scott to join Tawney. In this case, Greer came down on Lincoln's side, saying, "Lincoln's okay doing what he's doing. The blockade is constitutional, and it's not officially recognizing the Confederacy as an enemy nation."

Antonio Elmaleh: It's quite fascinating that again, this game of chess, but if you look at emancipation and the first conscription law, there's another law that struck me as being equally significant in terms of Lincoln's ability to get things done, and that is the establishment of a paper currency. The Union struggled certainly in the early years of the war to finance it, I think one of the solutions was to create what we now call "greenbacks." Could you briefly touch on how we got that done?

Jonathan White: Yes, there was a shortage of currency during the Civil War. A lot of people held onto their hard money because they were worried about the stability of the nation at this time. The problem was that the government needed money to be able to operate, and people needed money to be able to do things. So, the federal government in 1862 passed something called the Legal Tender Act. Again, as with all these other policies, this was a really controversial law because people were unsure about the confidence they would have in the money, they were unsure whether the federal government had the power to print money like this. So, it ended up leading to a number of cases in the state supreme courts and then ultimately to a case in the U.S. Supreme Court after the war.

I love to tell my students about Legal Tender and the Legal Tender Act of 186, because the money that goes back to that period is still good money. For instance, I collect some things from the Civil War, I have a twenty-five cent note from 1863, I think, and if I wanted to go in and spend it in a 7-Eleven, I could still spend it, it's still legal tender. I wouldn't be getting my money's worth out of it, because it's worth a lot more than a quarter, but the money that dates back to that period is still good money today.

At first, in order to try to assuage people's concerns about paper money they actually printed what were known as postal stamp currency, and they would print images of postage stamps on the currency because people knew that stamps had real intrinsic value, and so they hoped that maybe if there was a picture of a stamp on the money it would give people confidence that the money would carry its value.

Antonio Elmaleh: I'd like to spend a little bit of time discussing military tribunals.

Jonathan White: Sure. Military tribunals had been part of the American military experience going back to the Revolution. Civilians had been tried in military courts during the War of 1812 and during the Mexican-American War, and they emerged again during the Civil War. They first began during the Civil War in Missouri. Missouri was a place rife with guerrilla warfare and civil unrest and societal upheaval. Beginning in September of 1861, Union military authorities in Missouri began trying civilians and guerrillas and their aiders and abettors in military tribunals, they did this under a military order issued by a major general named John C. Freemont.

Freemont is famous today for being an explorer in California in the 1840s and then for being the first Republican candidate for President in 1856. He was a very politically-connected guy, and so Lincoln appointed him a major general and placed him out in Missouri, and when Freemont found all of this upheaval in Missouri, he thought, "Well I've got to deal with this in a pretty drastic way." So, trying civilians and irregular combatants in military courts was the solution he came up with.

Over the course of the next four years during the Civil War, nearly forty-three-hundred civilians and irregular combatants were tried in military tribunals. Again, as with everything else, this was really controversial. People looked at these trials, and more moderate and conservative Northerners said, "Just because you suspend the writ of habeas corpus and arrest people by the military doesn't mean that they lose all their other rights under the Bill of Rights, so people should still have a right to a civil trial."

Congress grappled with this issue for two years. For two years, Congress could not come up with a solution, and finally in 1863 they passed a law called the Habeas Corpus Act of 1863, and this law tried to regularize the process of, "How do we arrest people with the military and what can be done with them after they've been arrested?" What the law required was that if the military arrested someone they had to have their name put on a list, and the list had to be sent to the local federal court, and they either needed to be indicted for a crime or set free if they were willing to take an oath of allegiance. What I think Congress was trying to do was essentially stop using the military to try and convict people in military tribunals.

Lincoln signed this law but then I think he promptly ignored it. And for the duration of the war, even after Lincoln signed this law that essentially tried to move military detainees into civil courts, Lincoln allowed the military to keep trying people in military courts.

After the Civil War this became a major issue. A case came before the U.S. Supreme Court that was handed down in 1866, called "Ex Parte Milligan." In the Milligan case, the Supreme Court said, when the civil courts are open you can't try civilians in military tribunals. The case was actually handed down by a Justice of the court named David Davis. David Davis and Lincoln had been friends since the 1840s, and in 1862 Lincoln put him on the U.S. Supreme Court. Throughout the war Davis believed that Lincoln had been acting unconstitutionally and illegally in arresting and trying people in military courts, but Davis was very careful to never make a public pronouncement on that issue when he had the opportunity as a Judge, he chose not to say that Lincoln was acting unconstitutionally.

But after the war was over, after the emergency was past, David Davis wanted it to be written into Constitutional Law that you can't try civilians in military courts when there's a civil court in their jurisdiction that's functioning where they could be tried.

Antonio Elmaleh: It gets a little more complicated, doesn't it, when you start to look at the fact that civilians either during the war or certainly after the war actually sued for damages against these military commanders and instilled a level of fear that, "Oh my, if we rule against this person, they could come back at us later and basically wipe us out economically." How much of a chilling effect did this civil suit for damages as a result of being arrested or incarcerated, in some people's minds, illegally, affect military tribunals?

Jonathan White: It was a huge issue. For instance, John Merryman, the Baltimore County farmer, sued the military officer who had detained him at Fort McHenry for fifty thousand dollars. That's an incredible amount of money in 1862-63, when the suit was instituted. In that Habeas Corpus Act of 1863 Congress tried to deal with this issue, and so they did a couple things to try to protect military officers.

One is they said if these suits are instituted, they're going to be moved from state courts to federal courts, and the hope there was that federal judges would have the national interests in mind rather than state judges who are elected by local voters.

Then the other thing that the Habeas Corpus Act of 1863 did was it said that if you could produce an order from the President showing that you were authorized to arrest someone, then you could produce that in court in defense of your action and it would indemnify you, it would protect you from this sort of lawsuit. The problem is that in most cases military officers could not produce an order from the President saying, "Look, I was authorized to do this." So, these suits went through and caused tremendous trouble for military officers.

One of the more interesting suits was a guy named John McCall. He was arrested in 1865 in San Francisco because he apparently got drunk and went out and celebrated that Abraham Lincoln had been assassinated. So, the military officer in San Francisco, a guy named Irvin McDowell, had John McCall arrested and thrown in Alcatraz Island for disloyal speech. This guy was put at hard labor and he was an older man, and when he got out of prison he decided to sue General McDowell for false imprisonment and for assault and battery. The judge who presided over that case granted an award of, I want to say around six-hundred-and-fifty dollars, to John McCall from the general, and the judge said, "Look, what he said was a terrible thing to say, but Irvin McDowell could not produce an order from the President saying that he should be arrested, and therefore under the law John McCall is owed damages."

So military officers were in a very precarious position. They're trying to do things that they think are for the good of the Union, they're trying to protect public safety, and yet if they go overboard they can be personally liable.

Antonio Elmaleh: Given the extraordinary powers Lincoln had exercised as Commander in Chief in his dealings with the judiciary and especially the Supreme Court, I think we'd agree it's easy to see why so many people thought he was really a dictator. Do you agree that it is remarkable that he used his powers somewhat dictatorially and possibly illegally, yet at its very essence and in other areas of his leadership he was the exactly the opposite?

Jonathan White: He certainly had a very difficult situation, an unprecedented situation on his hands. I always marvel at how much he was able to juggle. Not only was he going through all of these issues at once, he held office hours like a college professor, and anyone who wanted to could show up at the White House, wait in line, and then go in and talk to him about what they were upset about on that given day. It's unbelievable the number of things that he was able to balance.

But back to your question, I think that on some level a lot of Americans cut him some slack for the ways that he may have gone a little too far because of the pressures and the problems that he was facing. In my books and articles I'm critical of Lincoln, for instance, for violating the Habeas Corpus Act of 1863, a law that he signed. And yet I'm understanding of the realities that he faced on the battlefield and in Washington, D.C.

The other thing that has helped his reputation recently, is that for a long time people looked at this issue of military arrests of civilians and they just assumed that most of the people who were arrested were Lincoln's political opponents and he was just arresting people to try to silence them. There was a historian named Mark Neely who won the Pulitzer Prize back in 1992 for a book called *The Fate of Liberty*. Neely spent years and years going through every scrap of paper that he could find at the National Archives relating to the arrests of civilians, and what Neely found was that Lincoln did arrest probably at least fourteen thousand people, but most of the people who were arrested were somehow either helping the Confederacy or hurting the Union war efforts, they were not just political opponents of Lincoln. I think that Neely's work has gone a long way to exonerating Lincoln for being a tyrant or a dictator. Lincoln never stopped elections from being held, and most of the people he arrested were people who would have been arrested anyway if the federal marshals had been up to the task, but there just were too many disloyal people.

Antonio Elmaleh: I think it's also critical to remember that these were uncharted waters. I think you said "extraordinary circumstances require extraordinary measures," and he was not shy or afraid to use them where he saw fit. So that context of being in this once-in-a-country's-history war, colored everything he did in terms of what he had to do to keep the Union together.

Jonathan White: I think that's right. And he always did try to connect what he did to the Constitution. The arguments that he made can be controverted, but he did try to connect his positions to the nation's fundamental law.

Antonio Elmaleh: Is there one revelation or finding your research has uncovered that opens up new fields of inquiry in this exhaustively studied subject?

Jonathan White: With each one of my books I always try to find a question or a topic that no one else has thought to write about, or that they've come to answers that I think are not necessarily the right ones. A lot of my books cover a bunch of different topics. I've written a history of dreams during the Civil War, which I think was something that no one else would ever really think to write about. And then I've written a lot about the civil liberties question; the civil liberties question has been dealt with a lot but what I've tried to do is get at the records that people often ignore, most of the time when people look at civil liberties questions they rely on published case records, what I've tried to do in my research is find things that add insight that most historians have not thought to look at before.

The book on Merryman, by finding records, letters that he wrote that no one had ever seen before, and manuscript court records that people had ignored. In that case I was able to explore why Merryman did what he did and the effects that it had on the court system in ways that people hadn't seen before.

And then I have a book on Union soldiers that deals with civil liberties, and I looked at soldiers who were court martialed for criticizing Lincoln and emancipation. In that case we tend to think most soldiers supported Lincoln, most soldiers supported emancipation, that's what most historians argue, and yet I was able to find this whole undercurrent of anti-emancipation, anti-Lincoln soldiers who vocally protested against him and were court martialed and punished for doing so.

I think the Civil War is one of these wonderful moments where there are so many records out there that have yet to be explored. There will always, I think, be something new for historians to find and to say about the war.

Antonio Elmaleh: And I'm very grateful for the work you've done because, as I said, our show is about uncovering little known facts about the Civil War. We try to go for, "Oh, I didn't know that," kind of moments. And yet there's so many myths and misunderstandings about it even one hundred and sixty years later. I'd like to wrap up with one final question, which is: if you could leave our listeners with one overriding thought for consideration about the subjects we've been discussing today, what would that be?

Jonathan White: I think that the issues that came up during the Civil War with the Supreme Court and also with civil liberties are perennial issues. Any time a nation's involved in war we deal with this tension between liberty, personal liberty on the one hand and national security on the other hand. Related to that, we deal with the question of, "How should the courts function in wartime?" That's an issue that's been prevalent during the War on Terror, especially ten to fifteen years ago when the Supreme Court was dealing with Guantanamo Bay cases. It's an issue that was enormous during the Civil War.

During the Civil War you had some judges like Roger Tawney who believed they needed to stand up and state very firmly when Lincoln was violating the Constitution even if it might hurt the war efforts. Then you had other judges like David Davis who during the war stayed quiet on these issues and only waited until after the war to decide that Lincoln was acting unconstitutionally.

I think the tensions that existed during the war are still with us today, and the more we study these issues in American history, I think the better we can understand them in our own time.

Antonio Elmaleh: And just as a side note, you mentioned Jose Padilla and the suit for damages, can you just quickly wrap that up because it goes to your point about how the implications of decisions made one hundred and sixty years ago are still playing out as we speak.

Jonathan White: Yes. Jose Padilla was a terrorist or a suspected terrorist about ten years ago, and he was arrested and he sued John Yoo. John Yoo was a lawyer in the justice department during the administration of George W. Bush. He sued John Yoo for damages, because John Yoo had written the so-called "Torture Memos" for the Bush administration. At the time that I wrote my book the case was still alive against John Yoo, Padilla's suit against Yoo. So, I thought that studying the damages cases and suits of the Civil War offered insights into the way that we still see people who are arrested, suing people who arrest them in the War on Terror.

Ultimately, the case I think was dropped or John Yoo won the case. But for a while he had to retain very high-powered lawyers to help protect him when he was being sued by people who had been arrested under his so-called Torture Memos.

Antonio Elmaleh: Amazing, just amazing to me how we continue to find reverberations and consequences of this event to our lives today. I'm afraid we have to wrap it up, before we do though, let me ask you Jon, are you writing any books or are there any publications we should keep our eyes out for?

Jonathan White: Yes, I'm writing a biography of a convicted slave trader during the Civil War named Appleton Oaksmith. I've written about three hundred pages and I have about a hundred to go. And then I'm working on an edited volume with a friend about Ex Parte Milligan, that 1866 case where the Supreme Court struck down Lincoln's habeas corpus policies during the Civil War. Those are the two things that are keeping me busy right now.

Antonio Elmaleh: When do you anticipate them coming out and who's publishing them, or do you have a publisher yet for them?

Jonathan White: I've not lined up publishers for either of them yet. I'm hoping that the Appleton Oaksmith book will reach a broader audience through a trade press. I'm writing it, it's an adventure story, this guy was a world traveler, he escaped from jail, he was a womanizer, he was almost kidnapped by the Lincoln administration when he was in Cuba at one point. He had really incredible adventures, so I'm hoping that could be a good TV miniseries, so I'm going to hopefully line up an agent for that one. And I imagine I'm two years away from publishing that one, and probably about three years away from publishing the Milligan one.

Antonio Elmaleh: Well, good luck with that and I'll look for it when it comes out in whatever form it does come out.

Jonathan White: Thank you.

Antonio Elmaleh: I'd like to thank my guest, Professor Jonathan White, for joining me for this highly informative and provocative discussion. Thanks again, Jon, for your time.

Jonathan White: Thank you so much for having me.

Antonio Elmaleh: And to our listeners, please join me for another installment of *Uncovering the Civil War*. Until then, stay safe and do good.

NINE

UNCOVERING THE MAN OF THE MIDDLE, RUTHERFORD B. HAYES

Guest: Dustin McLochlin

Antonio Elmaleh: Welcome everyone to another segment of *Uncovering The Civil War*. Today, my guest is Dustin McLochlin. He is a curator at the Rutherford B. Hayes Presidential Library and Museum, and has been with the museum since 2015. He received his PhD in policy history from Bowling Green University in 2014. Thanks for coming on the show, Dustin.

Dustin McLochlin: Yes, thank you for having me.

Antonio Elmaleh: Before we start, I'd like to see if we could provide a context for what we will discuss, and first off by mentioning a comment that our subject, Rutherford B. Hayes, was quote "a man of the middle." I would like to give a roadmap to our listeners of the topics that we will cover today: we will talk a lot about Hayes' role in the 1876 convention, the ultimate vote for the presidency, some of his policy initiatives, and try to get a better sense of who this man of the middle was. So, back to man of the middle, who said that, first of all?

Dustin McLochlin: Well, I've seen it written by Andrew Caton who wrote this book about Ohio and the history of its people, and he kind of uses notable Ohioans to highlight certain aspects of what Ohio was and the people that made Ohio, and he uses RBH a lot to point out a way that Ohioans saw themselves. And obviously when you talk about these things and generalities, they're always somewhat vague and ambiguous, as Hayes is sort of this guy with this high self-esteem, this exalted opinion of his talents, but really someone that tried to not ever come across in a way that would look as if he thought too highly of himself.

So throughout his life he established or placed himself within the middle of whatever he was operating in. Ohio is this sort of battleground in America, politically, and it is very much in the middle. No matter what is going on federally or overall, throughout the country, Ohio is sort of centrist in a lot of ways. And so RBH sort of exemplifies this, and I think that's what he was trying to get at when he was talking about Hayes in that way.

Antonio Elmaleh: During the war, did Hayes have any relationship or contact with Ulysses S. Grant?

Dustin McLochlin: Yes. Grant was out west to begin with, of course, and Hayes basically spent his whole time in what would become West Virginia and then Virginia as well. So later on when Grant made his way east, well obviously Hayes would have noted Grant, and I'm sure Grant would have taken note of Hayes, but Hayes actually fought under George Crook, and then George Crook was under Phillip Sheridan. So, they weren't directly connected.

Antonio Elmaleh: So, what did he do, how did he start in the Civil War? What rank, and I know he ascended to major generalship, but can you chart his rise through the army and then his political rise?

Dustin McLochlin: He comes in as a major. And he begins to train in 1861 right when the war is starting and goes in as a major. He's from the Cincinnati area at this time, and he joins the 23rd Regiment, Ohio

Volunteer Infantry, and as quickly as people are pushed out he moves up the ranks into eventually becoming a colonel. And then towards the end of the war, his last major battles are at the end of 1864, his last major battle is Cedar Creek in October of that year. And after that battle, where he's fighting along with Crook, he takes a real active role in the formulation of battle plans and kind of falls in a lot with the type of guys like Sheridan and Grant who were not timid, who were pretty aggressive in the way that they fought their battles. And after Cedar Creek ...

Antonio Elmaleh: Which was part of the Shenandoah campaign, wasn't it?

Dustin McLochlin: Absolutely, yes. And after Cedar Creek he is then awarded the brigadier general position, after which they actually moved him out further west and he doesn't fight another battle, but he is a brigadier general there toward the end. When he is mustered out in 1865 they gave him the rank of private major general, which is just an honorary title, but his last command was a brigadier general. He didn't see any battles as a general, either, so his last command in battle was as a colonel.

Antonio Elmaleh: So, he never fought or followed Crook into the Indian Wars either?

Dustin McLochlin: No, no. He was done in '65 and became a congressman and moved onto working with a joint committee between the House and Senate where he was on a library committee. So, he wasn't one of the big movers-or-shakers in Congress. He was a junior representative, as he notes in his own journal, but he found himself sympathetic to the radical Republicans. He writes very positively of Thaddeus Stevens, and even writes back home to one of his friends asking his friend to give him a cool, levelheaded position on where he should stand because he's so far into the radical Republican belief that he doesn't know if he's seeing things clearly anymore. He goes to the South and begins to push for or to explore the Freedmen's Bureau. And he does that for three years until he decides that he's had enough of being away from home, and he comes back to try to be governor of Ohio.

Antonio Elmaleh: In that time that he spent looking at the post-war South, what do you think he saw as far as the condition of the South, especially during the run up to the 1876 convention? Was he struck but anything particular that you can discern?

Dustin McLochlin: The thing is that up to the war he's growing this case, in his own mind, I guess, for abolition. And he's not raised by abolitionists by any stretch of the imagination. His uncle, Sardis, is an old Whig and really has an anti-abolitionist stance. And then his mother, it's hard to really get a grasp exactly what she believed. But he then goes off to Kenyon College in Gambier, Ohio, which has a large Southern faculty. But in Kenyon he's again getting back to that idea of the middle way or the man of the middle. He finds himself being an arbiter between revival groups in college that are North and South, and he's actually the guy that tries to make everyone work together there, especially when it comes to two literary clubs that were formed on their political leanings of the South versus the North.

And then when he becomes a lawyer, he starts to take on at least a couple of fugitive slave law cases to try to maintain the freedom of one escaped slave and one slave who was brought across the border by her owner. And then really starts to write a little bit more about slavery and says that slavery is the reason for the war even before the Emancipation Proclamation. And he's fighting in this war to, what he claims is, to end slavery; he says that's the true cause of the war, he says that the only way that this war can be ended is with the abolition of slavery or a complete crushing of all the rebels. He starts to believe very strongly in his feelings on slavery.

Once slavery ends it's a little bit harder to tell where he stands precisely on the issue. He believes in education, so he's a very strong advocate of providing education to everyone. He believes that that would be the best answer to fix all of the ills that are going on in the world. Maybe a little bit utopian, I guess, in the way that he views things, but he starts to take on this view that ending the war, we still have war powers going on, is the answer. And by ending the war, he makes the argument that the rebels would no longer have a reason to continue the atrocities that they're continuing, because they're committing these atrocities because the war powers are continuing.

So, he's a strong advocate to provide basic voting rights, civic rights to freed slaves. And he believes that education will hopefully bring the rest around, that's the short answer, I guess.

Antonio Elmaleh: And just to follow up quickly, what was the condition of the South in the run-up to the convention? What were his perceptions of the conditions of life in the South before he was nominated and then after he was eventually elected? Does he write about that at all, his observations traveling around, or no?

Dustin McLochlin: He doesn't spend a lot of time talking about that in particular, but I guess the answer is he doesn't really say a whole lot about it. He basically believes strongly that the only way to maintain any sort of progress down there is to provide basic voting rights. And then, as well, his idea is that what we have in the South, he always thinks legally as a lawyer and what he can do as a politician, and he believes that the best way to deal with the South is, of course, to ensure that the basic 13th, 14th, 15th Amendments are upheld. And he also thinks and hopes that he can bring the Southern Whigs into the Republican party. By rebuilding that Southern Whig foundation that that will cure whatever civil problems are happening in the South at the time. He's aware of the problems there. The states have been reconstructed to this point to, in essence, 1871 when the last representatives are seated from Georgia, and the war powers of reconstruction had ended. And there were enforcement acts that had to be passed to prevent some level of violence of going on there. He knows that that's happening, so his answers are a little bit less about how federal government can get involved, because he's a reconstructionist, and believes that the federal government only has so much say in those local areas. But he's thinking about ways that hopefully build up a strong state stance.

Antonio Elmaleh: I have two comments about your last answer. One is you mentioned that he refers to slavery as inefficient, it doesn't accomplish anything. There's no mention of the morality, the fundamental immorality of the system. So, my question is, was he deliberately avoiding discussing it since he was, at heart, an abolitionist? That's a question I'd like to see if you have any kind of a sense of, because so much about this man seems to be an enigma.

Dustin McLochlin: Yes, if you read some of his diaries he does make some negative comments that sound very paternalistic towards African Americans. So, he is a man of that time, I'm not going as far as to put him in with guys like Andrew Johnson or people like that, but I do think that he has this view that there is this gap between the white and the black race.

But morally I think that he does see something wrong with slavery. I know that I mentioned that in 1850, 1849, he makes that comment that slavery is an inefficient system, but he does come out and, as he gets older and as it's getting closer to the Civil War, make very strong comments about slavery. At one point, he gets word of a letter that James Garfield had written to his commander, Jacob Cox, and in this letter Garfield writes that the real enemies of the war are people like William Sherman who don't believe in the real cause of the war, which is to end slavery.

And Hayes writes in his journal that we have got to be careful about who's going to be in control of the military after the war because it cannot be people that don't understand the true cause of this war, which is to end slavery. So he does have a very strong feeling about the morality of slavery. And I think that as far as after the war, the question for him is less about what strong positions the government can take to help with the immorality of the injustices between the two races, and more about non-governmental ways that it can be fixed. And in his mind, it's things like education.

Antonio Elmaleh: But it strikes me, and I'm fresh off of another program where we talked a lot about the insurgency of returning ex-Confederate veterans and planters. Almost literally after the ink was dry at Appomattox in Durham Courthouse, there was a widespread and continuous reign of terror across the South, something like fifty thousand ex-slaves they estimated were killed between the beginning of the Emancipation and 1885. Was he naïve in understanding that? He wants to pull the Army out in favor of this very soft and progressive notion of educating people, believing that's how you'll right the wrongs and level the playing field. All this when every day blacks are being lynched and terrorized and all this other stuff. Was he naïve about that particular information about what was going on in the South? Or knew, but didn't feel he could address it except through the solution that he prescribed?

Dustin McLochlin: To start with, yes. Whenever I present information on this particular decision in 1877, my thought is that there was quite a high level of naivete there. Very naïve in the way that he thought or he hoped that he could reestablish a Southern Republican party, or rather establish because before they were Whigs, a Republican party in the South that would be based on white voters that could then help with ensuring the voting rights of African Americans too. Let's be honest here, this isn't out of any sort of racial progressive ideas, this is simply because they knew they'd be Republican voters, right? So, there is a level of naivete there.

The larger question, though, is the question of what Hayes was responsible for and what he could do. And this is a tough position to be in, right, because I'm the curator of the Hayes Museum so it sounds like no matter what I say it's a lot of defense for Hayes. But what I want to kind of explain is that after 1865, with the signing at Appomattox, there was this ending of outright battle, but it wasn't the end of war. The war powers were still in place for quite a few years afterwards, and there's the struggle between presidential reconstruction and then when Johnson showed to the radical Republicans that he wasn't quite doing what they thought he should do, there was this fight over that. Then we move into this era of congressional reconstruction. And what recent studies have looked at is that the only real way to maintain black civil rights or black voting rights after the war was through the presence of the military. Now there's this very difficult relationship between war powers and the Constitution, and the constitutional rights of federal and state rights.

As the Southern states are being reinstated into Congress, the war powers are ending and it's now based on other powers that the federal government can put together, if they even have the desire to maintain these rights. In 1871, Georgia seats its final representatives, or rather the final representatives of the Confederate States, to then end what would be the war powers. So, by the time that Hayes takes the reins, the only states that have Republican governors still in the state house is South Carolina and Louisiana, and the amount of troops in the South is at a very small number, I believe it was three thousand in the non-Texas South, that were still there. And Hayes really only had the choice with the two states of trying to maintain control over the state houses with the Army there, or whether he was going to tell the Army to return to their barracks. It wasn't as if there was this large-scale removal of the Army in the South. The same number of troops stayed there, they simply stopped propping up the Republican governments in those two state houses.

He had a few options, he could have decided that he was going to try to redraw or bring back all of the Reconstruction powers that had been diminished over the years. That could have been an option if he felt that he had the strength to do that. But he was an old Whig and he saw that Congress held a lot of the power. And so he wasn't going to be that strong guy to reinstate all of this Reconstruction that had been dismantled slowly over the past few years. And so he made that decision to stop having the troops maintain those state houses. And so it's more of a symbolic end of Reconstruction than a real end, but it was an end, nonetheless.

What I always try to think is that sometimes when we focus so heavily on this decision, which can happen a lot, and it's not to absolve Hayes because Hayes made a decision that shows that he's on the wrong side of history. But I think the bigger, more powerful thing to think about it is what kind of a problem was going on in society that people were tired of maintaining black rights in the South? In the 19th century there was this desire to end this bayonet rule; to slowly not care anymore about what was going on in the South.

Antonio Elmaleh: Exhaustion.

Dustin McLochlin: Yes, the exhaustion over it. And then into the 20th century, of course, we still have these problems today with incarceration and everything else that's being pulled out. I think the stronger thing is to think about what's going on as a society at the time then and today.

Antonio Elmaleh: I'd like to just follow-up with one observation, and again it's coming from another show we did, but the issue of the Army wasn't simply that Johnson wanted to pull it out so he's uniformly a bad guy, there were several other factors at work: namely, one, the government didn't have any money, it borrowed so much money to finance the war that they couldn't possibly keep what was rumored to be something like two hundred thousand troops that would have been needed to cover Texas to Virginia. There was just no way that they could do that.

And secondly, a lot of the enlistments were up, there was just no way you could convince some grizzled veteran who's put his life on the line in countless battles to then be convinced to go and police freed men trying to protect their lands from marauding KKK bands. It just wasn't going to fly. So my question really is, was he looking at the fact that the Army had to rethink its entire policy of how to effectively implement these reforms? And what they came up with was, let's have the army just walk all the black people to the voting booths, but to do that you have to have guns on the ground, and if you pull the guns out, that whole notion of education and the 13th, 14th, 15th Amendments, just goes out the window. It's great idealistically, but practically, there's no way to implement it. Do you have any sense that Hayes understood that?

Dustin McLochlin: I agree with you, that's all I can say to that. In his mind he does write in his journal after he's done, and he's thinking about his four years, he said that he had hoped that, when he made this decision to finally end what was going on in South Carolina and Louisiana, that he had hoped that the reason why there were these atrocities going on, was simply because war powers had not ended. And he had hoped that by ending the war powers, these sorts of atrocities would be lessened and then we could get back to a moment of normalcy, and maybe a moment where Southern white sympathizers to the Republican party for their economic policies and, etc., would then begin to try to vote Republican and hopefully bring blacks along.

I do agree that the idea of all this feels very naïve today and maybe was naïve then. I know a lot of people at the time were not necessarily happy with the decision, and some people felt like it was the only decision he had and it was the best decision. So, yes, I don't know. But I mean, when we were talking about the Army appropriations, as you mentioned, the Army starting to be reduced every year, Congress is trying to reduce the amount of money that's going to go to the Army. And of course, underneath all of this are Southern congressmen that are continually trying to defund the Army that is still present in the South.

Antonio Elmaleh: Oh, and by the way, there's this notion that as more troops are pulled out, more of them are white. And the ones who take up the slack are black.

Dustin McLochlin: Yes, that's right.

Antonio Elmaleh: That's bad, you've got a sheriff in town who's also got a bullseye around his neck, and the stories are quite frequent of just that happening to black occupation soldiers being murdered and god knows what else.

Dustin McLochlin: Yes, and up to that point, when we know they had enough men, they were trying to position black soldiers in places where they would not be in that dangerous position, but like you said, as the number of soldiers are dwindling, they're being put in really difficult spots.

Antonio Elmaleh: Right. Now take us to the 1876 campaign, and outline some of the hot button issues of that campaign for our listeners.

Dustin McLochlin: Yes, of course. Like we just discussed, Reconstruction is an issue, it's one of the most important issues. However, at this time, it's over a decade since the Civil War had ended. And a few other issues have cropped-up. One issue that never goes away, of course, is the currency question. So there is a strong interest by both parties about the presence of greenbacks that were printed in the Civil War and backed by nothing, the question of whether the currency should be reinstated within a gold standard or the presumption of a gold standard. And then of course the question of tariffs. And the silver issue, as to whether silver should be used as a currency.

And then the other new-ish topic that was really starting to take off was this question of civil service reform. So, Reconstruction, currency, and civil service are really the hot button issues, as well as the thing that Hayes wanted to highlight, which is "vote how you shot."

Antonio Elmaleh: And we'll actually get back to each of those policy initiatives later. I want to focus on the ultimate high drama of probably the most contested and controversial presidential election in our history. Will you describe what happened at that convention? How was Hayes chosen?

Dustin McLochlin: So, with the nomination there was one guy that really stuck out as the main guy, and his name was James Blaine from Maine. And James Blaine had quite a reputation. He kind of took the middle road in Congress. He sometimes sided with the radical Republicans, but he was somewhat moderate. And he was the front runner to take this nomination. The problem was that he didn't have enough support to get him over that delegate count. The other individuals that were possible candidates, there was Roscoe Conkling from New York, who becomes bigger than life here in the next few years, after this moment; Oliver P. Morton from Indiana who was this very strong radical Republican; and then Benjamin Bristow was thrown about as well since he was the Secretary of the Treasury that kind of undid the whiskey ring and went after some of the corruption in Grant's administration; and there was also John Hartranft from Pennsylvania, who was a favorite son candidate as well.

So, when they go into the nomination process, Hayes had sent representatives to feel things out; he felt somewhat confident, he was a third term governor from Ohio. He wasn't very well known but he was a good candidate because he was unknown and because he was from Ohio, to be specific. And then the fact that he had the Civil War record. As the voting's going, and Blaine has a very strong presence, a few things happen with Blaine. One, there's this strong question about what connection he has with some of these railroad contracts and some contracts that he had in his position. At one point they're looking through what connection he had to some of these corrupt railroad policies in the way that they're building and what kind of kickbacks he's getting, and he's trying to prove that he's not a part of that, but he fumbles that because he takes the documents and changes them in a way that makes him look better.

Antonio Elmaleh: That's not so good.

Dustin McLochlin: And then, I don't know if you remember from the 2016 election where Hillary Clinton fainted, I think she fainted or she had some spell where she looked like she was out of commission. Something similar to that happened to James Blaine when he was coming out of church, so people were questioning his health. And on the first four ballots, never quite gets enough delegates. So, it goes to a new round and they're starting to see who the other option was. Rutherford wrote a little bit later that he seems to be the second choice of everybody, and the delegates start to get together and they start to talk about, looking at the electoral mapping, that you need Ohio if you're going to win this election.

So, slowly, they start to move toward Hayes. Indiana is one of the first states to fold. They were propping up Oliver P. Morton because he was their favorite son, and so they start to move to Hayes, and then the real turn is when New York decides that they were going to switch to Hayes. And on the seventh ballot, Hayes jumps straight up and everyone sort of converges on him, and so Blaine is overtaken and Hayes becomes the nominee.

So he becomes the nominee, and after the Republican nomination, after he becomes the nominee, he writes a letter. And as you guys probably know, at this time the candidates themselves are very reluctant to get involved in the actual campaigning. So he writes a letter about his campaign pledges, and they include staying on the gold standard, they include civil service reform, he makes a vague reference to home rule in the South, so it looks as if he's done with the propping up any level of whatever Reconstruction is still taking place. And so those are his three big campaign promises.

Antonio Elmaleh: It actually interestingly dovetails into what I was going to ask you next, which is to outline briefly the action plans, but these are, I guess, more his inaugural plans than they are his plans prior to winning the nomination. But could we move to the election and that question of how the election was decided before we get to his actual plans for his administration?

Dustin McLochlin: So, the election, as the returns are coming in, they notice that Tilden has probably won. And so the Hayes's go to bed that night thinking that they had lost. Tilden had decided that he had won. But some Republicans noticed that it was really close in three key Southern states: Louisiana, Florida, and South Carolina. The returns were too close for Hayes to give up. And basically, how it turned out is that Hayes had one hundred and sixty-six electoral votes that looked pretty solid, Tilden had one hundred and eighty-four. And so if Hayes could have won and taken all of those final electoral votes, he would have one hundred and eighty-five and that would be the deciding number.

So, Republicans sent notice down to those returning boards that were held by Republicans and said, hold those states, if you hold them and they go to Hayes, then we win. So, they held them.

Antonio Elmaleh: How?

Dustin McLochlin: They don't call an exact winner yet, basically.

Antonio Elmaleh: I see. They don't throw in those returns.

Dustin McLochlin: Yes, they don't claim a winner. So, both parties send people down there to look at the voter returns. The Democrats send guys down to each state, so do the Republicans. They're looking through returns, through each of these districts, the Republicans are looking through and seeing where there has been voter intimidation perhaps or any kind of reason to throw out returns, disenfranchised black voters or whatever. Democrats are looking and claiming there's ballot-stuffing and some other stuff that's going on, there's shenanigans on the other side. And they both come to their own conclusion that they had won, of course. So, they send their returns back to D.C., with the Democrats saying we've won these states, and the Republicans saying they have won these states. And so there's nothing in the Constitution which determines how this should be counted, because the only thing that there is is that the president pro tem will count the returns. Not that he has the ability to declare a winner when he has two sets of returns in front of him.

So there's this fight over who's going to declare this. Hayes of course thinks, "Well, the president pro tem makes the decision," because that happens to be a Republican at that time, so that makes sense for him. And so, the Congress gets together and they start to try to come up with some sort of plan to get to the bottom of this. And they come up with this decision that they're going to create an electoral commission. And the electoral commission was going to consist of fifteen men, five from Congress, five from the Senate, five from the Supreme Court. The five from the House would be three Democrats to two Republicans because the Democrats control the house. It would be three Republicans to two Democrats from the Senate because the Republicans controlled the Senate. And then they would pick five Supreme Court Justices. So they pick two that lean Democrat, two that lean Republican, and then they were going to pick a fifth, a guy that would be a true neutral.

Antonio Elmaleh: Another man of the middle.

Dustin McLochlin: Yes, basically a guy that was going to be the one that makes the decision. I mean, at this point the other fourteen guys are just there. And so they pick David Davis from Illinois, who is a Democrat, but is connected to Lincoln. And there's this belief that he's going to be the guy that will be truly neutral and look at this from a nonpartisan viewpoint. The Democrats are actually much more supportive of this than the Republicans, and they vote in a higher percentage for the electoral commission than Republicans do. And they pass it, so this electoral commission is created to investigate these returns.

The Democrats from Illinois make a really bad decision in that they decide that they were going to appoint David Davis as a Senator from Illinois. Maybe they were trying to buy his vote, but he then takes the Senate position and resigns the electoral commission. So now, they're faced with having to find a new neutral fifth Justice and all of the Justices left are Republican. So, they pick Bradley, who they think is the least Republican of those remaining. Bradley takes it on and he does seem to relish in this idea of being the kingmaker.

There's this one quote from James Garfield, because Garfield was on the commission, and he says that when they were making their first decision from Florida about who these electoral votes were going to go to, Bradley starts to give this long speech. And he's talking and neither side knows which way he's going to go, and Garfield writes down that he was more stressed by this than he was at Chickamauga. The tension in the room was very strong, and Garfield writes that, finally, when Bradley said that he was going to go with Hayes, he said everyone in the room was relieved, even the Democrats, because they were sick of the tension. But nonetheless every time they went to each state, and Oregon, by the way, is also thrown in the mix, because they had a snafu with one of their electorates, but in each case on a vote of eight to seven, they voted for Hayes. So, it was a strictly partisan vote that gave Hayes the election.

Antonio Elmaleh: This kind of makes Bush-Gore look like a garden party.

Dustin McLochlin: Yes, exactly.

Antonio Elmaleh: And tell our listeners what the margin was, the final electoral margin.

Dustin McLochlin: It was one hundred and eighty-five to one hundred and eighty-four, so he won by one vote. And Tilden actually won the popular vote by about two hundred and fifty thousand votes. Although, at this point, who knows what the popular vote really was going to be because all of the things that were thrown out and the disenfranchisement and everything else, but the overall vote is Tilden won the popular vote.

And where the real controversy comes in, I mean that's controversial in and of itself because of the partisan nature of it, but where the real controversy comes in is that after the returns are in, after the electoral college, our electoral committee makes its decision. Some Southern Democrats decide they were going to filibuster the return, so that it could not be finalized. And that's where there were discussions between key Republicans and these Democrats to try to end the filibuster to seat Hayes. And often when you hear that phrase "Compromise of 1877," that's where this comes from. When Republicans basically use Hayes' nomination letter, which I told you about before, and make certain assurances to Democrats that if they stop the filibuster, that these things will occur. Lots of stuff has been written about this. C. Vann Woodward would add something about how the question would also come down to economic concerns and things that were going to be thrown the South's way. But because of these meetings and because of the way that the filibuster ended, it's often seen as this sort of backroom deal.

Antonio Elmaleh: And that the Democrats extracted a promise to remove the remaining troops, was that part of it?

Dustin McLochlin: That was part of it, yes, that's part of the narrative. And from my view, just going by the nomination letter that Hayes had written, I don't think it would have mattered. I think he was going to do that anyway. But that is one of the things they got. C. Vann Woodward would add that they would also provide some economic stimulus through railroads and things like that, too, which didn't actually come to pass, and Woodward has been taken to task on that. But his response is that, just because it didn't come to pass doesn't mean that this deal still wasn't promised.

Antonio Elmaleh: I'd like to turn to once he's inaugurated, and specifically his inaugural speech where he outlines his agenda for his administration. And if I'm correct, he outlines four specific policies and/or initiatives that he wants to embrace. I'd like to take them in order so you don't get lost, why don't we start with civil service reform?

Dustin McLochlin: Yes, he's a mild civil service reformer. He believes that it needs to happen, and he's actually the first President where this starts to actually come together. And he calls for civil service reform into a system where you put in place individuals who help you get elected, so it's not based on merit, it's not based on abilities, it's simply based on taking care of your people. So, his way of doing that is to focus a little bit more on some merit, rather than just who got him elected. He also refuses to put in his own family members. Matter of fact, he has a fight with, I think, his brother-in-law because his brother-in-law wants to be put into a very small position and Hayes refuses to do that.

But his most monumental moment is when he decides to attack the New York Custom House, which was really held and controlled by Roscoe Conkling, who I mentioned earlier. And Conkling had in place, one of his right-hand men, Chester Arthur, who was running the Custom House. And Hayes looked at that Custom House and thought that it needed reform. He begins to try to put in his own men there. And he actually nominates Teddy Roosevelt Sr. to be that new Custom House head, and Congress turns that down. Conkling actually turns the tables on Hayes and says that you need to let these people's terms end, you're only doing this as your own means of taking care of your men. And so that gets shot down by Congress, but then he waits for Congress to go on break and he puts in his own guys anyway. And that doesn't get overturned.

He does kick Arthur out of the New York Custom House. That's a big symbolic win for him, because one, it's not just a civil service reform moment, this is a factional "my part of the Republican party versus Conkling's," but there's also the fact that seventy percent of the customs income that the federal government is getting, is coming through New York. So, it's also a big symbolic win, too.

Antonio Elmaleh: I'd like to mention, I don't know whether you've thought about this, but Hayes' successor, James Garfield, was hounded by a deluded office seeker who claims that he'd been promised, I don't know, the ambassadorship to France, or something. And Garfield wasn't rude to him, but he basically blew him off, and as he's walking up the steps at some building, this fellow pulls out a gun and shoots him in the back and assassinates him. Have you ever thought about if Hayes been reelected, he might have taken that bullet?

Dustin McLochlin: Yes, who knows? If he would have been very active in trying to get Hayes elected, it might have been Hayes. Hayes did have some bullet holes go through windows when he was inside the White House. But the other irony, where I thought you might have been heading with that, was Arthur, who was the impediment or one of the main actors in the patronage side of things being Conkling's right hand man, when Garfield is shot he becomes President, of course. And he's the one that signs the Pendleton Act, which begins to unravel the patronage system.

Antonio Elmaleh: Strange bedfellows.

Dustin McLochlin: Yes.

Antonio Elmaleh: We talked about civil service reform; next, Hayes outlines in his inaugural address a plan for infrastructure spending for the South. Can you comment on that policy, what became of it?

Dustin McLochlin: Yes, not much came of it, and it's interesting. There was this big push and nothing ever really comes from it. He often gets maligned in some of the scholarship because he's friendly with Tom Scott who was the railroad tycoon, and when the great railroad strike breaks out in 1877, Hayes, whether he's naïve or whether he wittingly does this or not, he breaks the strike and comes in on the side of big business. So, he's seen as palling around with Tom Scott and doing things for the railroad industry, but as far as appropriations and stuff and ability to build that up, that never really comes to pass.

Antonio Elmaleh: Too bad, too. We've been talking about infrastructure which is kind of like the bête noire, every administration trots out its grand proposals, and we have the bridges and roads that we have today as proof of how successful that's been. [Laughter] And finally, and perhaps more enigmatically, he made the case for a constitutional amendment to limit the presidency to a single six-year term. So, do you have any notion of what his rationale for that was?

Dustin McLochlin: Yes, this goes back to his civil service reform stuff. One thing I neglected to mention is that when he wrote his nomination letter, after he was nominated from the Republican convention, he says he's only going to serve one term. He claims that he wants to be a one-term President, and he and James Polk are the only two to make that claim and stick to it. He believed that the first year of the Presidency all you were trying to do is get reelected, which meant that you were doing things like putting the people in positions that could help you in the future, fulfilling those patronage claims so that you could then reestablish yourself for reelection. And he thought, "Well, in order for me to truly accomplish what I want to accomplish, I can't be bogged down with that," so he was going to only serve the one term. But his view was that four years isn't quite enough to do all of that, and he did not believe in reelection, so he advocated for that one six-year term.

Antonio Elmaleh: It's a fascinating position to take, but it kind of offers up an intriguing, and I know you don't like the supposition school of history, or the "what if", but do you have a sense of whether he really wanted to be President? I mean, given this man of the middle, and straddling all these seemingly disparate positions and all of the things we've talked about, do you have a sense that he didn't have that classic, burning, politician's desire in their gut to do this? To win, and then stay in power until the crows come home, you know?

Dustin McLochlin: Yes, I don't think so at all. I think that he was a very ambitious man. I do think that whatever he did he wanted to stick out and be the best at whatever he did. Valedictorian in school, he was always trying to get the promotions in the military, although he did make some claim that he'd rather be a good colonel than one of the generals. But he always sort of had this view of himself as being the best. So any individual that's pushing to be President obviously has some level of strong ambition. But I think you're right. I think that considering the fact that he quit halfway through his second term as congressman because he didn't want to be away from his family anymore, and then he came back home and ran for governor, and the fact that he was so willing to make that one-term pledge, and then the fact that there were some people that were pushing him to go back on that pledge and run for a second term and he never wavered, he never wavered that he was going to run again. So yes, he has the ambition, there's no way you try to become all of those things that he became without that ambition. But at the same time I think that he was perfectly fine being more of an administrator as President and then quietly moving away from it.

Antonio Elmaleh: So, you don't see him doing a political calculation, "What are my chances of being reelected? Do I want to go through that whole battle?" Or he just wanted to be done with the whole thing?

Dustin McLochlin: There is that chance that he might have been doing the calculation. You get the feeling, and this is something some of his biographers have written about too, that considering the way that he was elected and the fact that even his own, like Roscoe Conkling, called him a fraud, called him Ruther Fraud Hayes, the fact that he came in with a really difficult position at the beginning, and then slowly found a way to try to bring some respectability back to the White House, at least that's the way he would say it.

Grant had the problems with the scandals, and I know that Grant biographers are arguing back-and-forth about whether Grant was a drunk or not, but the fact that that was some of the public perception, and then Hayes makes the decision to not serve alcohol in the White

House, not only because he wanted to differentiate himself from Grant but also because of the growing number of prohibitionists that might have been in the Republican party. In his mind maybe, again like you said we don't try to speculate, but in his mind maybe he thought that he had a shot at reelection now that four years had passed and he had cemented himself there.

But regardless, what we know from what he writes is that he's ready to gear up and go home, he's ready to retire and he's ready to be done with that public life.

Antonio Elmaleh: Earlier in the show I alluded to his relationship or perhaps no relationship with Grant. But I'd like to flash forward to the campaign. Did he have any contact with Grant during the campaign? Grant had to loom large as a two-term incumbent, even though he had all these rumors or actual corruption things going on and made the decision not to run again, which he probably regretted. But do you have a sense of Hayes steering clear of offending him, or in any way, shape, or form doing anything that would have suggested that he prefer Grant just not be a factor in this at all?

Dustin McLochlin: I've often thought about that, how weird that was, because a lot of Hayes' stance had some connection to differentiating himself from Grant. And then Grant, when we get to the actual election crisis part of things, Grant is actually making comments that this needs to end because Tilden's the true winner and let's just give this to Tilden. So, it doesn't seem as if Grant is all that invested in Hayes' presidency. Hayes has some policies that look like they might be repudiations of Grant. But after the dust is all settled and Hayes is determined the winner, there was a moment there where the inauguration was going to be on Monday, but Grant's term was going to end on Saturday. So, there was going to be a full day where there was technically no president.

So, Grant has Hayes over for dinner in the White House, and then surprises him by taking him into the Red Room, having him sworn in as president basically a couple of days early, and then he has the big inauguration one day early, on Sunday. So, it seems, if there was any sort of discontent, they at least made up a little bit there at the end. And then later on, when Grant is writing his memoirs as he was dying, he makes very fond comments about Hayes in the war. And then Hayes writes in his journal about how that impacted him and how wonderful it was to read those things. So as far as the campaign itself, there wasn't a whole lot of common ground, but later in life they had a mutual respect.

Antonio Elmaleh: I think we both would agree that what very often drives history is money. Beneath the rhetoric and the flag-waving and all the highfalutin' philosophical arguments, there's always money operating somewhere behind the scenes. Do you have a sense of what Hayes' concerns with the currency were? And could you share those with our listeners.

Dustin McLochlin: Hayes had a strong conviction that the currency should be backed by gold. As you know, from the Civil War, there was the printing of greenbacks which were not based on gold. So for years after the Civil War there's this battle over whether money needs to be backed by gold anymore or to kind of have a free-floating currency. And the stance from the federal government was often to try to get things back on gold and to resume that, whether that was through taking greenbacks out of circulation or trying to build up the gold reserves. In 1875 there was the Resumption Act that was passed, which basically said within a couple of years there should be the resumption of money being backed by gold. And Hayes was a big supporter of this because internationally, in Europe, this was the system, it was the gold standard. And he felt if these loans were going to be paid back, they needed to be backed by the honorable currency system; you cannot pay back loans based on money you're printing. He had a very strong feeling on that.

And so in his administration, John Sherman, his Secretary of Treasury, acquires large reserves of gold and does resume having the government back on the gold standard. The irony of that is that at the same time that's taking place, there's also this movement within the government to start printing silver at a limited level, and to put it into the currency. Hayes wasn't necessarily against that, but he felt that if you were going to print silver it could not have a fixed rate with gold because those two currencies would then fluctuate on how much they were worth, and you could not do that if there was a fixed ratio of silver to gold. So, they passed this limited coinage of silver, the Bland-Allison Act, and then Hayes vetoes the act. The veto then gets overturned and it does go into effect.

So even though the Hayes administration was the one that resumed the gold standard, it's also the one that saw, once again, a resumption of gold in the currency as well. I guess one of the ironies of is after he vetoes that silver act, he's the first one to receive the silver coin off the press. So, he takes the first silver coin even though he vetoes it.

Antonio Elmaleh: He should have given it to James Garfield.

Dustin McLochlin: McKinley actually votes for it as well, and McKinley is one of his best friends.

Antonio Elmaleh: There you go. In an earlier program we also discussed the currency crisis, it was a panic actually, a small one, that I think occurred in 1865. I mean were people just panicked, like in 2008. It happened then, but that's now. And boy, people sure have a short-term memory, but it was very clear from that crisis that the confidence in having enough gold to back up the debt of the government was a very, very iffy proposition. Had those fears been allayed by the time that Hayes took office?

Dustin McLochlin: Well, in 1873 there was another panic. And one of the arguments that people would make is that the reason why that was exacerbated is because there was some level of deflation. So basically both sides of the argument had an argument to be made as to why their side was right, maybe that was part of it.

Antonio Elmaleh: And then he makes a statement, and this probably relates back to, well I'll just ask you to comment on it, the statement he makes, "He serves his party best who serves his country best." It's a strange syntax. What's he really trying to say, here?

Dustin McLochlin: Yes, the phrase actually comes from Carl Schurz, and he uses it. The phrase in his speech is, "he serves his party best who serves his country best." This is after the Civil War and there's this view that the South is Democrat and North is Republican, and he's arguing that we need to stop thinking in partisan terms and in what you can do to help your party succeed; rather what you need to focus on is what is going to help the country. And if you do that from your partisan standpoint you're going to help your party anyway because you are going to be the one that is putting your country first. So it's a very, like you said, an interesting way to basically say stop worrying about partisanship, worry about your country, and oh, by the way, it's going to help your party anyway.

Antonio Elmaleh: I wanted to close with some general comments, so let me start by saying that Hayes seems to be a man who's trapped between passionate progressivism and somehow maintaining the balance of the system. And so this notion, a man of the middle, is that a mirror of what they were talking about more on a political level, that there was a war going on within himself? Which side of the coin was he going to fall on, or did he feel he didn't have to ever make that choice? I know that's all subjective and very suppositional, but have you thought about why this man seems to be such an enigma doing some things that are very progressive and then pulling troops out of the war as part of a compromise, for example?

Dustin McLochlin: Yes, that's one of the questions that I'm most interested in. My feeling is that Hayes is, like you said, a man of the middle. He sees himself, in multiple situations, on the side of the conventional wisdom of the moment that he's in. The fugitive slave law is, from what we can tell, unpopular in Ohio overall, based on congressional voting and voting for candidates, we see that the fugitive slave law was not particularity popular in Ohio. And Hayes was a lawyer that, at least on two notable occasions, was willing to put his reputation on the line to defend fugitive slaves. Historically, looking back, that puts him in a very positive light. Fighting in the Civil War his journal entry shows very clearly that he's fighting this to end slavery. Again, that puts him in a very, from an historical, and modern standpoint, in such a good light.

Later on, when he's in his post-Presidency, going back to what I mentioned about probably his naïve view that education is the answer to everything, he begins to support education funds for black students to help them to receive education through the Slater Fund and through other activities. And so again, he views this in a way that, from a modern standpoint, is very positive.

But again, when he becomes president, he does the thing that probably follows the flow that is the easiest answer to an issue, going with the flow of what's been going on, again. So again, from a federal standpoint, he seems to be following the conventional wisdom of that time. And from that, he's clearly on the wrong side of history. I get this feeling that Hayes himself is maintaining his particular path of kind of being emblematic of the conventional wisdom that he's in, but from an historical memory standpoint, he is on both sides of that memory.

Antonio Elmaleh: If there's one overriding impression or thought or memory or image you have of Rutherford B. Hayes that you could leave our listeners with, what would it be?

Dustin McLochlin: What I find the most interesting about Hayes, going back to all this discussion about how he's the man of the middle, he also is very representative of the natural flows that all men of his generation, or many men of his generation, seem to go through. Which is that as his moment was passing, as the Civil War had moved on, as Reconstruction had ended, as his Presidency had come to a close, he really started to reflect on the changes that were going on in the United States, just moving into the Gilded Age and this different view of what it was that drove Americans. And he starts to write in his journal very provocative things about how he laments how the nation has moved towards the rich. He says that the government of the United States is for the rich and by the rich, and has very negative things to say about how the striving for money, for riches, is taking over. Not just the way Americans operate, but the way that the government is in the hands of that.

So it's just an interesting thing, I guess, as you go through and you look at Hayes' life. From this individual that is raised in Ohio with these views that were not necessarily for abolition, and slowly moves toward abolition, and slowly moves in these other ways, and then makes a decision that's always going to be with him regardless of how he might want to justify it or how impactful that decision was when he became President, towards at the end having some very strong views as a guy lamenting the way that his country's changing. And I find those changes and those evolutions in his thought to be very interesting and intriguing.

Antonio Elmaleh: Well, thank you for that. I think that's really powerful because it suggests that that progressive, populist viewpoint surfaces again in the sunset of his life.

Dustin, before we sign off, could you share some information with our listeners about the Rutherford B. Hayes Presidential Museum and Library? Where it is, how to find it, things like that?

Dustin McLochlin: Yes, the estate is located in Fremont, Ohio. It's called Spiegel Grove, and it's about twenty-five acres of grounds, and within the grounds we have the library and museum. And we also have his home where he retired and lived for about the last twenty years of his life. And he's buried here with his wife, Lucy, as well as one of his sons and his wife. And we're open nine to five Monday through Sunday, so every day except for in some of the winter months, January, February, March, where we close on Mondays. But we are open all year 'round, and come on out if you're driving on 80, 90, the interstate that goes north through the United States, it's right off the interstate.

Antonio Elmaleh: I think one other detail, which I thought was fascinating, and perhaps you could just quickly opine on it, is that it's the last private Presidential library. Could you talk a little bit about why that's significant and what that actually means?

Dustin McLochlin: Well, we're state-owned by the state of Ohio. We actually opened in 1916, and this library was opened for the purposes of the study of Hayes' papers, making it the first Presidential library to be opened in the way that we view presidential libraries today, which is for the purpose of study. And we just celebrated our centennial in 2016, of course, and that was a fun year and we redid the museum. Yes, we predate the federal library system, so when Franklin Roosevelt Museum was being created they actually looked to this site here to determine how they wanted to create theirs.

Antonio Elmaleh: Well, thank you for that.

Dustin McLochlin: Yes, no problem.

Antonio Elmaleh: And unfortunately, we've run out of time. I'd like to thank my guest, Dustin McLochlin, for coming on the show and helping us uncover new and provocative insight into the life and career of a man of the middle, Rutherford B. Hayes. Thank you, Dustin.

Dustin McLochlin: Thank you for having me.

Antonio Elmaleh: And to all our listeners, let me thank you for taking the time, and having the curiosity to listen to another segment of *Uncovering the Civil War*. Please come back again. Until then, be safe and do good.

TEN

UNCOVERING THE UNION OCCUPATION OF THE SOUTH, PARTS I & II

Guest: Gregory Downs

PART I

Antonio Elmaleh: Welcome everyone, to another segment of *Uncovering the Civil War*. Today my guest is Greg Downs. Greg Downs is a professor of history at the University of California at Davis and the author of two books on the Civil War and Reconstruction history, including the recent *After Appomattox: Military Occupation and the Ends of War*, as well as a book of short stories.

With Kate Masur, Greg is co-author of the first-ever *National Parks Service Theme Study on Reconstruction*, and co-editor of the first ever *National Parks Service Handbook on Reconstruction*. Their efforts, along with politicians and South Carolinians, helped inspire President Barack Obama to create the first site dedicated to Reconstruction in Beaufort, South Carolina.

He, along with Scott Nesbit, is also creator of a digital history site, Mapping Occupation. He's currently finishing a book on the US Civil War, Cuba, and Spain, entitled *The Second American Revolution*.

Welcome, Greg.

Greg Downs: Thank you so much for having me.

Antonio Elmaleh: My pleasure. Before we begin, let me attempt to set the context for what is an enormously and intensely complicated subject by offering one little-known fact, as well as give you some idea of the topics we'll cover. The Civil War is officially acknowledged to have ended on February 4, 1871 when Homer Miller became the first US Senator from a former Confederate state, Georgia, to be sworn into office. He served all of a week. Historical consensus, if there is such a thing, observes that Reconstruction ended in 1876 with the election of Rutherford B. Hayes. Here are some of the topics we will discuss: deployment of the US Army as an army of Southern occupation; the Freedmen's Bureau; the significance of the struggle between Congress and the presidency over who controls war powers and making peace; the insurgency of planters and ex-Confederate soldiers which subverted and prevented the implementation of the 13th, 14th, and 15th Amendments; what those Amendments stipulated and tried to accomplish; and the impeachment of Andrew Johnson.

Okay, Greg, why was Appomattox not the end of the war, as popular opinion holds?

Greg Downs: Well, there's a couple of reasons why we should be wary of the idea of Appomattox as the end of the war.

One reason turns on basic military facts. Lee's surrender at Appomattox was not the surrender of "the" Confederate Army, it was the surrender of "a" Confederate army. Many others remained in the field at the time that Lee and Grant meet in Appomattox Court House in April 1865. In North Carolina, Joseph Johnston is commanding quite a large Confederate army. There are other, smaller commands spread across the United States. And it's for this reason that we have things like Juneteenth, the acknowledgement of the surrender of Texas to the United States in June 1856, two months after the Appomattox ceremony. So even on a very basic level, did the war end at Appomattox? The answer has to be "no" because there remains fighting and engagement and negotiation between military commands across the Confederacy.

But the key point that I make in After Appomattox is that there's a bigger reason why Appomattox didn't end the war, and that's because the United States decided that it would not end the war. In this sense, that if we see Appomattox as the dawning of peace, we're reading our contemporary views back onto the 19th century and misunderstanding how policymakers, politicians, and generals understood what took place at Appomattox. In the days before the surrender ceremony, Robert E. Lee had asked Grant for peace in written communications and Grant consistently rejected that, denied that he had the power to make peace, and had told his generals that he took Lee's request for peace as a signal that they were going to have to fight because he believed that Lee should have known that it was impossible for him to grant peace. Repeatedly Grant says, "I cannot grant you peace, but I will accept surrender." And he's willing to fight based upon the differences between those words. Only when Lee accepts that all he can obtain is surrender do they meet at Appomattox.

Why does he think those two words mean such different things? For Grant, surrender was a simple military operation, an important and profound one of course, but a relatively simple military operation. The Confederate soldiers would lay down their arms, the US Army would grant them parole to return home, and on promise of good behavior they wouldn't be molested or interfered with. But peace meant something else. What he understood was that peace meant a restoration of normal time.

The Army had been operating in the Confederate States with powers that it could never have in Pennsylvania or Massachusetts or California, in states in a position of peace. The Army had taken over court trials because freed people were excluded from giving testimony. The Army had arrested and displaced local officials. Soon after Appomattox, the Army would arrest a series of Southern state governors.

This can't happen in a normal state of peacetime. No matter how much the current administration might have a conflict of words with Governor Brown in California where I live, there's no conceivable way in which the Army is going to march into Sacramento and arrest him.

But in the weeks after Appomattox, the Army does march into different state capitals and arrest those governors. Why can they do that? Because they're still at war.

And Grant knows that if they turn over those powers of war, if they restore a period of peace, that that will guarantee a persistence, quite possibly a legal persistence, of slavery if the 13th Amendment hadn't been ratified, and certainly a persistence of a ruthless caste system over ex-slaves in the South in which they would not be allowed to practice their civil rights. So, he knows that he has to preserve the state of war in order to permit the administration in Washington D.C. to figure out what they're going to do in the Confederate States.

Antonio Elmaleh: That's really amazing, and we'll cover some of the implications and some of the distinctions of war powers versus making peace, and then some of the irony that is attached to that.

What do you think Lincoln's vision of Reconstruction was?

Greg Downs: Well, this is one of the great mysteries of historical scholarship, especially since there are enough tantalizing hints that one can support whatever narrative you end up with, and yet there's enough mystery that no one can ever know a final truth. So it's the perfect thing for historians to debate about since there's evidence of everything and proof of nothing.

My own belief is that it's rooted in a couple of things that are underestimated in the historical record. When we think about what Lincoln would have done, we emphasize his efforts in Louisiana and his Louisiana plan, which was a relatively mild and soft plan for bringing the state back in. And we also emphasize the language at the conclusion of his second inaugural, language about mercy. In the process, it's too easy to read over the prelude to that closing of the second inaugural, which is about the ways that slavery had built the wealth and power of the country and the kinds of demands that would be put on the country to atone for it.

But for me, when I tried to look at what Lincoln was working on in the last days, I looked at the kinds of directives he was giving to his Secretary of War, Edwin Stanton. Stanton is creating plans for what the military's role will be in regulating the Southern states, and Lincoln is reinforcing through Stanton to his generals that they cannot resolve political questions. They can't make peace, they can only accept surrender. This is why Grant is so clear, both because Grant is an intelligent person but also because he has understood these are the orders from Washington D.C.

So if we work forward in this way, what we see is the Lincoln administration preparing to do quite a bit of what the Johnson administration does after his assassination: to install military governors over Southern states; to delay resolutions of political questions until practices on the ground have been established and guaranteed, both the end of slavery and the ratification of the 13th Amendment; and some kinds of civil rights for freed people. If you go any farther than that you get into extrapolations about how Lincoln would have responded to what happened on the ground, and that's a great mystery. So all I know is that the plans he had established become the initial plans for the Johnson administration because they're carried out by the most important architect of Reconstruction policy which is Edwin Stanton, the Secretary of War.

Antonio Elmaleh: That's interesting. So, we don't have a real sense of what he was thinking. We have these sort of glimpses, and they're, again, historical conjecture which is great to debate but don't really advance understanding of what was really going on.

Can you comment on Lincoln and Grant's fears of the vast guerrilla war they were concerned about unleashing by sending the ex-Confederate Armies home if the terms of surrender were too stiff, too punitive?

Greg Downs: That's exactly right, and it's something that's easy for us to overlook in asking why they didn't demand more. They were both careful readers of other civil wars. In fact, many of the people in the Army and in Congress made quite elaborate comparisons between the US Civil War and the ends of the English Civil Wars, the end of the French Revolution, and the Austrian response to the

Hungarian uprisings in 1848 in Russia and Poland. So, they're quite aware of the idea that a civil war can end in an ongoing cycle of civil war. They also draw on the history of Mexico. They even have a term that they use to describe this outcome of civil wars in which they never quite end, which they called "Mexicanization," the idea that in the aftermath of a civil war every political conflict will lead to some kind of coup or uprising.

So they're very concerned about this possibility, and they're also highly aware of the size and nature of the Confederate States. It' a vast territory, an area that includes all kinds of mountains and hollows and places that would be hard to regulate. Grant, when he meets with Lee after the surrender ceremony, asks Lee would he tell Confederates to stop fighting and to accept the terms of the end of the war, and Lee won't do it. And he says to Grant that he expects Grant will have to march two or three times across the entirety of the Confederacy before people learn of the impact of the war's end. Grant is very disturbed by this idea of a constant Civil War and guerrilla action.

When Sherman accepts the surrender from the other major Confederate Army near Durham, North Carolina a few weeks later, this is foremost in his mind precisely because in the interim Jefferson Davis went on the run from Richmond. Davis had been trying to plot out some kind of guerrilla war, and he asks Confederate General Joseph Johnston to disband his men and send them into the mountains to fight a guerrilla war. Johnston won't do it. But it's this fear that leads Sherman in a panic to offer what Grant would not, peace instead of simply surrender in his hopes of preventing a guerrilla war. When his offer goes to Washington D.C., however, President Johnson and the entire cabinet, from the most radical to the most conservative members, reject it. This is how we know that Appomattox wasn't the end of the war and that the war couldn't end in April of 1865. It's presented as an option to the president's cabinet, and they unanimously reject the idea of peace. They send Grant there to dissolve this understanding and to impose upon the Confederates solely a claim of surrender so that they can preserve these rights.

Sherman in response says, "What is going to become of us? Don't we know what happens in other periods at the end of wartime, and what will we do against the guerrilla insurgency gathered everywhere?" It's a huge fear of theirs that if they press too hard they'll inspire this guerrilla insurgency. Now, historians have wrestled between saying this is an insurgency that they successfully prevent from being launched to more recent work, coming both from scholars working on freed people like Julia Saville as well as scholars centered on army and military comparisons like Mark Grimsley, that there was a guerrilla warfare. That we should think of what happens in the South and the violence against both freed people and against the US Army in the South as a kind of insurgency that takes different forms and that it is often not aimed at overthrowing the government in Washington, but like other insurgencies they're looking to create political situations through violence.

So in this sense they may have prevented one kind of guerrilla warfare, but these scholars have asked us to inquire whether in fact there was a different kind of guerrilla warfare throughout the South in the years after Appomattox. The kind of warfare seen in one congressman's claim that fifty thousand African American men are murdered in the South in the twenty-five years after the Emancipation Proclamation.

Antonio Elmaleh: What was the Freedmen's Bureau? Just a brief description of what it was and what was it intended to do.

Greg Downs: The Freedmen's Bureau comes from an act of Congress to try to regulate the end of slavery and the development of new legal and labor relations on the ground in the former Confederate States. It came out of the American Freedmen's Inquiry Commission, a group that had toured the South and suggested the challenges that were going to be faced in navigating this transition from slavery to freedom. The Bureau doesn't only regulate freedmen, it also has power over white refugees, the white Southerners who had fled from their homes because of attacks by Confederates repressing those who didn't support the Confederate cause. As well as over abandoned land, lands that had been left by planters fleeing the US Army.

And so the Freedmen's Bureau had power to regulate court hearings involving freed people because they're excluded from testifying in civil and criminal cases in many of the Southern states, to help to set contracts and to negotiate between planters and tenants, and to provide certain amounts of rations of food or assistance in housing. As well as help navigate the creation of schools, mostly by missionary organizations but also working through the Freedmen's Bureau, and hospitals. And for a time it also looked like the Freedmen's Bureau would play a key a role in turning those abandoned lands over to freed people in the ultimate hope of re-creating agricultural life in the South in the form that it was in the North, of small family farms farmed by freed people rather than vast plantations. That doesn't happen for reasons that we'll go into.

But in many ways it's easy to overstate what the Freedmen's Bureau is, because as a matter of fact the Freedmen's Bureau is not able to sustain its own bureaucracy and it exists as an adjunct of the Army. It's a way of organizing a part of what the Army does, but it quickly becomes simply another tab of Army officers and company commanders located in the South rather than a bureaucracy of its own.

Antonio Elmaleh: And we will cover the ultimate fate of the Freedmen's Bureau in the context of the general evolution or devolution of Reconstruction later in the show.

There's a man named Benzoni who offered a novel solution to this central question: if practical freedom depended on the proximity of soldiers to enforce it, what would happen if/when the Army went home? Can you outline Benzoni's solution? I think it's quite inspired, albeit it didn't happen.

Greg Downs: It's really an interesting "what if". A lot of the "what if's" we get are about Reconstruction. I mean there's no moment in American history where we spend more time wondering what else might have happened, and where we spend more time in the counterfactual. But as in any discussion of counterfactuals, most of the time the counterfactuals we suggest have basic practical problems or, really, emerge from a later vision, not from that time period. But what's interesting about Benzoni is you see something that does emerge as a seemingly realistic and American solution, from a commander on the ground thinking in practical terms. He believes the US Army could transition out of active duty by creating colonies of former soldiers in Southern states and redistributing land to them.

Now, again, like the hope of redistributing land to freed people, this question of where the land would come from is a major question. But it's an open one at the time he's writing. He's looking to the way Alexander Hamilton had, in the country's founding, looked back at Roman imperial models: at the end of their service you put soldiers as farmers on the frontier so they would be a first wave of defense. And Hamilton had looked to this in the settlement of what's now our Midwest and was then the Northwest: the idea that if you put soldiers there as farmers, they would be a first line of defense.

Benzoni says it's a second founding. This isn't the language he uses, but he's thinking in those terms back to the nation's founding. What if we use that as a model and we create two hundred thousand colony soldiers across the South out of a million men, most of whom who will soon be demobilized from the Army. Put them in as small farmers on the ground, re-create a society based on small farmers, but settle people with known loyalty to the United States in and among them. And he says they would both help break up the plantations and create a new culture in the South, but they would also be a reserve force that the United States could call in if threatened again.

So it is a sort of remarkably creative and yet still deeply American way of resolving what he saw as a basic problem: freed people knew their rights but could not defend them without having some kind of force in the area. And he's already saying, even within months of Lee's surrender, that the force of active duty soldiers is not going to last very long and we have two choices: figure out another way to provide force, or wrestle with the fact that their rights won't be defended and won't be meaningful once we're gone.

Antonio Elmaleh: Well, first of all, what happened to his proposal?

Greg Downs: It doesn't go anywhere for a variety of reasons. A key one is the inability to access sufficient amounts of land that would make possible either wide scale redistribution to freed people or to soldiers. And instead of inability what I should say is unwillingness, as over the course of the summer of 1865 Andrew Johnson restores a great deal of land to planters who have asked for pardon. And many people, including the commander of the Freedmen's Bureau and various congressmen, ask Johnson to, as he's issuing pardons, make them contingent upon setting aside certain amounts of land, either for the government or for freed people. But Johnson doesn't do this and so over the course of 1865, by the winter of 1865 to 1866, most of the land of the former Confederate planters has been restored to them and they hold title to it. That makes Benzoni's idea of taking two hundred thousand people and giving them, say, one hundred and sixty acres each, or even forty acres each, impossible. Access to that amount of land had been largely taken off the table by Andrew Johnson's decision to restore unimpeded title of it to people he pardoned.

Antonio Elmaleh: Can you describe the insurgency in your book? I think it deserves some serious attention on the program.

Greg Downs: Yes, there's often a view, especially in popular culture, that after Appomattox there was peace. And we see this in the way that we talk about the Civil War and then Reconstruction, as if the Civil War gets resolved and everybody takes an exhale and then things get messed up by Reconstruction. But in fact, once we understand that these two things are deeply intertwined, that they're not separable in that way, we can start to ask, as a lot of scholars have done, we can examine what's going on in these months right as Confederate surrender happens and after.

And what we see there is a resistance to accepting the end of the war. We see this in symbolic ways in which, upon returning to their towns, former Confederate soldiers wear buttons, wear their uniforms. The US Army bans this in a series of Southern towns as a way of signaling that they shouldn't embrace their Confederate service in the months right after. We see it in a growing series of attacks upon slaves in the spring of 1865, documented recently by Savolia Glenn among others; in raids in South Carolina against freed people claiming their freedom; and in attacks by both regular and irregular bands of Confederates that are attacks against freed people's self-assertion, starting during the war and continuing straight after the war.

And we see it in campaigns of violence, mostly disorganized but very focused in their impact in the summer of 1865. As the US Army moves into the former Confederate States very often they're attacked, including active duty US soldiers as well as former soldiers, black and white as well as freed people. And so what we see in the descriptions from both Army officers on the ground riding back to Washington and from travelers is a campaign of murder and terror from the beginning.

It's in this sense that we can think of an insurgency. It's not that the insurgency begins in response to Reconstruction, but the insurgency is a natural outgrowth of the resistance to federal power and its uses to transform the relations of slavery. And it's that resistance that had driven the Civil War, and that is not extinguished at Appomattox but is pushed into different form.

Antonio Elmaleh: Given this notion about the Army being a police force and then the resulting attacks on occupying soldiers as well as freed slaves, why was the occupation Army predominantly black? It seems almost like inviting the very retaliation Grant and Lincoln and other politicians were so terrified of.

Greg Downs: There are certain windows in time and certain places where a majority of the US Army stationed in the South is black. On the whole, for much of the time of the occupation the majority of the active dury soldiers on the ground are white. But it is true that black soldiers play an important role and that role grows over time. This then becomes a center of former Confederate complaints about so-called domination.

So understanding who's on the ground is something that I spent a lot of time working through materials in the National Archives, to try and figure out who's there, how long are they there, where are they, things that we should have known about occupation but we really didn't. And one of the things that I found shaped the period is we have two impulses working in contradiction, both of which are logical but which are hard to sustain together.

And one is, as you said, a recognition coming out of Appomattox and then the surrender near Durham, North Carolina that the Army was going to have to assume a responsibility in the South because there was no legitimate normal civil government the Army could work through. They could, if they wanted to, work through and choose to work through judges and sheriffs, but they didn't have to. But that meant that if the US didn't recognize local law as having a normal status, who was going to regulate them? The Army was the only possibly answer, there was no other institution with the size, the organization, or the credibility to do that. And so that's what helped to push the Army out into the countryside in the days after surrender.

But at the same time you've got an enormous upswell of petitions from enlisted men in the Army asking to go home, and this begins even before Appomattox. And they say, "We enlisted for," as many of them did, "three years of the duration of the war. Isn't this the end of the war, shouldn't we go home?" And the Army has two responses, one of which is, "Legally and technically, no, it's not the end of the war. It won't be the end of the war until Congress or the president determines it's the end of the war, and so you can still be held to that. We have this power to make you stay in the Army."

But at the same time the Army recognizes that it's going to need to demobilize people for two reasons: one, politically, it'll create a huge political backlash if a million people are still held in service over the winter; and two, financially, the US government had challenges in raising money in the early months of 1865 and that propelled a series of cost-cutting plans that were in process even before the Confederates surrendered. And so those two pieces: "How do we save money?

We've got to cut our expenses on soldiers," and "How do we respond to all these congressmen pushing to say, 'My men want to come home in time to plant their crops.'" These both lead to one answer, which is to reduce the number of people in the Army. But the impulse to occupy the South suggests that there needs to be some people still left in the Army, something more than its 1850s extremely low levels of membership of service.

So in the face of that, the Army is looking to see, "Who do we have to demobilize politically and who can we keep in?" And black soldiers – the USCI, US Colored Infantry, and the US Colored Cavalry, which combined make up what we refer to as the USCT, the US Colored Troops – A), have less political muscle to demobilize, but also B), most of them are not asking to be demobilized but in fact are eager to serve in occupation duty and eager to stay in the Army, both because they understand what's going to transpire and how central the Army will be, and because they understand that the Army offers both wages and protection at a moment when they understand those things will be in short supply in the South.

Antonio Elmaleh: One other observation, which is a lot of these black soldiers also come from the very areas that they're going to have to effectively police, so they understand literally the ground that they're watching. Their neighborhood, so to speak.

Greg Downs: Absolutely. As you know, there is a core of free black men in the North who enlist in these units, but over the course of 1864 and into early 1865 increasingly large numbers of ex-slaves form the basis of what will be about one hundred and eighty thousand soldiers in the US Colored Troops in the US Army.

Antonio Elmaleh: I want you to reiterate a statistic for our listeners because I think it bears repeating, and it's this: how many ex-slaves and black soldiers were murdered during Reconstruction?

Greg Downs: We don't have the exact answer. It's one of the things that would be fascinating to figure out, though it would take a lot of work in county courthouse records, some of which of course burned in fires or were flooded. But twenty-five years after the Emancipation Proclamation, a congressmen, surveying both Army reports that had been produced on the ground in the South as well as other reports after Reconstruction, had estimated that fifty thousand black men had been murdered in the South in the twenty-five years between 1863 and 1888. Could we document that number precisely? No. And how should we understand what percentage of those were political murders as opposed to other kinds of murders? These are open questions.

Phil Sheridan, a major general who is an extraordinarily effective military commander in the US Army and one of Grant's most respected and beloved subordinates, assumes a crucial role in the Army in Reconstruction. And when he is sent to Louisiana to observe the downfall of Reconstruction in early 1875 he tries to compile reports of what he says are political murders. And he argues there were, I think the number is on the order of two thousand, politically-focused murders of African Americans between 1865 and the end of 1874 with thousands of other people wounded, and that's just one state. In Texas the numbers that people tried to compile later suggest that they're even higher. So you can start to imagine why fifty thousand might be a reasonable number, even if we can't absolutely nail it down and say, "This is a precise count."

Antonio Elmaleh: One thing to remember is whether they were political murders or not, it's still the price tag of the insurgency.

Greg Downs: That's right. Sheridan was especially interested. Remember, his two thousand is from one state, Louisiana, and it's for half of that time period, 1865 to 1874. So if you simply doubled the time period and then multiplied across the Confederate States you'd be getting a number close to fifty thousand, although that's not precisely how the congressman's estimate was reached.

But you're absolutely right. We had organized murders of political leaders during Reconstruction that we can document. Many, many, many of them. We also have things like, "What do we do with people who are attacked or murdered for demanding a better labor contract? Is that something different than people who are attacked or murdered for organizing the Republican Party?" Or should we see this as part of this overall effort to assert an absolute right of planters, not of white people generally but of planters specifically, to make the rules upon which the American South will be governed? And those rules are political and economic and social and cultural, but they together are aimed to support this claim of power. So you're right that—

Antonio Elmaleh: Bear in mind also, I think, the wider the net of the type of killings that took place, the greater the terror that it induced.

Greg Downs: That's right.

Antonio Elmaleh: So breaking it down into neat little pockets is almost beside the point. If the point was to terrorize and essentially scare away, or worse, hold on to ex-slaves and return them to slavery, then the more terrified they are of doing anything else, the more it accomplishes certain people's aim. I think one way or another it accomplishes the one thing that an insurgency always does, which is create this sense of terror that it could come from anywhere, from anyone, you don't know who your enemy is, and on and on and on. And we've certainly seen that in some of the wars we've fought overseas, Vietnam being, I think, a very strong case in point.

Greg Downs: And I should also add that along with murder, scholars have been interested more recently in starting to excavate campaigns of rape and of understanding the rape of freed women in these massacres as part of a deliberate effort with its own analogies to other campaigns of rape, especially in the Balkans, but also in other parts of the world as part of the tools that insurgencies use to try to inspire terror in the population. And so then when people like Hannah Rosen look at places like the Memphis massacre, they say let's make sure that we're capturing not just the people murdered in the massacre in Memphis in 1866, but also what might unite the sexual assaults in that massacre by white Memphians upon freed women. And to see those not as some other category but as you said, part of this overall effort to terrorize people into submission.

Kidada Williams has been doing something similar on the impacts of the attacks upon children and looking at the testimony of people who were children during Reconstruction and the impact of witnessing these kind of assaults, of seeing their mother raped by Klansmen, of seeing their fathers assaulted, as a way of sort of imagining the role of trauma as a kind of goal of an insurgency, to traumatize people into silence or into flight.

Antonio Elmaleh: I wanted to add one more follow-up to the fact that Johnson essentially kicked a lot of the legs out of the whole idea of redistributing land by a sweep of a pen, returning almost half of the land seized just because it was a sop to the planters. But let me ask you this: he also declared peace in 1866. What was the fallout of that declaration?

Greg Downs: It's a very good question, and to get to it I want to give a little bit of background on how to understand both what Johnson was doing and why it matters, because it's confusing in ways that I think sometimes baffle not just the general public, but even scholars. And one of the arguments that I make in my book is that Johnson actually matters quite a bit less than we think. We've talked about the what if's of Reconstruction and one of those what if's is what if Johnson wasn't president? And I think that there's something very alluring, but also limiting, in ascribing the problems of Reconstruction to Johnson. Some of those are factual, which I'll get to in a second, but conceptually built into that seems to be a premise that if only we had a better president it would have been easy or straightforward. And I think there's nothing in looking at other efforts to remake society through occupations, there's nothing to suggest that that's true. There are examples where it works, but not where it's simple, fast, obvious, or accomplished without massive expenditures and commitment.

So I do resist a little bit when scholars, including great scholars, say that Andrew Johnson is the reason why Reconstruction ground to a halt.

There are actually a lot of reasons to suspect that Johnson, though he hates Reconstruction, has much less impact on it than we think. So let me lay out that timeline and then we'll get to the declaration of peace.

One of the ironies of Johnson's role in restoring land – which is an area where he does have power and where one could imagine a different president acting differently, so it's a serious and legitimate hypothetical – one of the odd things Johnson does when he becomes president is he, in certain ways, makes Lincoln's plans more radical. Lincoln had plans to exempt high civil and military officers from his declaration of general amnesty, and that declaration of general amnesty would have restored for most of them either their title or their right to go to court to regain their title to land. But Johnson, when he looks at that list, adds another group that will be exempted from the general amnesty, and that's large planters.

So what he does then at the start of the post-surrender period is to say planters who have over a certain number of acres are automatically withheld from this general amnesty. That's what puts their land at risk. And so the reason why Johnson's pardons matter so much is because he had exempted those planters from the general amnesty. It's very possible to imagine Lincoln – in fact we can see the plans at work in the Lincoln administration – simply including them under general amnesty. And that means that large amounts of the land that Johnson will return in August, September, October, November of 1865 would have been off the table in April or May.

So in this way, even this sort of one area that Johnson is responsible for, a cataclysmic reduction of the possibility of Reconstruction, perversely he's also responsible for making that redistribution a possibility in the summer. As we then walk forward with Johnson, what's interesting is when we separate his rhetoric from his actions he's often more wary of interfering with Reconstruction than his language suggests.

So, in the fall of 1865 Johnson is talking about states' rights. In fact, he's talking about them from the moment the war ends. But as a series of very smart lawyers realize, he's not actually acting upon a belief that the former Confederate states have any rights. He's not only supporting military governors but he's sending direct orders, often framed as strong requests, to state constitutional conventions in the South insisting that they eliminate slavery, that they repudiate Confederate debt, strongly suggesting they permit testimony by freed people in civil and criminal cases. And so, he is not at all acting as if these former Confederate states are real states, because he would never do this to Pennsylvania or Kentucky or Ohio.

So he's supporting the Army in many ways – not in every way – and he's also supporting the idea that the federal government has special control over the Southern states. In April 1866 he does go to rhetorical war with Congress over Reconstruction and over the question of what will happen when Confederate states come back and when Confederate states will be readmitted to Congress, and this creates a severe break. But there, the impact of his actions is mitigated by the fact that Congress just overrides his veto. But they do have to rewrite the Freedmen's Bureau Bill narrowly when he vetoes it, in order to get a supermajority. The Civil Rights Act, when he vetoes that, they override it immediately. Johnson's statements are outrageous and abhorrent in that he's kind of claiming that any rights given to black people constitute a denial of rights to whites, but the impact of those is really quite small.

And then, in April 1866, he issues, as you point out, a proclamation of peace, and this sometimes will be referred to in later Supreme Court cases as the day the Civil War ended because he seems to embrace that, though it's also confusing because he exempts Texas from the order. So in this sense, this creates its own confusion. But what does this proclamation actually mean? Salmon P. Chase, the Chief Justice of the US Supreme Court, had refused to have Supreme Court Justices go to sit in the Confederate states – which in those days they did, they would sit on the circuit courts – on the grounds that the military was in charge and Supreme Court Justices should not be regulated by the military. So if the military was in charge, the Supreme Court Justices should simply leave it to them.

He goes to Johnson and he says, "I saw in your proclamation that you suggest it's peacetime, but you did not say that a general writ of habeas corpus was assured," which is the right to go to court to demand charges or to be released, "and you didn't say that courts were supreme over military law in the South. I've written up this little order for you, and if you do that, then I will encourage justices to go into the South and sit on circuits." Johnson doesn't do it. Why? Because he knows it's not the end of the war, and he knows that because he is receiving reports from military commanders saying the moment that you give courts power over us, they're going to arrest every soldier in the South. This was already happening in Kentucky, which was not covered by the same kinds of wartime power.

So Johnson wants to say it's peacetime, but he doesn't want to act like it's peacetime because he knows the implications of this. In August he extends that proclamation to Texas and in the face of this Grant says, "We should act as if it would be better not to use the powers of war to take control of places or to intervene, but in an emergency you have to do what you have to do." He also suggests, "And we all know what's going to happen in December." And in fact, what happens in December of 1866 is Congress says, "Congress makes war and Congress ends war" and the president's declaration of the end of the war does not actually end the war. And so in the winter of 1866 to '67, between December 1866 and March 1867, Congress declares that the war continues. It's this sense that gets us to the moment that you used in your introduction, the idea that the war doesn't actually end until 1871. And that emerges from Congress's claim that it has the power to declare an end to the war.

So Johnson wants to give big speeches, he wants to claim this role as the defender of states and the defender of peace, and he wants to mess with Congress but he's actually, behind the scenes, much more guarded than we might think. That's what saves his presidency during impeachment, that he takes his hands off the Army after acting against Military Reconstruction, which I'm sure we'll get into.

And it also mitigates the impact of the proclamations you asked about. It turns out they matter more for the language than for the fact. For legal scholars they have a huge impact because later the

Supreme Court will say, "We have to date the end of the Civil War from somewhere, and we're going to date it to those proclamations," as a way of deciding lots of cases that come out. But then they always say, "This is a legal fiction, and as a political question only Congress can determine when the war ends."

Antonio Elmaleh: So he's traded a certain amount of political posturing and image. It doesn't sound like a great trade for Andrew Johnson. It certainly explains his baffling behavior more clearly, so thank you for that.

What was the significance of Mississippi's state government authorizing a militia and Johnson allowing it to proceed? And just for clarification, when did that take place?

Greg Downs: Now this is a place where Johnson's role matters. In the spring of 1865, when he first assumes office, many Republicans actually think that he'll be bolder than Lincoln, both because he included large planters among the group who was excluded from the amnesty proclamation, and also because he had then cracked down, in quite tough terms, in Tennessee as military governor. And he had repeatedly said that his job was to make treason odious, to make Confederates suffer so that no one would ever rise up again.

But there are a couple of "hopes" that take center the month after surrender. One is black suffrage, which people hope Johnson will include in his proclamation and say the new states will be remade with black voting. He doesn't do this; he could have, he doesn't. I think it's quite unlikely that Lincoln would have done it either. And in fact, people like Salmon Chase and others who are lobbying for this are lobbying specifically because they think Lincoln's death gives them this window they wouldn't have had if Lincoln survived.

But the other hope goes to the relationship of the new state governments being built in the South in the months after surrender.

Carl Schurz was a German revolutionary who had been minister to Spain in the early years of the war and lobbied for European support for the United States, and then came back and became a general, partly because of his ability to mobilize German-American immigrant soldiers both into the Republican Party in the 1850s and into the US Army in the 1860s. Schurz goes on an observational tour of the South and there he writes about the conditions that he sees on the ground about extraordinary violence against freed people and about the determination, the ways that these new Southern state governments are asserting their power over their states and over freedmen.

It's late summer of 1865 as he's making his tour. When he gets to Mississippi, he sees that the Mississippi government has called up its militia and he believes this militia is going to be turned into simply a force of repressing freed people. So he writes to Johnson asking Johnson's permission to block it. Instead, Johnson authorizes it. This represents a moment when radical and even moderate Republicans start to turn and see that Johnson won't be the ally that they had hoped. Because to them, to give state militias the power to intervene is to create two sets of authority on the ground: the US Army interpreting federal law and federal policy, and these militias, which are going to be speaking to quite different goals of what kind of society they want to remake.

Now, I think it's an interesting question to ponder what Lincoln would have done under those circumstances. Certainly, it's conceivable that Lincoln would have imagined not permitting those states to organize militias, but I'm not so sure he would have given a different answer. Johnson does it in part because he says, "This is what we used to do in Tennessee when we were worried about slave uprisings," and so in that sense he seems to welcome the idea of militia as ways of keeping black people in line. It's hard to conceive this is the way that Lincoln would have justified it. But it's also quite hard to know whether Lincoln would have acted differently.

What it does is create a confidence in those Southern state governments in the summer - fall of 1865 that they're actually in charge. And this Johnson comes to regret, even on his own limited terms, because some of them start refusing to make the concessions that he demands of them: to acknowledge the end of slavery, to affirmatively wipe slavery out of their state laws, and to accept the 13th Amendment which would end slavery for the nation.

Antonio Elmaleh: So he tips his hand, effectively, early on in a concrete way, rather than some kind of posturing or smoke-and-mirrors way.

Greg Downs: That's right. It is a moment that shows where his sympathies lie that go beyond the pardons, and it shocks Schurz who believes that he really has Johnson's ear. One of the things that's interesting about Johnson in this early period is he's extremely effective at convincing people that he agrees with them without actually agreeing with them or committing to follow through on it. So for the first four months or so when he's in office both conservatives and radicals think that he's really on their side, and it's only with these acts in the late summer in August, September 1865 that Republicans start realizing how opposed to them he actually is. The militia and the land return are the key ways in which they come to understand this.

Antonio Elmaleh: You write extensively on the irony of Republican strategy to prolong the war in order to establish a lasting peace. Could you explain why so much of the struggle between Congress and Andrew Johnson resided in the question of who controlled the government's war powers authority, as opposed to what basis to admit Confederate states back into the Union?

Greg Downs: Yes, it's a challenging question and I'll do my best to explain it in a way that'll make sense to laypeople. Even a lot of historians struggle to understand what legal scholars mean by war power and why it's important to them and why it's such a crucial part of Constitutional history, in part because our Constitutional framework is premised upon limits to federal power even now, and yet in wartime every administration has gone beyond those limits. And so for legal theorists, war exists as this defined period of time in which the normal rules don't apply.

Francis Lieber, was a German theorist who wrote the code of war for the Army, brilliantly described by John Fabian Witt as one of the great books ever written about war power. Lieber writes that saving the country is the ultimate requirement of the federal government, and this sort of establishes a line. Supreme Court Justice Jackson, I believe, in the 20th century, will say that the Constitution's not a suicide pact. Lincoln, in more colloquial language, will say that he knows he can do things in wartime that he can't do in peacetime, and that he doesn't accept peacetime limits in wartime. But he says, and I'm not going to get his quote exactly right, that he no more accepts the idea that because he can't do certain things in peacetime, he can't do them in war than he would accept the idea that because he shouldn't take a certain medicine when he's well, therefore he shouldn't take it when he's sick. It's a discrete period of time when you're able to go beyond normal limits.

And almost everything that the US government does during Reconstruction depends upon those special powers. They're arresting governors, they're imposing new laws on states, General Sheridan changes jury terms in Louisiana and Texas. These are things that the federal government and especially the Army can't do in normal time: taking control of cases, hearing cases in their own court. And what causes the disagreement is that both Democrats and Republicans generally accept once it's peacetime these things can't happen, so the question of what's possible depends on whether or not it's wartime or peacetime.

Now to us, we associate war-making powers with the president. We live in an era in which very few wars have explicit Congressional declarations of war –there are general authorizations, of course, that do help to establish these principles. Some legal scholars have wondered whether there'll ever be another declaration of war again or whether Congress has sought to cede that power to the president so that it can critique it rather than be responsible for it. But who knows? Predictions are hard, especially about the future. But so, in this sense we become very normalized to the idea that wartime authority is executive authority.

But many of the Republicans had not believed that. In fact, many of them were former Whigs who had argued that ultimate authority resides in Congress rather than in the president. They see Andrew Johnson as trying to revive an old Jacksonian Democrat claim that the president has particular powers over Congress as a particular representative of the people. And so, along with their fight over Reconstruction, they're reenacting these 1830s, 1840s fights over who's paramount: Congress or the president. And they believe that while the president is the Commander-in-Chief of the Army, Congress is the body in charge of determining when they're at war. This had created problems even with Lincoln during the war, when Lincoln had argued Congress was exceeding its powers and infringing on his as Commander-in-Chief.

It's this that becomes the center of the fight between the Republicans and Johnson, and what enables the Republicans to hold together. Often we portray them as dividing between conservatives and moderates, and sometimes that's true. But even as they disagree on specific policy: on black votes in 1865 into early 1866, on enforcement acts in 1870 and into 1871 through 1875 – even as they disagree on what they should do, they largely agree on the idea that they have to hold on to the power to do it. And so again and again Congressional Republicans mobilize themselves to say, "We have the power to declare when the war is over, and on that power turns our ability to do whatever we decide to do in the South."

Antonio Elmaleh: Which goes back to an initial point in our conversation about continuing to prolong the war in order to create a lasting peace farther down the road.

Greg Downs: Throughout the period, Southern Democrats, both those coming into Congress and from the outside, say, "All we need for peace is to withdraw the Army and to take your hands off." And Republicans repeatedly answer – and go on answering, even into the 1870s and 1880s, after the so-called Compromise of 1876 and so on – Republicans repeatedly answer that this is the peace that the British put on India after the Mutiny of 1857, or the peace the Russians put on Poland after their uprising, or the peace that Austria put on Hungary, or the peace that the English put on Ireland. This is the peace of oppression, and that actual peace depends upon limiting that oppression and limiting the ability of Southern planters to exclude freedmen from political power and political participation and the impact that that'll have on their economic power and economic growth.

So what this turns on is: what's going to be peace? Is peace going to be the planters back in charge and no longer rebelling against the US government? That can be attained pretty quickly. Or is peace going to be the creation of a new kind of society in which freed people have defensible rights? And that's much more problematic. Even in the late 1860s, after years of these fights, a group of some relatively moderate Republicans, like William Fessenden, argue that they're going too fast in restoring peace precisely because they make this distinction between wartime and peacetime, that once they give up this power they'll never be able to get it back. And what will they do then when the planters rebel?

And over the early 1870s, as the Ku Klux Klan and then other insurgent movements capture parts of the South, Republicans repeatedly debate, "What can we do in peacetime to resist this? And if those powers aren't enough, should we reconsider whether or not the war has actually ended?" And even in 1875 you get large numbers of Republicans saying, "We thought the war was over but we were wrong, and we know we were wrong because we need those powers now to restore peace and order in the South."

Antonio Elmaleh: It's just amazing. Can you offer us a brief synopsis of the 13th, 14th, and 15th Amendments for our listeners?

Greg Downs: These are, Republicans repeatedly say, the ultimate fruits of the war. These three amendments, each finally ratified after Confederate surrender but ratified through war powers, remake the Constitution. Many legal scholars call them a second American Revolution or even a second founding, and argue that we should see these three amendments, especially the 14th, as making in some ways a second Constitution, that we live in a new Constitutional order created by the Civil War and by the continued use of war powers in the years after Appomattox. But why do they think so, and how does this help us to understand both what our relationship is now to our first founding, to Philadelphia and the creation of the Constitution, and how does this helps us understand what the war did and did not accomplish?

The 13th Amendment is passed, is demonstrated ably, with some historical nitpicking. It –

Antonio Elmaleh: Daniel Day-Lewis did a great job, right?

Greg Downs: That's right, in the movie Lincoln. It's passed after the 1864 presidential election in the short session of Congress between December of 1864 and March 1865, and the 13th Amendment ends slavery. So it moves from emancipation, freeing individual slaves, to abolition, ending the law of slavery and overriding any efforts to bring it back. In this sense, it ends. It passes Congress, and this part of the story, the story that the movie was interested in, ends before Lincoln's assassination or before Appomattox.

But one thing that the movie, then as it looks forward into the challenges and dilemmas of Reconstruction, seems to contract those challenges to the leadership during the short session of Congress that finally passes the 13th Amendment. But what that misses is a basic question of Constitutional law: how do amendments become law? Not when they pass Congress, but when they're ratified by the states.

And this poses immediately all kinds of dilemmas. How are you going to get a supermajority of state ratifications? Who counts? Do the former Southern rebel states count? Do they count if they vote "yes?" Do they count if they vote "no?" Who's going to determine the fraction that are necessary?

Antonio Elmaleh: Let me just ask you this question: in January of 1865 they're not former states. They're Confederate states.

Greg Downs: That's right. They're ...

Antonio Elmaleh: They're still Confederate states, so that argument kind of disappears.

Greg Downs: This might be where the surrenders at Appomattox and Durham change that calculation, because in the time the Northern states start ratifying it, conditions in the South have shifted and now they're in a period of occupation. So it is an interesting question. What would have happened if surrender had been delayed six months or nine months or a year or something and if the supermajority of US states had approved it, not counting the Confederate states?

In the situation they do face, Johnson demands, or all but demands, sometimes with a veneer of volunteerism, that Confederate states pass the 13th Amendment. And so they then count toward the ratification of the 13th Amendment. And he sends those "suggestions" through military governors stationed in those states. So when later Confederate sympathizers would say that the states were coerced into passing the 13th Amendment, that's absolutely true, and it's a signal of how challenging it was. Even this first step required military force, threats of sustaining martial law occupation forever, in order to get a simple acknowledgement.

Then when Congress comes in in December 1865, the first time they meet after the assassination of Lincoln, a number of ideas are circulating about what's next. They can see the problem of simply abolishing slavery, as it doesn't establish the condition of former slaves. So, what are their rights? States are creating explicitly racial distinctions of rights. In some states they used to have, before the Civil War or during and up until surrender, a set of laws that treated free black people as a separate caste. And they simply then incorporated all the freed slaves into these separate castes. Some states prohibit freed slaves from owning certain types of property, from testifying, and impose different punishments upon ex-slaves than they do upon whites.

So what does freedom actually mean? The 14th Amendment does many things, but one of the crucial things it does is establish the rights of Americans. Some are specific to citizens, some more general to residents in the United States. And so when we think of due process, equal protection under the law, privileges and immunities less often invoked now, these matter now because of the 14th Amendment. The 14th Amendment establishes that you, as an American citizen and in some other groups, have protection against the state government treating you disparately based on race or color or a few other conditions.

So this emerges from their awareness of what's going on in the Southern states and from questions that are bubbling up in Southern state courts such as, "Are freed people citizens?" Slaves weren't citizens. And could they deny freed people offices on the ground that they hadn't established US citizenship for long enough?

Something that'll circulate with the election of the first African American US senator, Hiram Revels, in response to the "too quick" claims: Congress adds to the 14th Amendment the idea of natural-born citizenship, in order to sweep away contestations over whether slaves were citizens of the United States. This changes the country permanently, as we see in our ongoing debates about the citizenship of children born in the United States to parents who are not US citizens. An outgrowth of the Civil War, and one especially tied to the ways that planters had tried to use citizenship claims against ex-slaves.

And there are some other aspects. The 14th Amendment promises that they'll never pay Confederate war debt, and it does a complex dance around the question of representation in Congress and who can vote. That has its own long explanation. But anyway, Congress creates the 14th Amendment and it tells the Confederate states, "You have to pass this, too." And this message is communicated through Congress, but with the understanding that if they don't pass it they'll stay under military law. And then, even after saying this, Congress says, "But even if you do pass it, we're still not promising to put you back into peacetime. We're just saying we're not even going to lift until you pass it." And this is a fight at the end of the 1866 session. Is it a promise, is it terms of peace to Southern states: "Pass the 14th Amendment and you're in?" Or is it simply a statement of, "This is a threshold you have to do before we even consider you."?

Johnson urges the Southern states not to pass it. They don't, and that's what then helps to propel Congress in December 1866 to take control of Reconstruction, put the South in a state of war, and there they put as an explicit term that the new state governments will have to pass the 14th Amendment. What the 14th Amendment promises is not just that the federal government can't take those things away but also your state government can't, and in fact, the state governments have been much more commonly the site of this kind of repression and of this kind of differentiation.

And then the 15th Amendment emerges out of the question of the vote. Black men were enfranchised in former Confederate states in 1867 after the Military Reconstruction Act, but there are concerns that it'll be stripped away. The 15th Amendment emerges as a resolution to that, saying that the right to vote can't be taken away based on race, color, or previous condition of servitude. And once again Congress tells the remaining states – not all of them have been brought back into Congress at this point in 1869 — that they have to pass the 15th Amendment if they want peacetime in their state.

So we've got military power that remakes the Constitution in order to create the set of legal rights that most Americans understand themselves as living under today. In this sense, we really should think about this remaking of the Constitution as a kind of second founding in two ways: one, we should contemplate what they meant by it; and two, we should have our doubts about how much the first founders can tell us, because what they created was a Constitution that failed and had to be remade by force in order to sustain and create the country that we live in.

Antonio Elmaleh: If I may interject also, it strikes me that these amendments are actually what Lincoln was referring to without knowing it, a new birth of freedom.

Greg Downs: Certainly, it's crucial for us to think through that observation. And I'm not sure. Predicting Lincoln's view of different Constitutional amendments devised after his death is challenging. Obviously, we know he supported the 13th, and it's interesting to contemplate how he would have responded to the others. But I think, at least on the level of theme, certainly they fit in with this idea of a new birth of freedom. They're central to it. Our right to due process is central to what Americans think of as what it means to be free, and that right is created in Reconstruction.

Antonio Elmaleh: Yes. That's well said.

Well, that's all the time we have for this edition of *Uncovering the Civil War*. We've covered a lot of ground in Part One of our discussion about Reconstruction and we will continue our discussion with Professor Gregory Downs at the University of California Davis in our next podcast of *Uncovering the Civil War*. I'd like to thank Greg for joining us and sharing with our listeners his expertise and thoughts about Reconstruction. I look forward to Part Two of our discussion. I'd like to thank our listeners for joining us today. Until then, be safe and do good.

PART II

Antonio Elmaleh: Welcome to another edition of *Uncovering the Civil War*. We're going to continue our discussion with Professor Gregory Downs, Professor of History at the University of California, Davis. Welcome back, Professor Downs.

Greg Downs: Thank you so much for having me.

Antonio Elmaleh: My pleasure. Now, we covered a lot of topics in our previous discussion about Reconstruction. I'd like to pick up where we left off, if that's all right. Tell us about the shift in strategy of the U.S. Army from policing the South to escorting freed men to the ballot box, and what the importance of that shift meant.

Greg Downs: Most Army officials, including those who strongly support the goals of Reconstruction, work to find an exit strategy where the Army's not responsible for everything. In this way it mirrors the actions of many military commanders in occupation who've come to doubt whether or not they'll ever have the kind of force and support they need to accomplish their goals, and in the face of being told "expansive goals with minimal force" are to argue about how the Army can extricate itself from this impossible predicament.

For them, supporting state government that will be receptive to free people becomes a highly alluring outcome and a way of helping moderate Northerners who share many of the racial prejudices of the time, and many of whom were doubtful about black male suffrage come to support the idea that black men can vote as the only way out. Either occupy forever or give black men the vote and then they can make their own government and then the Army can start to withdraw and retreat.

As these new states make courts in which black people can testify, the Army no longer has to take control of court cases. Their hope is that these new states will create militias and police forces that can enforce the law, but this turns out to be almost impossible on the ground. So over the course of the '60s and '70s, Republican Southern state governments are asking the Army for support and the Army's uncertain of how much they can or should do.

On election days in the 1870s, the Army is often stationed in county seats where they will be available, if there is a request from a US marshal or a US judge, to offer their help and counterweight against the organized bands of White Leagues and White Lines and other insurgent groups trying to terrorize black people away from the polls. This creates all kinds of controversy in and of itself, not least because it's also being used on the ground in New York City. And so it suggests the idea of the Army as a kind of national police force at election time. That understandably makes people nervous.

But the counterargument the Republicans make is that in the face of the numbers and violence and weaponry of white Southerners and of their willingness to use force, the freed men are being presented either with not voting or with launching an all-out race war in the South, which in many places they know they'll lose. And so the only alternative to that, they argue, is for the Army to be stationed near polling places. But this is an extremely controversial issue in Northern politics, not to mention among white Southern Democrats.

Antonio Elmaleh: If I may interject, also it's not exactly the same situation but there are definitely parallels and you cite this in your book, the 101st Airborne was stationed in Little Rock to allow a black girl to enter school because the fear was she wouldn't even make it past the front door. Again, I think it was Eisenhower who called out the troops to enforce that, and then again in the Mississippi case, I think it was James Meredith, the Army was called out to guarantee that these people would have the right to enroll in the state schools.

We see that tool being wielded even into our generation or certainly in our lifetime as well. So it just speaks to the resonance of all these issues, to what's going on now, as well as what was going on then.

Greg Downs: When Eisenhower was contemplating how to respond in Little Rock, one of his attorneys answers the question of what power the president has to use the Army domestically. And this is something that is up in the air at the end of Reconstruction. In 1878 and 1879, Democrats in the Congress pass laws that seem to limit what the Army can do and who they can respond to. One of these we now call the Posse Comitatus Act. It's an amendment to another bill, but the Posse Comitatus Act continues to limit when the president can deploy the Army inside the United States and to what end.

This came up during Katrina, where the question was whether or not President Bush had received the proper form of request. The way that the law is written suggests, and the way it refers to older laws from the nation's founding, that the request needs to come either from a governor, if the legislature's out of session, or from the legislature, if the legislature's in session. The president can use the Army to defend state governments but not against state governments, and in part this comes from Democrats' efforts to stop Reconstruction in 1878-1879.

But the Civil Rights Act of 1866 had built upon – in one of the sort of genius moments of Republicans' understanding of the legal system – it builds upon the Fugitive Slave Law of 1850, where Southern clans or politicians had written into the federal law a right of the US marshals and US judges to call upon a posse to enforce acts of US court order.

In the 1850s, Caleb Cushing, a cabinet member, had written an argument that federal judges and marshals could call upon the Army to enforce their orders and this is part of the way that Army and Navy soldiers, officers and sailors are utilized to march Anthony Burns, a runaway slave, from the court house in Boston through crowds of thousands of angry Bostonians to waiting ships to take him back to slavery in Virginia.

Well, Republicans see that Southern politicians have expanded the power of the federal government incredibly to protect slavery, in some ways the most significant expansion of federal power in the antebellum United States, and they turned that power against slavery. The 1866 Civil Rights Act is modeled on the Fugitive Slave Act on the grounds that they will catch planters in their own support for massively expanding the powers of federal government and force them to admit that they want a big strong government when they can use it for slavery, and they hate a strong central government when it's used against slavery.

Well, in a convoluted set of legal maneuverings, the 1866 Act is divided in the federal code and it survives, the seeds of it survive, a series of efforts to undo the powers of Reconstruction. And Eisenhower's lawyers point to it specifically as the authorization. Why can Eisenhower send the 101st into Little Rock? Because he's doing it in order to enforce a federal court order.

This then becomes also the model for Kennedy, that they can use the Army in this way, because they're not just sending them in, they're sending them in to enforce a federal court order. The Fugitive Slave Act and the Civil Rights Act of 1866 had written this into the national compromise.

We still see questions about what the Army can do and under what circumstances in the very contemporary debate about the use of the Army at the border and an initial claim by the President that he was going to send the Army to the border to enforce the law and what looked like, you know, not being privy to actual internal documents, but what looked like an immediate reaction against that by Army attorneys who have long argued that they cannot be used in that way because of the Posse Comitatus Act. They can only be used domestically in these situations involving either a request from a legislature, or a request from a governor, or to enforce a federal court order, or a certain small number of other emergencies. They can't normally be used for law enforcement without those.

What ended up happening was something much more in keeping with the post-Posse-Comitatus-Act regime, which is that the White House made a request to governors to call out the National Guard. And in this sense the response on the border fit within post-Posse-Comitatus limits, that Army can't be used normally to enforce the law.

In this way, we still see both Reconstruction and the battle to undo Reconstruction shape what the government can and can't do, especially in relation to its use of the Army.

Antonio Elmaleh: It's just mind-boggling, the complexity and the resonance of all these issues to what's going on now. Would you spend a few moments describing the Panic of 1865 and why it is so crucial to understanding one of the reasons for drawing troops out of the South?

Greg Downs: One of the things that is easy to overlook in the story of Reconstruction is the way that finances shaped what the federal government is doing, and shaped Republican sense of the possibility. And so because the US wins the Civil War and because it issues billions of dollars of loans to pay for a war that totaled nearly six billion dollars in 1860s money, we can assume that they had resolved by 1865 the financial challenges of the war and so therefore were operating on a kind of open playing field.

In fact, what happens in March of 1865 is something that creates a mild but meaningful financial panic. It's not something akin to the great panics and depressions of US history of 1873 or 1929 or 2008, but it is an important moment for shaping Reconstruction. What happened is that the crisis goes into convoluted questions about the relationship between the price of gold relative to the dollar, where the dollar had floated free of an absolute relationship to the price of gold. So we had what's called a "floating currency" during the Civil War, and it broke the association between the price of gold and value of the dollar. And this shaped the government's ability to issue new loans that it's promising to pay off at certain interest rates over the next five to twenty years.

What happens in March of 1865 is that gold prices relative to the dollar drop by about fifty percent over the month of March, and it seems like in certain ways it could be a good thing. But because the US government is selling its bonds in dollars but suggesting that it's going to pay off the interest in gold, what people are really buying is not so much an interest rate but a gold premium. When that gold premium dropped in March, then it essentially cuts in half the promised rate of return of the most popular loan that the US government uses. Very quickly some of the loans that the government is selling actually dropped below their face value on the resale market.

Meaning, that if you bought them for a dollar, people are re-selling them on the resale market for ninety-eight or ninety-nine cents. What that means is people who want to buy those loans can buy them more cheaply in private markets than they can from the government, and that makes the government panic that they're not going to be able to sell these loans. And if they can't sell the loans, they're not going to have money coming in.

This creates a mild but meaningful financial panic in which railway shares, petroleum, pork, tobacco, cotton, all things the government is a key purchaser of, their value drops by about twenty percent in late March of 1865. At this point the US government is facing a massive daily shortfall. They need to pay bills of about four million dollars a day. They have a one hundred million dollar cash deficit. They're going to pay those bills by selling the loans, and if the loans don't come in then what are they going to do?

It's this financial fear that, for all of the expertise devoted to financing the war, that it might all come to naught right at the end, right in the weeks when Grant is trying to pen Lee in, leading up to the surrender at Appomattox.

What the government does is two things. First of all, it tries to manipulate the gold market, and so it sends its agents out to secretly start buying up gold to shore up its price. They're basically gaming the price of gold in order to increase the value of the loans they want to sell so people will start buying them again. The government spends tens of millions of dollars in March and April to try and shore up the price of gold secretly, because they know that if word gets out that the reason why gold is holding its value is because the government's doing it, that this will cause a second crash.

What it also leads to is a series of panicky worries in the Treasury Department that gets communicated to the War Department and to Lincoln's White House, that the federal government won't be able to keep paying its soldiers for long. This creates a sort of step-up on the pressure of the generals to corral the Confederacy. Some panicky people say, "If we don't get them to surrender soon, we'll have to sue them for peace by the summertime if we can't pay our bills." Others say, "Even if we get them to surrender, we're going to have these major bills," and this creates the impetus to developing plans to start sending men home as quickly as possible.

Antonio Elmaleh: That, and also there's going to be a massive desire to get home and not be a policeman in the South. Was it in your book you mentioned something like two hundred thousand troops were needed, or estimated to be needed, to effectively enforce Reconstruction? And what was the Occupation Army at its height, eight-five thousand, I mean not even half, something like that.

Greg Downs: There's different estimates that are out there, and then there's also some social-scientific work on size of occupying forces, so that I think somewhere between – if you look at cautious, relatively moderate generals like George Meade, the place where he starts saying, "Wait a minute, you're taking men away too fast," is where it crosses around a hundred thousand. And The Army and Navy Journal and some others had estimated a hundred thousand as the number of people to have in Southern states.

That might be too low, and it might well be that estimates closer to two hundred thousand are more realistic for what the government was asking of the Army, but it's somewhere in that ballpark. You wouldn't have needed a whole million men in the Army, but you would have needed something much larger than the 1850s US Army to enforce it.

What we get in the demobilization is that so many people are demobilized from the Army that by the fall of 1865, Meade, a moderate, not a radical by any stretch, is saying, "We don't have enough people." Then you get another wave of demobilization on top of that, so the Army in the South drops from a hundred and twenty thousand to eighty thousand to quickly half of that. So that's when you start having generals saying, "I can't do the things you're telling me to do. I can't protect this countryside with the small number of people that we've got."

What's interesting is that the overall numbers of the Army continue to drop. Even when Congress passes Military Reconstruction, they don't deploy that many more soldiers into the Army. There's fewer people on the ground during Military Reconstruction than during the early months of Johnson's occupation in the summer and fall and winter of 1865. Everybody by that point has accepted the idea that the Army is too small but they're not going to add to the Army.

Antonio Elmaleh: Doesn't it also have the inadvertent consequence of enlivening the insurgency because they're not stupid, they can see, "Well, they're reducing the police force, so we're going to have more, we're going to become more bold in our terror campaign, with far fewer consequences." It had the unintended effect of actually intensifying the insurgency.

Greg Downs: Absolutely. Many officers say that former Confederates understand that they've lost the war, but they need to be reminded and kept in fear and the only way to be kept in fear is by the presence of soldiers. They say this repeatedly and they also say that what's happening over 1865 and 1866 means that for most Southerners those soldiers were very visible in the summer of 1865 in almost every county seat, and are somewhat visible in the fall and winter of 1865.

But by the spring of 1866, many commanders in many states have centralized their forces in a small number of cities in the hopes that they can send them by railroad if they get word from somewhere out in the countryside. Instead of the Army being a visible presence, and a presence that freed people can get to and to state their situation, now the Army becomes something out of sight, something in a capital city or in a railroad hub. And for freed people, without access to money for the railroad or without horses, they're really almost impossible to reach.

That definitely empowers white Southern insurgents to feel like they can act to regain control. As long as they keep out of the headlines, the Army literally would not know what's going on in the countryside, which is at the heart of Southern society. It's built and made from the countryside, not from the cities, because of the way that plantation agriculture had shaped the South.

Antonio Elmaleh: So much of history – if you peel away the flag, you peel away the ideology, there's always money somewhere at the bottom, driving something fundamental in the collision.

Can you explain the relationship or the parallel of the women's suffrage movement, the right of women to have the vote, with the right of freed slaves to have the right to vote?

Greg Downs: This is a profound story and one that many people don't know. The historians have done a lot of work to excavate it. Women's suffrage had, in large measure, learned organizing and developed their organizing skills in their central roles in the anti-slavery movement. And in many ways the women's rights movement and the anti-slavery movement were part of a combined –sometimes tenuously – but a combined project in the 1840s and 1850s.

Frederick Douglass is at Seneca Falls during the convention on women's rights that leads to a Declaration of Sentiment. Many of the people, of the women leaders at Seneca Falls, had been at many, many, many different anti-slavery conventions and had been central players in organizing and keeping anti-slavery afloat. There's a strong sense among many people that these two questions are intertwined, that they're both issues in which an unfair power is reserved for a small group of people, over both slaves and women, especially married women, and that a liberatory effort should work in both directions to emancipate slaves but also, in the language of women's rights' advocates, to emancipate women, especially married women.

In many states, their rights disappeared under their husbands' with marriage. They lost legal standing not just to vote but to even act as a legal actor. For this reason many women's rights' advocates are crucial in pushing forward black suffrage as a solution to the war, but they also hope that they'll be able to use the expansion of the vote to black men as a wedge to raise a broader conversation about the expansion of the vote to women.

In 1865, leaders, especially Wendell Phillips, but through him Frederick Douglass and others, and Charles Sumner and others, people who had supported women's suffrage, come to the conclusion that they have a chance for black male suffrage but only if they're willing to step away from women's suffrage – not to say that it's wrong that women should vote, but that this is the time for black male voting and women's voting will come later.

As this happens, this leads to two interesting effects. For Democrats who don't want black men to vote, they grab onto the women's issue as a way of sabotaging the whole project and so every time black male voting comes up in Washington, D.C. where Congress has the power to legislate Military Reconstruction in the debates over the 14th and 15th Amendments, Democrats who had never supported women's suffrage suddenly offer amendments saying, "Expand the vote to women, too." What they hope to do is to sabotage the whole project.

In the face of this, many Republicans who had supported women's suffrage now vote against it, saying, "We have to take what we can get and women's suffrage will not fly, politically." This in turn alienates leaders of the women's suffrage movement, people like Elizabeth Cady Stanton and Susan B. Anthony, who had always argued that the two, black male suffrage and women's suffrage, were intertwined. And now they see that their moment is passing.

In the face of these crises, isolated prominent anti-slavery movements, some of them defunded where money is withheld from them if they continue to argue for women's suffrage as they go around the country speaking, start to make alliances, especially in Kansas with Conservative Democrats who are trying to use women's suffrage to block black suffrage. This creates this historic fracture between women's rights and black rights in the 1860s and leads to a falling out between people like Stanton and Frederick Douglass, who had long been allies but now find themselves aligned on opposite sides.

Historians have long wrestled with, "Should we see this division as reflecting women's suffrage's racism?" In fact, it's a largely middle class, white, Northern movement. "Or should we see this as reflecting their extremely limited options in a world that they see is turning against them?" We do have to remember that they were right to hear people saying "just wait a while" as meaning "wait forever." It'll be fifty years between the 15th Amendment and the 19th Amendment and a large number of the women's rights advocates who had fought to inject women's voting rights into the 15th Amendment would be in the grave years before the extension of votes to women in the 19th Amendment.

This should be a break on our understanding of Reconstruction as a complete overhaul of American society and to understand how, even though it had all these many implications, it turned upon the questions that had caused the Civil War: the questions of slavery and what was to become of the former slaves. And in that sense it got separated from other swirling hopes for a broader reconstitution of American society.

Antonio Elmaleh: It's more like an expansion of a specific part of the population's expansion of rights, but not a universal expansion of rights that would be a more profound change, if it had occurred.

Greg Downs: That's right. It's a bitter irony to many of the women's rights leaders that the first time the word "male" is used in the Constitution occurs in the Reconstruction Amendment. The moment when they believe they're seeing a possibility of tearing down male supremacy they come to believe is a moment of reasserting male supremacy.

Antonio Elmaleh: Can you describe Johnson's impeachment and why it failed to convict him?

Greg Downs: There had been a bubbling effort to impeach Johnson from his vetoes in 1866 of the Freedman's Bureau Bill and of the

Civil Rights Bill, but Republican leadership had kept that down on the grounds that impeachment would weaken them politically and distract them from what they're trying to accomplish with remaking the South. The push, what moved Republicans towards impeachment, is Johnson's acts toward Reconstruction.

After the Military Reconstruction Act, Johnson accepts Grant's suggestions of whom to appoint to oversee the different Southern military districts in 1867 and appoints a number of figures who'll be bold and radical leaders: Phil Sheridan over Louisiana and Texas, and Dan Sickles over the Carolinas. When they begin to intervene dramatically, arresting officials, making new laws, Johnson acts against both of them. Sickles resigns in order to answer the charges, Johnson replaces Sheridan and another commander.

This creates an immediate backlash in Congress. At the same time, Congress had tried to protect Secretary of War Edwin Stanton by an act called the Tenure of Office Act that suggested that a President needed Congressional approval to fire members of his cabinet. When he fires Stanton as Secretary of War in order to undermine the Reconstruction efforts that Stanton is defending in the South, then Congress votes to impeach. The Articles of Impeachment pass the House and they're sent to the Senate.

There, Johnson's extraordinarily able lawyers delay long enough to let the momentum dissipate and, in that time, they successfully convince him not to destroy his own case and, having made these actions of appointing new commanders in the South, now to keep his hands off. As the Senate is wrestling with how to handle the impeachment trial and wrestling with the evidence, Johnson stops interfering in the South and a series of Southern states complete Reconstruction and present themselves.

And so then what Johnson's lawyers are able to say is – separate from the legal questions which are complicated – they're able to convince a handful of Republicans that Johnson has decided to keep his hands off the South and so what are they really going to gain? By this and by legends of bribery and of other kinds of chicanery, Johnson is able to very narrowly prevail in the Senate and to hold onto his office but is reduced to a mere figurehead over the last months of his Presidency. And it's quite likely that even if he had been impeached, if he had been convicted and removed, that the practical difference would have been minimal.

Antonio Elmaleh: It's fascinating, the rope-a-dope that he's doing. To our point earlier in the show, this guy is a complete enigma. He's here, then he's there, which side is he on? "Well, I'm over here today, but guess what folks, I was just kidding," and nobody can pin him down. Everybody's in uncharted territory, basically recreating a new country out of the ruins of the Civil War. Nobody's ever done that before, so this fellow is charged with, number one, filling the giant's shoes with Abe Lincoln, and, two, navigating this insanely complicated maze of decision-making that nobody's ever faced before.

It sheds a different kind of a light, certainly for me, on him as a President, because I know he's universally reviled.

Greg Downs: I mean, I think he's clearly the worst President in US history and none of what I say is meant to mitigate that, but only to explain sometimes the logic of what he was doing – or in attributing too much power to him, we've mistaken the question of why Reconstruction turned out to be a disappointment. One of the things that I often wonder is how different it would have been if Lincoln had lived. It would have been different in some ways, but it wouldn't have been easy. We could have had, you know, Lincoln and Napoleon and George Washington and Martin Luther King together sitting over the country, and it was still never going to be easy. Sometimes we attribute every fault of this to Johnson and that reinforces the idea that there was an easy solution.

The other interesting thing about Johnson is that he was very savvy about saying wild and extravagant things but also understanding how politics work. In one sense, he's a disastrous politician in the sense that he goes to war with Congress, but in another sense he's not a fool. He's playing for a crowd that he thinks is going to be against Reconstruction.

He can't believe it's popular and he misjudges the populace dramatically on that, but he's also very adept at separating his language from his own actions.

Sometimes historians read his language as proof of what he did, rather than to look at his own ability to read policy, to read complex legal documents, and to isolate. He's nobody's dummy. He was not educated, he only learned to read as an adult. He married his teacher, an older woman who had taught him to read. He's not an educated person but he's extremely shrewd in certain ways, even if he's on the wrong side of history and the wrong side of the politics of the day.

Antonio Elmaleh: Yes. You write very powerfully about the many ironies and contradictions that Reconstruction provoked. Here are two things that struck me. The first one is: the end of slavery had the perverse effect of expanding the political power of the South; and the second one is: expanding the right to vote, instead of having a purifying effect on expanding Democracy, had the unintended effect of intensifying and accelerating violence and chaos.

Would you care to comment on the end of slavery having the perverse effect of expanding the South's political power and, you know, if you feel like also talking a little bit about how expanding democracy actually accelerated chaos?

Greg Downs: This turns upon the question of the relationship of the end of slavery and the political power nationally of the Southern states. It turns upon something that historians and legal scholars know well but the public often misunderstands, which is the Three-Fifths Clause of the Constitution – so often invoked as a sign of the relative worth, in an abstract or ethical sense, of enslaved people but in fact it emerged in the Constitution as a way of resolving the question of how much do slaves count toward either the taxes or the representation of the states where slaves are held.

The irony of this, from our perspective, is that the people who are calling for slaves to count as a hundred percent were not anti-slavery people but planters. Because if they could count their slaves as people, whole people, then they would get more congressmen and maximize their power. And the people who hated slavery the most wanted slaves to count as zero because they understood it not as an ethical debate about slaves' personhood but as a debate about the power of slave owners. And so the more slaves counted, the more power slave owners have.

Well, one of the ironies of the end of slavery is that it offered the possibility that planters would get a substantial bonus in representation by moving four million slaves from three-fifths of a person to a hundred percent. It would expand the political power of the South. And so if planters could prevent black people from voting but count them as free people, they would have more congressmen and more electoral votes than they would have otherwise.

This creates the series of crises that shaped the 14th Amendment, that shaped the question of seating congressmen from rebel states, and eventually shaped the outcome in the 15th Amendment. But you do have to say that Southern planter politicians who recognized this in the 1860s were able to achieve their goal eventually by the 1890s. And then, by disenfranchising freed people and African American men, they were able to count them for representation without having to listen to their votes. And so that's why Jim Crow expands Southern planter influence upon national politics – in some ways, not in all.

That's the answer to why this irony, that one potential outcome of the war that all Republicans feared was that it would expand the power of planter politicians in the South, why they tried so hard and why people opposed black male suffrage or who were Jim Crow, deeply racist, and come to support black male suffrage, as the only way to avert that catastrophe. In terms of the overall relationship, their hope, as they enfranchise black men, is that this creates peace, that it moves what had been a large scale fight on the ground between vigilante groups – eventually the Ku Klux Klan and black organized union leagues – that it turns those from fights through violence to fights through politics.

In the end, as happens often in democratization, what it does is instead of removing violence from the fight it moves the violence into politics. We really should think of the politics of the South in the 1860s into the 1890s as a para-military politics: as a politics where people win through violence and the violence structures the tools and the ways people understand and think about politics.

It was this that leads Ulysses S. Grant, after his time in the White House, to say privately that they made a mistake. And the mistake that they made was expanding, giving the vote to anyone, and that rather than enfranchising freedmen they should have disenfranchised Confederates and not let anyone vote in the South for ten years while the military held the ground. Instead of solving the violence politics had accelerated it and the solution was not to let anyone vote, but he also said, "No one would have dared to suggest this because it was counter to popular opinion and people wouldn't have supported it."

Antonio Elmaleh: Yes, didn't he also say something to the effect that, "We didn't use enough force?"

Greg Downs: Right, that's right.

Antonio Elmaleh: Can you just touch on that briefly?

Greg Downs: Grant had hoped that, after surrender, white Southerners had accepted the end of the war, but he becomes convinced, both in his time remaining as commander and then as president, that white Southerners had not accepted the lessons of the war. It's for this reason that he continued to think about the use of the Army in the South, both against the Ku Klux Klan in the early 1870s and then to consider utilizing the Army again in 1875 in response to General Phil Sheridan's judgment that it would take the Army to pacify the South in the midst of violent elections in the middle of the 1870s. And he becomes convinced that white Southerners have never accepted the end of the war or the results of the war.

Antonio Elmaleh: I think in the last part of our program, I'd like to focus a little bit on the resonance of all these issues to our country today, and let me start by pointing out to our listeners that the state legislature in South Carolina just either drafted or passed a measure to either authorize or discuss the possibility of seceding from the Union.

This is in 2018 and a hundred and eighty years after the war. The issue is still alive and well in some ways.

My question is: do you think it's safe to say that the North won the Civil War, but the South won the peace of the next hundred years?

Greg Downs: Famously, the novelist and former Freedman's Bureau official and judge, Albion Tourgee said, "The South surrendered at Appomattox and the North has been surrendering ever since," which captures that view of what was lost. And there are good reasons to contemplate that idea, among the most powerful of which are the near complete assertion of not just the white Southern power but really a white Southern planter power in the 1890s and 1900s: disenfranchisement, Jim Crow, and the real evacuation and hollowing out of that Constitutional revolution, making the guarantees of the 14th Amendment simply parchment guarantees, things that had little meaning in practicality.

For this reason, and then the success of white Southerners in spreading a cultural version of this view – not only in celebrating racism and helping to make racism a sort of common aspect of American popular culture, from everything from Gone With the Wind to Walt Disney – but specifically to romanticize. I mean that even white Northerners had always been interested in racist betrayals of African Americans. But what white Southerners successfully do in late 19th, early 20th century is to celebrate the plantation culture and to kind of create a "moonlight and magnolia" vision of the white Southern plantations. And then they sort of tinge their fall with a kind of regret.

We see this in Birth of a Nation and the novel it's based on, Thomas Dixon's The Clansman; Gone with the Wind; Song of the South; real landmarks of American popular culture that are rooted in this kind of evocation. A wistful evocation of plantation slavery as a place of graciousness.

Antonio Elmaleh: It's a lost cause, so to speak

Greg Downs: That's right, and especially a kind of lost cause. David Blight most famously, among many others, has argued about the eclipse of Civil War memory and the triumph of Southern reconciliationist vision, in which the white South accepted that secession was wrong and the white North accepted that Reconstruction was wrong. And all those things feed into the question as you posed it, and yet I, myself, would resist that formulation. I do think that the gains of Reconstruction were real, even if some of them were fleeting, and some of them were less fleeting than we might think.

For one thing, if we think about what was possible even early in the war, it's conceivable to imagine that some people were free, emancipation without abolition, that some slaves were freed but not all and that slavery itself endured. It's possible to imagine that if we had had some kind of armistice and a negotiating out of terms, that even if Confederate states had been convinced to end legal slavery, they would have established and demanded some kind of apprenticeship system, on a massive scale like you see in the British Caribbean or later in Spanish Emancipation. Years of apprenticeship, of "free womb" laws in which babies born become free at the age of eighteen – but people aren't free.

Those were very live possibilities in the 1860s, but then Reconstruction kills slavery. It's also, even after that, imaginable to have a system in which explicit legal caste is invoked, that rights are denied to people not just because of their color and a way that people understand but by law.

People compare the American South to Apartheid South Africa and these are interesting comparisons, but there's also this interesting divergence. They have to go to lengths in the American South to enforce segregation. They don't elsewhere because some of those legal constraints remain, and the legal caste system that would have been invoked, even with the limits of the 14th Amendment and its application, would have been even worse. That's why it's off the table or delayed or transformed by the 14th Amendment. It takes longer and it takes more creativity to establish this ultimate separation.

Then finally, when we look at what did happen in Reconstruction, I think that there's a lot of reasons to see it as a success even if it can't be delivery of a paradigm. One is education, right? The literacy levels were extremely low among slaves because they were, in many states, outlawed to learn to read. A massive movement is education – those education systems are under-funded, are poorly treated – but they still have a huge impact. And in a society absent Reconstruction they might never have existed at all.

South Carolina had no public schools for anybody, white or black, until Reconstruction. Reconstruction creates the first-ever statewide public school for white people in South Carolina. It creates, like I say, imperfect schools but schools that transform. There's also a surprising amount of property accumulation throughout the 19th century, so that black people are able to acquire – not the sort of dream of small holders in the midwest, of small family farms that are independent and self-sufficient – but significant amounts of property over the 1870s and 1880s, sometimes even deeper.

Then there's been some interesting work on the legal system that, as much as the legal system of Jim Crow was largely imbalanced against black people, new work by Melissa Milewski and others, and ongoing work by Dylan Penningroth, have explored the ways that African Americans in the South continue to use the legal system. It's balanced against them but it's not closed; it's unfair but it's not non-existent. Those can seem like small windows until we think about what it means to not have them.

I think to assess Reconstruction we have to measure it not against our dream of the world that we wish had been made, but against other post-emancipation societies. And, compared to ex-slaves elsewhere, Reconstruction actually looked both somewhat effective in raising the status and possibilities of ex-slaves and in diminishing the political power of planters.

As Thaddeus Stevens said, in talking about why he was willing to support acts that he knew were imperfect, "It's because he lives among men and not angels." Compared to an angelic society, Reconstruction's a failure. But compared to our actual history of what happens at the end of slavery or the actual history of other moments of American intervention, in many ways it's a dramatic success. And a success that we can read in the determination of white Southerners to tear down as much as they can of it and to discredit it as much as they can.

Antonio Elmaleh: I think it was Ted Kennedy who said that if you want to be in the game of politics, you've got to come to grips with the fact that it's a game of inches. If you move the ball down the field in a lifetime, a few inches or a foot, that's considered a success in the context of the rate of change that it takes to get anything moving and then implemented and then finally integrated into the society at large.

I think what you're saying is that it's unfair to measure Reconstruction against the visions that its proponents had, and instead measure it against the practical obstacles it faced, the enormous challenges and difficulties that it posed, and realize that these changes are not just revolutionary they're enduring to this day. Is that fair?

Greg Downs: Along with the paraphrase you had of Kennedy, it seems clearly true that another way of saying it is, and I'm going to get the translation slightly wrong but, "Politics is a slow and boring boring of hard wood," that politics and political change happens slowly and it might not happen anyway.

The second myth that can be built into the ways that people fantasize about politics is that you get to do a victory lap, that you pass something and then it's over. And I think what's even more dismaying for Americans about Reconstruction is that enormous things were passed – and then torn down. And Americans tend to incorporate the nation's history and its failings by thinking about a narrative of progress, "Things were bad and now we're getting better and they will be better."

Reconstruction really threatens that. It threatens it because of its successes and it threatens it because it shows those successes weren't sustainable. I think it's very dismaying, not only looking backward but looking forward from now, for people to contemplate the things that they take as rights that were established – whether constitutional rights or voting rights or programs that people think of as entitlements like Social Security or something – these aren't chiseled in stone and haven't come down from Sinai but they are things that have to be defended.

The people who want to retain them have to defend them, and I think that Americans have not been good about remembering that. And the American Left has often done better at articulating bold visions of change than of articulating the need to stay focused on the slow and boring work of sustaining and defending that change.

Antonio Elmaleh: That's well said and I think I certainly appreciate that clarity as someone who studies history and has to come to grips with what our expectations are and what we fervently hope will happen, against what's happening now and what kind of progress, if any, is being made. It tests all of our resolve on all levels.

In closing, I'd like to ask you this one final question and that is: do you have one thought, observation, or even a question you'd like to leave with our listeners as a result of your work?

Greg Downs: I think on Reconstruction, one thing that I've asked people is "What did they learn about it?" It's been interesting to hear not only people, especially of an older generation recount being taught myths of Reconstruction, corruption, and so on, but it's been very striking to me with my students of how often the answer is nothing.

They're no longer being taught the sort of myths of a bad Reconstruction, but they're also often not being taught anything at all. And I guess if I were to leave people with a question on that aspect of Reconstruction, of how we think about it in our present day, it would be why do they think that is? Why do they think that Reconstruction, and we've made huge advances against slavery and the Civil War and re-thinking the founding, why does Reconstruction, in some ways, seem like the thing that can't be talked about?

I think the other question I would leave is more of a historical question, though, a counter-history. We've talked before about the what ifs of Reconstruction. And I would ask people what happens if we think about what should have been done as a process in Reconstruction, as a policy, rather than what we wish were the outcome?

People find it easy to articulate the outcome they wanted and very hard to articulate how they would have gotten there and protected that outcome. That reveals how easy it is for all of us to kind of think of the law as a magic wand: "I'll make this law..." But they made great laws, they just didn't make them stick. And in that sense, how can Reconstruction help us to develop the capacity to separate our hopes for outcomes from our understanding of the processes that it'll take to make them so?

There are lots of reasons to study history but a lesson that I articulate to my students all the time is that aside from understanding your past and the way the past features in present day conversations, history is, in some ways, a long and dismaying understanding of the importance of things that people find really boring, especially when they're in their teens and twenties, like process, like bureaucracy, like sustaining rather than building anew...

Antonio Elmaleh: Like it being a game of inches as opposed to long strides.

Greg Downs: That's right. I think I would ask them that if they could, instead of looking backward and saying "It should have ended with this," to say "How would you have run a process?" Even if you were a dictator and could do anything you want, what are the process and policies you would use? And how does flipping the question that way help us to process the kind of policy debates that circulate around us all the time, not just in this political moment but four years ago or eight years ago or eighteen years ago.

What would it mean if we could talk more about politics in those terms? Like you say, of inches, of bureaucracies, of policies, rather than simply of aspiration?

Antonio Elmaleh: I think you hit the nail on the head. You know, we're used to drama, we're used to sweeping resolution. All our movies and our pop culture teach us to expect that in the end there's going to be some kind of a neat wrapping-up of all these conflicting forces and whatever the outcome is, it's what we hope it would be. But it's so fundamentally a myth, an illusion that does the very thing it's not supposed to do, which is to reinforce a set of unreal expectations on how life works, how things work.

Greg Downs: Right.

Antonio Elmaleh: That's a disservice of education, and I don't know what the answer is. I've thought about this a lot and I think, just to blow my own horn, one of the reasons this show exists is to try to just peel away some of the easy assumptions and myths that have been made about this most, to me, critical and profound event in our history and to really look at it in the context of, "Okay, let's strip away what we thought it was about, let's strip away what we learned in history, if we ever did."

But then how much time do they spend on Reconstruction? I mean it's appalling, and let's look at the complexities of what people were facing, the challenges of, and the complications of, literally, remaking a country out of the shambles of seven hundred and fifty thousand people killed, and to do that, I don't know what that takes. Courage? Curiosity? Something.

Greg Downs: I do think this conversation was really, in a lot of ways, a model of how to, as you say, avoid some of the shortcuts that keep us from thinking, and to kind of think about how real historical inquiry leads to more thinking, not less, right? And how to cultivate that habit: the only answer I know goes back to the same issue. It's by doing.

Antonio Elmaleh: Doing the work. We've reached the end of the line for today. I'd like to thank Professor Greg Downs for a powerful and illuminating discussion. Many thanks to you, Greg.

Greg Downs: Well, thank you so much for having me and for all of your excellent questions.

Antonio Elmaleh: You're very welcome, but before we go, please remind our listeners about your newest book and when you anticipate it coming out. We'll be sure to look for it when it does.

Greg Downs: I'm working on a short book called *The Second American Revolution* that is a group of essays that aim to help us think about the Civil War and Reconstruction as a revolution, both in the terms that we talked about today, how the transformation of the Constitution was itself an act of revolution that depended upon the force of the Army and the force of martial law, but also in two other ways:

By thinking about the ways the Civil War emerges out of revolutionary currents in Cuba and in Spain, and of exiles from there who come to the US in the 1840s and 1850s and participated in the heightening of political conflict in the US.

Then to think about how the outcome of the US was revolutionary, and again by looking at Cuba and Spain and the way there that insurgents and republicans and revolutionaries try to use the Civil War to create new societies where they are. An insurgency in Cuba leads to what's called the Ten Years' War and the declaration of a forgotten First Spanish Republic led by an historian, of all people, for a time in early 1870s Spain, and one that really uses Lincoln as well as his contemporary, Mexican President Benito Juarez, as models of a new order.

If we were to ask in what ways the Civil War changed the world, one of my suggestions in this book to answer that is we should be looking at those places, Cuba and Spain and Mexico, as places where people are really looking at the Civil War and Reconstruction as a model of how do you sustain a republic in a world that seems to be turning back toward monarchies or dictatorships.

I hope that it'll be available in late 2019.

Antonio Elmaleh: Well, as I said, we will look for it, we will talk about it on the show, certainly mention it to our listeners, and again thank you for coming on the show. It's been really, really wonderful.

To our listeners, many thanks for taking the time and having the curiosity to listen in on another segment of *Uncovering the Civil War*. I hope you'll come back again. Until then, be safe and do good.

ELEVEN

UNCOVERING EDWIN STANTON

Guest: William Marvel

Antonio Elmaleh: Hello, everyone. Welcome to another episode of *Uncovering the Civil War*. This is your host, Antonio Elmaleh. Today, my guest is William Marvel, an independent scholar specializing in mid-nineteenth century American history with eighteen published books so far, mostly about the Civil War and related topics. His latest book is *Lincoln's Mercenaries: Economic Motivation Among Union Soldiers During the Civil War*. It's due to be published in November 2018 by Louisiana State University Press. Welcome, Mr. Marvel.

William Marvel: Thank you for having me.

Antonio Elmaleh: You're very welcome. Today, our topic for discussion is Mr. Marvel's book *Lincoln's Autocrat: The Life of Edwin Stanton*, and more specifically Stanton's tenure as Lincoln's secretary of war.

Would you like to start us off with a brief, and this is a tall order I know, a brief summary of Stanton's life prior to serving in Lincoln's cabinet?

William Marvel: Sure. Well first of all his name was Edwin M. Stanton, and he was born in Steubenville, Ohio, and his father died when he was quite young. His mother was dependent on friends and relatives for income for quite some time thereafter. He, after a brief apprenticeship in merchandising, went into reading the law with a local attorney and became a lawyer. After a few years practicing in Steubenville and affiliating with politicians in that community, he moved to Pittsburgh and got more interested in corporate law, then finally moved to Washington and started practicing there. That's where he became available for various administrations to appoint to their cabinets.

Antonio Elmaleh: That's pretty good considering it encapsulates, what, forty-five years? Describe how Stanton was able to get appointed to Lincoln's cabinet from attorney general in Buchanan's when the two presidents were so vastly different in policy, style, and temperament.

William Marvel: Stanton, as always, was covering both sides of the fence. When he was still in Buchanan's cabinet he befriended William Seward, the secretary of state-to-be for Lincoln and at that time thought to be the power behind the throne, and he began feeding him inside information from the administration – basically, betraying the president he was serving and ingratiating himself to Seward sufficiently that he was able to start doing legal work for the government under the Lincoln Administration. Then when Simon Cameron, the secretary of war under Lincoln, proved to be inefficient and undesirable, Seward and Chase together – Salmon P. Chase had been a friend of Stanton's in Ohio – suggested him as a replacement. He was accepted.

Antonio Elmaleh: You talk about this two-faced, duplicitous character, and we'll focus on that quite a bit over the course of this show. Can you tell me about the various moves Stanton made to take control of the War Department once Lincoln appointed him secretary of war when Cameron resigned, I think in disgrace?

William Marvel: More or less, yes. It was sort of covered up, and he was appointed minister to Russia as a...

Antonio Elmaleh: Off to Siberia.

William Marvel: It was the consolation prize. Stanton, after having befriended the General-in-Chief George McClellan, immediately turned hostile to McClellan and began forcing distance between McClellan and the president by interposing himself between the two. Not long after he took over the War Office he issued decrees to the media, to the newspapers, basically criminalizing the reporting of information and essentially setting himself up as the arbiter of what was publishable and what was not. Then he took the Telegraph Office away from McClellan, out of the Army headquarters, and installed it in the office next to his own in the War Department, so he could monitor all the conversation through the telegraph. Thereafter, McClellan was forced to communicate with Washington and the president through Stanton.

He basically started taking control of all the means of communication. He was very good at that. He appointed his friends as assistants and clerks in the War Department. They served him more than they did the War Department in some cases.

Antonio Elmaleh: I have a note here that he also established the Judge Advocate General, and established military tribunals to supersede the court system. Can you speak briefly to that?

William Marvel: The Judge Advocate General whom he chose was Joseph Holt, who was another somewhat duplicitous character who had served in the Buchanan Administration. This was a little later in the war. Stanton installed him, I think, September 3, 1862, which was what, almost eight months after he entered the War Office. He appointed him, or rather suggested him to the President to appoint, because he wanted to get Fitz John Porter court-martialed, and he, on the very day he called Holt into his office to interview him for that appointment, had received information that led him to believe that he could probably court-martial Porter, sort of in lieu of McClellan. They had been collaborators in the Buchanan Administration and they remained collaborators as long as Stanton was in the War Office.

Antonio Elmaleh: The Civil War is by no means a popular war. Significant resistance and sedition certainly were not uncommon amongst border states and anywhere where people were considered sympathetic to slavery, even if they were in a Northern state. You make the point that Stanton made the war even more unpopular by trashing the Fourth, Fifth, and Sixth Amendments to the Constitution. Can you give us some further background or detail on that? It's quite revealing.

William Marvel: Well, he was instrumental, with Senator Henry Wilson, in coming up with legislation in Congress, often through the Military Affairs Committee, that was then passed and signed by the president and that he then used to punish those who disagreed with him. As you say, there was a great deal of resistance, especially after there was an effort to change the focus of the war from simply restoring the Union to making it an abolition war.

By the summer of 1862, it was obvious that that was happening. Some of the legislation that was passed included the Amendment to the Militia Act, which allowed certain changes in the recruiting process, but also it allowed the president to decree, or at least the executive department to decree, certain speech illegal and to arrest and confine people for what they called "discouraging enlistments," which could mean anything from criticizing the politics of the administration to saying, "Well, you fellows are not enlisting for patriotism, you're enlisting for the bounties." That legislation was imposed during the first draft in August of 1862, the Militia Draft. It was heavily enforced, and arbitrarily enforced, and that was a very effective means of silencing any opposition.

Stanton probably knew that it was really unconstitutional, but he was intent on protecting his office and the administration now that he was loyal to that administration, at least on the face of it.

Antonio Elmaleh: Arresting somebody and putting them in prison. In Stanton's War Department, a lot of those folks never went to trial. That wasn't the point. The point was to just get rid of them and get them into a controlled environment where they could be watched. People would languish in jail without a trial, it was effectively a jail sentence without actually being convicted. Would you agree with that?

William Marvel: That's certainly true. I mean, the editor at the Dubuque Herald was arrested and brought to Washington from Iowa by a Republican operative who happened to be a marshal for Iowa. Stanton knew all about it, and he actually authorized his arrest before he released the pronunciamento that declared what this editor had written to be illegal. This editor, Dennis Mahoney, stayed in jail for many weeks. His newspaper, of course, languished. He was in hard economic times anyway. He was always struggling, he had to sell his newspaper in order to save any of his fortune such as it was, and only then was he released from prison when he was no longer capable of publishing criticism of the administration.

Antonio Elmaleh: In that light, can you offer us a little insight as to why it was important or significant to have military tribunals rather than civil courts adjudicate some of these cases? Can you shed some light on why that method was chosen and why it was effective?

William Marvel: It was chosen, and it was effective, simply because it was much easier to obtain a conviction. It was essentially a court-martial of civilians. You had officers in the Army who were often hostile to the politics of the people who were under trial. You had officers whose careers depended on what Stanton might do for them or might not do for them; he was known to summarily muster soldiers and officers out of the Army whom he didn't like.

In a case like Fitz John Porter, for instance, all he had to do was appoint the right officers. People in the old Army knew who was hostile to whom, and they knew what officers were malleable in principle. You appoint the right people, you get the conviction you want, especially with a Judge Advocate General like Holt.

Unfortunately, we still don't recognize how unconstitutional that is, because we seem to put up with it. For instance, in the Guantanamo Base trials, those are essentially military tribunals and they're held on leased US property. Given the 1866 Supreme Court decision, they should be unconstitutional. They were declared so, but this was after the war and Stanton and Holt still tried to try ex-confederates though this method, even after the case was decided, but they failed in their effort.

Antonio Elmaleh: Without getting too lost in the weeds over details on this, am I correct in stating that rules of evidence in military tribunals are very different than in a civil court?

William Marvel: They are different, and a lot of rules and procedure are different. You have the president of the court, they're called judges, all of the people sitting on the court. But in the case of Porter, for instance, you had one officer who was a judge on the court who stepped down from the court to testify against the defendant, and then went back on the court and declared him guilty. Furthermore, that officer was himself partly responsible for the defeat for which Porter was being tried.

Antonio Elmaleh: Good Lord, bald-faced, as they say.

William Marvel: Yes.

Antonio Elmaleh: Stanton's hypocrisy and his meanness and his bullying are legendary, and I'm still baffled by how he went from being a, I don't know if he was a champion for McClellan, but he certainly at least publicly supported him. Why did he make the switch from being a supporter to an unabashed opponent of his, seeking at every turn to diminish his power as general-in-chief?

William Marvel: Well, that was his way. He was not, I don't think, a sincere supporter of McClellan ever. McClellan simply happened to be in a place of power and Stanton sought him out because he needed people in places of government power in order to get the legal work that he was then looking for. In fact, what he started doing with McClellan was legal work for the Army. That was his purpose in, well I guess you could say, sucking-up to the Buchanan administration, the attorney general, so he could get legal work. Then that attorney general suggested him as his own replacement when he was promoted. He did the same thing in the Lincoln Administration. He sought out his friends and made new friends. He was as any sycophant would be, he simply followed the power.

Then, when he suddenly had more power than McClellan, he immediately turned on him because McClellan was the only person, the only other person, who could challenge his authority. McClellan had essentially dominated Cameron because Cameron did very little in the War Department. McClellan had his own way and Stanton wanted to be sure that that didn't happen to him. He was just hopelessly treacherous in that way.

Antonio Elmaleh: None of this was policy-driven, in other words. He had no guiding policy that might've also dictated loyalty. It seemed as if, as you say, he was just like a golem: wherever the power was, he sought it. History can't accept "what ifs," but I wonder would he have endorsed a pro-slavery general if it had suited his political control?

William Marvel: He certainly would've. He certainly would have because he supported the pro-slavery candidate for President in 1860, he supported Breckenridge, the Kentuckian who was essentially the slave power candidate, as did Holt, I believe. It was not a matter of principle that led him to his policy actions. His policy was power and is power, and as long as he could exercise power under Lincoln, he remained loyal to Lincoln.

Antonio Elmaleh: That kind of leads me to my next question which is, was Lincoln onto Stanton's two-faced character flaws? If he was, why did he tolerate them, since that was not his character at all?

William Marvel: Well, if you believe Gideon Welles, who was rather conservative himself and as a consequence has suffered some lack of credibility among certain scholars, Lincoln did catch on to him. There was one instance in a Cabinet meeting where Stanton had said one thing before the Cabinet meeting and he said something else during the meeting in Lincoln's presence. Welles described the President looking kind of critically on him, scowling at him, as though he recognized the duplicity, and it's quite possible that Lincoln did.

I mean, Lincoln was not the god that people assume. He was somewhat pragmatic and he was probably willing to allow character flaws among his cabinet members – I mean, we all have them – so long as they didn't become crucial in the management of the department, as long as they didn't adversely affect the management of the department.

I think Stanton's control over the employees in the War Department was such that even if there had been some adverse impact he wouldn't have been able to hide it. Lincoln, I think, was willing to have Stanton be his defender, or anyone else be his defender, who was flawed personally so long as it wasn't obvious politically. At least during Lincoln's time it didn't become all that obvious politically, at least within Lincoln's realm.

Antonio Elmaleh: That's very, very, very pragmatic.

William Marvel: Yes.

Antonio Elmaleh: Well, in a time of crisis it's hard to debate who has the luxury to have ideal people working to meet the crisis. We'll cover that later in the show. Apparently, Stanton's temper was legendary as well. He would fly off, and apparently he hated the fact that Lincoln was this inveterate jokester. Can you tell our listeners a little bit about some of the instances you cite in your book where he just completely goes crazy with anger about it?

William Marvel: Well, the instance that comes to mind, the most credible instance that's reported by someone else who was there, was during the discussion of moving the 11th and 12th Corps from the Army of the Potomac to Chattanooga. Stanton had, on his own, gathered some generals, quartermasters, some railroad executives, and was having a late night meeting at the White House. In fact, he had Lincoln roused from bed and brought in for it, to discuss this potential reinforcement of Chattanooga when it was under siege. In the middle of it Lincoln started telling a joke. One of the witnesses said, "This is no time for jokes nor no time for stories."

Other instances where Stanton turned on different people, including Lincoln, I think are sometimes apocryphal, like the instance on the hotel steps in Cincinnati during the McCormick Reaper trial before the war when they were both lawyers for the defendant. Stanton ostensibly insulted Lincoln; I don't frankly think that happened. There are other instances with Lincoln, such as the night of the, I don't know if it was the presidential election or one of the important state elections in 1864 where Lincoln was telling a story, and Charles Dana said that Stanton took him into another room and raged about it.

Stanton's temper, I think, was histrionic. I think he flew off the handle at people he thought he could cow, and then he immediately apologized to people who stood up to him. To people who had any authority over him he was entirely obsequious. His legendary temper, I think, was more along the lines of Andrew Jackson's, which may have been more convincing but also often artificial.

Antonio Elmaleh: It was a calculated device to get an effect rather than sincerely felt. Did your research ever uncover anything that might've revealed Stanton's desire to be president? It's well-known and well-documented in books like *Team of Rivals*, Doris Kearns' book about the Lincoln cabinet, that Lee Seward and Salmon P. Chase harbored serious aspirations, and in Chase's case they never abated. Seward, I think, became quite a devoted and appreciative part of the administration. To repeat the question, do you have anything in your research to suggest that Stanton, as well, might've desired to be president?

William Marvel: Nothing credible. Stanton was, I think, afraid of running for office because in order to do so you had to stake out your ground, you had to take a position on different issues. He was so accustomed to slide-hitting from one side of an issue to the other, as his interests dictated, that he never ran for office after the county attorney. He ran for prosecutor of Harrison County, Ohio, and served as prosecutor for a term, and after that he never ran for office. My suspicion is that he knew that he wouldn't be able to keep a straight face. Essentially, he wouldn't be able to maintain a course of policies because people would be able to contradict him with his own statements.

Some of his own correspondence indicates that he's writing to one conservative senator and praising him for a conservative speech on, I think it was the Oregon Controversy, and then he writes to a liberal senator who held the opposite viewpoint and he praises him for his speech. That sort of person is very much afraid of having to take a stand in public, and he would've had to do that to be president. I don't think he wanted that nearly so much as he wanted a lifetime sinecure. He was looking for work when he came into the War Department, and after he left the War Department he spent the rest of his life basically hoping for a lifetime appointment.

Antonio Elmaleh: The US Army had, I think, something like sixteen thousand men in 1860. By 1865 something like three million had served or were in uniform. Stanton had such an iron grip on all the war-related efforts, recruiting, the press, communications, supply infrastructure. As such, I think it's obvious that the opportunity for graft and kickbacks and corruption was enormous. Many people helped themselves freely to the low-lying fruit. In your research did you ever come to believe that Stanton ever profited financially from the enormous power he wielded?

William Marvel: Well, I've run across, of course, numerous accusations. I think, for instance, Montgomery Blair, the postmaster general under Lincoln, opposed Stanton's appointment to the War Department partly for that reason; he believed that Stanton had taken a bribe. Whether he took bribes earlier on, I don't know, but I'm quite sure that he didn't in office. For a couple of reasons: one, his fortunes diminished rapidly while he was in office instead of multiplying as Holt's did; he was basically not a pauper but he had very little money when the war ended. The other thing, I think, was he was deathly afraid of being found out. That would've been of course the end of everything for him. He wouldn't have been able to get a job anywhere after that, because he really wasn't much a lawyer anymore.

Antonio Elmaleh: When you look at it, again, it's not driven by any kind of morality as it is by practical consideration: he didn't want to be found out is not the most character-inspired reason to be honest.

William Marvel: I have a hard time thinking of Stanton as moral in any sense.

Antonio Elmaleh: I get that from your book. I want to go back to this relationship between Lincoln and Stanton and just probe it a little bit more deeply. I don't even know quite how to do that except to ask if it reveals a dark side of Lincoln's character that he didn't want to show to people because he was too busy trying to present an image of leadership? Or was it simply just a practical, "This is a guy who gets things done. I need somebody who will get his hands dirty and I'm not going to do it, it's not in my nature to be vindictive or to be a bully." Maybe it's both? Do you have any sense of what it said about Lincoln's character to have such an obvious cretin – I guess is a good word, I don't know, you tell me – like Stanton in his Cabinet?

William Marvel: I probably suffer as much as anyone from the childhood-imbued bias about Lincoln. I really revered him as a child. As much as I've read about the administration and Lincoln since, it's difficult to really think of Lincoln as approving of such behavior as Stanton's. At the same time, I'm not sure that he knew exactly how duplicitous Stanton was. I don't think he knew, for instance, that Stanton was willing to sacrifice Lincoln, if necessary, to remain in some sort of executive administration if the election of 1864 went the wrong way. At the same time, as I've said, Lincoln was pragmatic and was happy, I think, to have Stanton sort of operate his propaganda organization through Holt, especially at election times.

For instance, when Stanton was trying to promote the idea that the Democrats and McClellan were really trying to betray the Union to the Confederacy, Lincoln had no belief in that whatsoever. He pretty much ignored the argument but he allowed the trials, the show trials that Stanton organized to go on. He didn't criticize the media coverage of it. He was intent on winning the election, and probably mostly for altruistic reasons as much as his own ego.

Antonio Elmaleh: In that light I recall, and I can't recall the specifics which is why I'd like to ask you, that there was an election in New

Hampshire, of all places, that might speak to this idea of propaganda. Can you refresh my memory and our listeners'?

William Marvel: I think you're talking about – we have to remember that I haven't read this book in three years myself – but New Hampshire, as now, since 1920 New Hampshire has had the first primary in the presidential season. In the 1860s it had the first of the annual state elections. It was sort of the bellwether of what was going to happen nationally. You've heard that phrase, "As goes Maine, so goes the nation," well, that really applied to New Hampshire in the 1860s because our March town meetings included most state elections if there was no presidential election. If they went Republican, you could hope that the next state elections would be influenced thereby. It was important how New Hampshire went.

In the spring of 1864 there was a fear, and a justifiable fear, that New Hampshire would go Democratic. Stanton allowed the governor of the state to say that New Hampshire's draft quota, under the recently announced draft, had been met. It had not. They both knew it. That word went out, the elections happened, and they went Republican. Then immediately thereafter, Stanton and the governor started working together to make sure that quota was met. So they weren't caught at it, they began offering phenomenal bounties for the raising of a new cavalry regiment. The state was not only paying a three hundred dollar bounty on its own, it was paying the federal bounty of three hundred dollars in advance on Stanton's authority; the federal government was later going to reimburse that.

The federal government, meanwhile, wouldn't pay that bounty in advance because they knew that there were so many deserters who would just take it and run, and that's exactly what happened. I think the first New Hampshire cavalry ended up with a thirty-two percent desertion rate, and that's largely because of this bounty funding that was meant basically to cover up their little scheme.

Antonio Elmaleh: In that light, if you could explain briefly the distinction between the bounty and the substitute, the payment for the substitute, for our listeners?

William Marvel: A substitute was a man who enlisted for someone who had been drafted. Under the substitute law, the substitute had to be ineligible for the draft himself; he either had to be underage or had to be an alien or he had to fit one of the economic exemptions for the draft. Then the principle, the person who had been drafted, would pay this person a certain amount of money – sometimes the community would kick in a small amount of it, but the state never did. If you voluntarily enlisted and were eligible for enlistment for draft, then you would get a bounty, almost always at the end of the war, from your town, sometimes from your county, from your state, and then from the federal government. By 1864, those bounties were rising up to a total of nine hundred, one thousand, twelve hundred, fifteen hundred dollars at a time when thee hundred dollars was the average laborer's annual wage.

Antonio Elmaleh: I think it testifies to the unpopularity of the draft. People were desperate to find a way not to serve, which, again, speaks to it was not an overwhelmingly popular war by any stretch.

William Marvel: Well, the substitute costs, yes, speak to the unpopularity of the draft. The substitute fees and the bounties together speak to the overall unpopularity of the war itself, at least for the individual.

Antonio Elmaleh: I want to double back on a point about this relationship between Lincoln and Stanton. There was a bond between these two men, I'm not sure what it was, but there was some kind of a strange bond if Stanton was possible of having a bond. It's a supposition, but do you think they both shared grief, and that maybe that shared grief may have played a role in this strange connection between them? Can you elaborate on that, or do you think that's just stretching or reaching?

William Marvel: I think, of course in Lincoln's case, the grief was genuine. I think it probably was in Stanton's as well. The one arena in which he did seem to be sincere in his affections was his household. At the same time, Stanton was willing to exploit sympathy for his child who died in 1862 shortly after Lincoln's son Willie died. He basically pleaded with McClellan at one point when McClellan was on to him and said, "As the father of a child who, I'm going to watch my child die tonight." Then McClellan responded with what seemed to me like genuine sympathy, which Stanton took advantage of.

I doubt, really, that the bond was mutual. I think that Lincoln probably was sympathetic towards Stanton over that death, but the legend of the bond between them is really a manufactured myth manufactured by Stanton himself. He is the one who started, right after Lincoln's death, claiming to James Ashley of Ohio, a radical congressman, that Lincoln had begged him not to resign. Stanton said he had threatened to resign and Lincoln looked at him with tears in his eyes and said, "You can't, you can't," and made some soliloquy in praise of Stanton. This was out of Stanton's mouth.

Lincoln to Stanton was, toward the end of the administration, really just his political protector. I mean, this idea that Stanton took part in the Lincoln assassination is so ridiculous precisely because Lincoln was the last friend that Stanton had in the government, in the cabinet at least.

Antonio Elmaleh: He was also his meal ticket. His patron. Why would you kill the source of your power?

William Marvel: Exactly, exactly.

Antonio Elmaleh: In reading your book it's hard to like this guy. I don't come away professing to like him, but I wonder: he was always sickly and he suffered personal loss in terms of the loss of his children and other members of his family. He was also in constant pain from a knee injury and he suffered from terrible bouts of asthma. On some level there's no wonder the guy had a scowl on his face, because he couldn't breathe and he was in pain all the time. Do you give any credence or any weight to those two physical realities of his life to attribute to his sour disposition, or am I stretching?

William Marvel: Given my own level of arthritic pain, of course I have some sympathy with people who lived before the age of Advil, but many people had lost wives and children, including Lincoln, and many people suffered chronic pain and chronic illness without becoming these, well, I hesitate to say "ogre," but I can't think of a synonym at the moment. No, my sympathy for Stanton is more on focusing on his obvious lack of self-confidence. He obviously didn't think much of himself because he couldn't stand up for himself, he just had no backbone until he was on top of the pile. Then he was cruel to those below him. Those are …

Antonio Elmaleh: And out of control.

William Marvel: Right. Those are characteristics that are very difficult to be sympathetic with.

Antonio Elmaleh: I agree with that. In the context of Lincoln's death you write about the scene across the street from Ford's Theater, and the famous line that is supposed to have been uttered by Stanton, "Now he belongs to the ages," and I think you come away thinking that maybe he didn't quite say that? Can you fill our listeners in on what the confusion around that is? It certainly paints him in noble light standing with tears streaming down his cheeks, uttering this immortal phrase.

William Marvel: Oftentimes when I come on a famous incident like that I will begin researching the historiography. Although I don't remember the exact historiography of that particular incident, no one mentioned it at the time. There were no letters from people like John Hay or Robert Lincoln or anyone else who was present that that happened. The people who were there, who did leave records, don't mention it in contemporaneous records. There was a doctor who, I think twenty years later, wrote an account that he claimed Stanton had ordered him to write. He was an Army surgeon and in it I think he may have mentioned something, some phrase, similar to that. Not sure. I do know that by the 1890s, people who had been present, and in some cases I don't think were present, were claiming that they heard him say this.

One of them was the, I've forgotten his name, he was a veteran reserve corps soldier who had lost his feet or his legs and he was the stenographer – Tanner, probably James Tanner, he was a corporal in the Veteran Reserve Corps. He took down the testimony that – of course Stanton was interviewing people there – I think by the end of his life he was saying, "Yes, I was within ten feet of him when he said this." Oftentimes those late blooming stories tend to be directed more at indicating how close the author of the story was to an important event in history than they reflect history itself.

Because of that largely, and because of the melodramatic nature of it, I pretty much doubt that it happened. One surgeon who was there said when he said Lincoln died, Stanton went over and closed the shade.

Antonio Elmaleh: In the context of the assassination and its aftermath you write extensively about how Stanton and Joseph Holt treated the trials of the indicted conspirators. Can you shed a little light for our listeners on what was controversial about how all that, all those prosecutions went down?

William Marvel: Well, they were all tried en masse, the eight, and of course it was a military commission because they needed a conviction. They didn't want any inconvenient rules of evidence being played by the defense attorneys, but there was a desire to firmly associate the assassination plot with the Confederate government. Now, you had at least one former Confederate soldier, an escaped prisoner who was involved in the assassination, the one who attacked William Seward. Booth himself was a sympathizer, but he had never been in any military service. There was no real governmental connection, but there was a desire to make one. You had to convict these people – it was mainly for popular, political effect – you had to put them away or execute them.

This was the first in a long series of efforts to associate the Confederate government with the assassination. One of the witnesses who helped hang Mary Surratt himself appears to have been an early conspirator, and yet Holt not only ignored his part in the plot but got him a government job afterward and kept him in employ for several years.

It was just part and parcel of an effort that included forged documents and con artists who either perjured themselves or sought other perjurers for Holt to try to connect the Confederate government officially with the assassination.

Antonio Elmaleh: Well, this is an interesting point, because I wonder what was to be gained politically from ascribing this horrendous closure to the war to a government that was already defeated, unless it was just pure, out-and-out rage and avenging revenge?

William Marvel: There was a definite political element to it, because...

Antonio Elmaleh: I don't understand, what did they gain from that?

William Marvel: As you mentioned, there was a great deal of, well, I wouldn't call it sympathy with the South or the Confederacy in the North, but there was a lot of conservative thought that the South had been pushed into secession, and Northern Democrats and Southern Democrats could very well combine and outnumber Northern Republicans since there were no Southern Republicans.

1865 was the end of the war but it was not the end of the United States, and it was not the end of US politics. I think those two in particular were worried personally that if the Democrats came back to power, they might be the ones going before military commissions. It was crucial to demonize the South because that also demonized any support they had among the Democrats in the North, and it precluded any immediate restoration of political rights to Southern Democrats. It was sort of the, what do they call it, the "long game" they were playing.

Antonio Elmaleh: A preemptive strike. Yes, well, that makes a lot of sense. It's not in our agenda today to cover the stormy outcome of Stanton's tenure in the Johnson administration, we'd have to devote another program probably, but I would like to have you briefly describe for us how Johnson forced Stanton out of his position in the cabinet.

William Marvel: Well, it was becoming increasingly obvious that Stanton was not only an unfriendly spirit in the middle of the administration but was disloyal to the administration. Stanton served three presidents and he betrayed all of them at one time or another, Johnson most of all and most of the time. He was basically the radical Republican's cat's paw in the administration, he was their spy, and at one point Johnson finally asked him to resign. Stanton declined to do it. Johnson bounced him out of the office, and the Congress came in on Stanton's behalf and had him reinstated. Then finally, after the passage of the Tenure of Office Act by Congress to protect Stanton in particular, Johnson fired him again, which most presidents have the right to fire their cabinet officers. Congress denied Johnson this right. That was why he was impeached, but when impeachment failed then Stanton saw the handwriting on the wall and he resigned.

Antonio Elmaleh: It's like that vignette about, "Now he belongs to the ages." I remember early on hearing, understanding the story was Stanton actually locked himself in his office to just...

William Marvel: Well, he did that at one point.

Antonio Elmaleh: Oh, he did?

William Marvel: Yes, he spent weeks in the War Office, but then finally he started going back to work and opening the doors and going home. Then, after a while, Johnson fired him again. At one point a guard at the War Department said that he took Mrs. Stanton a note from Stanton asking for, I don't know, some bedding or something. She told him to tell him to come home and get it himself, she was kind of sick of it.

Antonio Elmaleh: Stanton was a lifelong attorney, and is was no secret, as you mentioned earlier in the program, that he wished to finish out his career in a lifetime government appointment. His days as a practicing attorney were over, he couldn't drum up the business, he still needed money, etc. etc., but he had an overweening lifetime ambition. Can you tell our listeners what happened to Stanton when Grant succeeded Johnson as president?

William Marvel: Stanton immediately started truckling to him as he had before. He engaged other emissaries, a certain bishop whose name escapes me at the moment, to go to Grant and basically beg for an appointment. He was disappointed that he wasn't named to Grant's cabinet. When Grant first had a chance to appoint Stanton to the Supreme Court, he declined. I think Grant knew exactly what sort of character Stanton was, and he didn't want anything to do with him. As Stanton was growing weaker, and as another Supreme Court justice was ready to resign, radical Republicans in Congress started pressuring Grant. Finally, he appointed Stanton thinking perhaps he wasn't going to live that much longer, and in fact he didn't. Shortly, days after the, maybe only a couple days, I don't remember exactly, after they delivered the appointment to him, he died of probably congestive heart failure as a result of his asthma. It allowed Grant to solve that political pressure without having to burden the Court with someone quite as duplicitous as Edwin Stanton.

Antonio Elmaleh: You could look at it and say, "History's ruthless, he got what he wanted but never lived to enjoy it."

William Marvel: Justice prevails sometimes.

Antonio Elmaleh: I'd like to finish with, well, two things. One, I want to make an observation. I was struck by a comparison that came to me in reading your book between Stanton and George C. Marshall. It seems that history always produces exactly who and what is needed to overcome great crises. Very often, sometimes they're cretins, but they get it done. Some, like Marshall, turn out to be extraordinarily dignified. I mean, Marshall was a lifetime soldier whose ambition was to serve on the battlefield, and he ended up running the entire war effort for Franklin Roosevelt. He was behind a desk and managing global armies in the defeat of fascism in both Germany and Japan. He was very much someone that Roosevelt turned to to get the job done. Marshall succeeded brilliantly I believe, not only that but also helped to restore former enemies like Germany and rebuild their economies with the Marshall Plan. The list of his achievements is pretty extraordinary. More importantly, his character was so unimpeachable that I think in one vote, I can't remember over what it was, he got a unanimous support from the entire committee, most of whom was initially hostile to whatever it was he was advocating for. He walked away totally vindicated.

Now, you contrast that with Stanton and you come away with two very different personalities, but history pushed them into these roles and, good or bad, ugly or admirable, they did what had to be done. Can you comment on that, is that fair a comparison?

William Marvel: I would say no, partly because it's so unpleasant to hear Edwin Stanton mentioned in the same sentence as George C. Marshall. I don't view Stanton as having been the organizer of victory, as William Seward called him. In fact, I think Stanton helped almost immediately after coming into office to hurt the war effort, perhaps to the point of prolonging the war significantly. He had no sooner taken office then he stopped the recruiting of soldiers in the entire country just at the moment when McClellan was calling for reinforcements saying he didn't have enough men. Whether he did that to stymie McClellan, I don't know, or if he did it because he was gullible enough to believe that recent victories indicated the war was essentially over. I think that his failure there created the situation a month and a half later where Stonewall Jackson threw Washington into a tizzy and took troops away from McClellan just as he was converging on Richmond.

I think Stanton went a long way toward prolonging the war and hampering the war effort by creating jealousies and mistrust among generals in the Army through the War Department. Others I think could have done the same job of organization, you only have to be OCD to do what Stanton did in terms of organization.

No, I don't consider it a fair comparison. The argument that Stanton was the organizer of victory was really an argument made by those who praised him in gravestone biographies and historians who have not looked any deeper into the subject.

Antonio Elmaleh: So much for my stab at an insightful concession.

William Marvel: Sorry.

Antonio Elmaleh: That's okay. I like to close my program with a question for all our guests which is this: what enduring thought or image would you like to leave with listeners after today's discussion?

William Marvel: Since we're talking about Stanton, I guess I would hope that people would consider the real Stanton whom I think I have come closer to than earlier students of his life, and ask themselves what that says about the virtual myth of perfection about Lincoln himself. I think our image of Lincoln is so reverential that it can't be entirely accurate, and yet renowned historians today still follow that same conclusion. I think it needs to be reexamined, and Stanton is the perfect vehicle for that reexamination.

Antonio Elmaleh: I think as a follow-up to that, do you see other members of the cabinet that would've also betrayed that same strange dichotomy that would've indicated a less than reverential approach to Lincoln's leadership?

William Marvel: How about John P. Usher? I think he was secretary of, the fall of the house of Usher. He was instrumental in taking bribes for Indian agencies, he was involved in the Transcontinental Railroad, I think he profited from that. So did Lincoln, by the way, although somewhat tangentially. Usher I think was your typical scheming hand-out palm-up politician. Why he chose him for his cabinet, I have no idea.

Antonio Elmaleh: That's pretty interesting to see how it rebounds onto Lincoln, that you'd like our listeners to think about that more deeply. I think we're out of time here, so I'd like to thank you, William Marvel, for a fascinating and hopefully illuminating discussion about certainly one of the Civil War's most controversial figures. Thanks again for joining us.

William Marvel: Thank you, I'm glad my phone battery lasted.

Antonio Elmaleh: Before we go, could you tell us a little bit about your upcoming book and what it's about, because we'd like to certainly announce it to our listeners in advance of its publication?

William Marvel: Well, the short form would be it's an examination of just how many poor people, for lack of a better term, people from the lower end of the economic scale, ended up in the Union Army, and why. It deals with what appears to be an indication that many Union soldiers, a great many, went into the Army because of the money, and not just during the high bounty period in the later half of the war, but from the very outset. I mean, some of the regiments that were most heavily composed of men of poorer circumstances were from the very outset of the war when there was a major recession going on that most historians appear to have missed.

Antonio Elmaleh: I take it you're not into hagiography?

William Marvel: No.

Antonio Elmaleh: That's a mild understatement. Again, thank you for joining us, I've had a good time talking with you.

William Marvel: Thank you.

Antonio Elmaleh: Next, I'd like to thank our listeners for taking the time and having the curiosity to listen in. Please, be sure to tune into another episode of *Uncovering the Civil War*. Until then, be safe and do good.

TWELVE

UNCOVERING RECONSTRUCTION

Guest: Eric Foner

Antonio Elmaleh: Welcome everyone to another episode of *Uncovering the Civil War*. This is your host, Antonio Elmaleh. Today I am pleased to welcome Eric Foner to the program. Eric is the DeWitt Clinton Professor Emeritus of Columbia University and one of the nation's most prominent historians. He specializes in and has written many books on Civil War, Reconstruction, and slavery. His book, *The Fiery Trial: Abraham Lincoln and American Slavery* won the Pulitzer, Bancroft, and Lincoln Prizes in 2011. His latest book, *The Second Founding: How the Civil War and Reconstruction Remade the Constitution*, will appear in September of 2019. Welcome, Eric.

Eric Foner: Thank you for having me.

Antonio Elmaleh: Before we begin, I'd like to try to set the stage for this rather monumental, very dense and often misunderstood period of our history by discussing three dates: January 1st, 1863, the date the Emancipation Proclamation was formally issued; February 4th, 1871, the date the Civil War officially ended when one Homer Miller was sworn in as United States Senator from the ex-Confederate State of Georgia; and March 5th, 1877, the date Rutherford B. Hayes was sworn in as President of the United States, as well as a commonly held date for the end of Reconstruction. My first question goes really back to the Emancipation and to Lincoln. Is there any hard evidence of Lincoln's vision of what Reconstruction ought to be like?

Eric Foner: Well, that's a question historians have been debating for a long time. Lincoln, during the Civil War, put forward policies toward Reconstruction. He had a Proclamation of Amnesty and Reconstruction at the end of 1863. Lincoln understood that if you begin with, as you said, January 1st, 1863, that emancipation meant there was going have to be a fundamental change in Southern society and indeed American society. Once he made the end of slavery a purpose of the war with the Emancipation Proclamation, that guaranteed that something of Reconstruction would have to happen because slavery was a total institution. It was a system of labor, of politics, of race relations, of social relations. If you eliminate that, you're going to have to rebuild the society.

But Lincoln, of course, was killed before Reconstruction got going and most of what he did in relation to that during the war were war measures. He was trying to bring Southern states back into the Union; therefore, he offered them lenient terms to come back. This was not a blueprint for the postwar world. It was part of his effort to win the war: if you could detach a Southern state from the Confederacy, that would be better than winning a battle, you know?

I think it's not "history" to think about what Lincoln might have done. This is counter-factual, as we call it. People debate it all the time and whenever I lecture on Reconstruction and the Civil War they ask me, "What would Lincoln have done?" And I can speculate, but that's not really history. Lincoln did not live to work out a clear policy on Reconstruction. The one thing I would say, though, that I can be fairly confident about, is Lincoln would never have gotten himself into the fix his successor, Andrew Johnson did: completely alienated from Congress, alienated from Northern public opinion and the Republican Party, coming within one vote of being removed from office via impeachment.

Lincoln was far too good a politician, far too rooted in the Republican Party, with far too good a sense of Northern public sentiment, to ever land in the situation that Johnson did.

Antonio Elmaleh: Yet he was his running mate, which was an interesting fact more than any other background.

Eric Foner: Back then, and maybe now, people were put on the ballot as vice presidential candidates not because anyone expects them to become president, but because they will pick up a bloc of votes from somewhere, or appeal to a body of voters. For example, Johnson was a Southern Democrat from Tennessee, a Unionist, a strong opponent of the Confederacy, and he was put on the ticket as a symbol of the Republican Party's desire after the war to appeal to these pro-Union white Southerners whose numbers they perhaps exaggerated a bit.

Lincoln was a young guy in his 50s. Nowadays, most of our presidents and presidential candidates seem to be in their 70s. No one expected Lincoln to die in his second term as President. His first vice president, Hannibal Hamlin, had no connection to the administration at all. When Lincoln issued the Emancipation Proclamation, Hamlin send him a note saying, "Oh, this is a great idea, good work." He'd never heard of it before, and he's the vice president. Vice presidents didn't have much of a role in government back then unless the president happened to die in office.

Antonio Elmaleh: Conversely, what do you think was Andrew Johnson's vision of Reconstruction?

Eric Foner: Well, we know the answer to that because Johnson tried to implement it. Johnson was deeply racist. He was a strong Unionist, of course, but he didn't think that black people should have any role in government. They should basically go back to work after the war was over. Of course, they're free now, they should get paid some kind of wages, but he didn't support civil rights/political rights for blacks.

So he put into practice an all-white Reconstruction policy in 1865, setting in motion the establishment of new governments in the South elected only by whites. And these new Johnson governments passed a bunch of laws which we call "the black codes" to force African Americans back to work on the plantations. And if they didn't, they would be arrested, accused of vagrancy, auctioned off to labor for someone who could pay their fine. It was an attempt to get the plantation system going again.

This was not what black people or many Northerners thought the emancipation of the slaves ought to involve. At the very least, in order to involve what Northerners called a free labor system where people competed in the labor market, if you didn't want to work on a plantation, go and find some other job — but not have the law or the sheriff force you back to work on a year-long contract and if you try to leave you're arrested. Johnson's plan very quickly fell apart and alienated the North and led Congress over the course of 1866 and '67 to try to formulate its own plan of Reconstruction because Johnson was obviously…let me just put it this way, sometimes we Americans get stuck with a president who is obviously unfit for the office. It's been …

Antonio Elmaleh: Oh, really?

Eric Foner: Yes, it happens sometimes. Johnson was one of those guys, unfit, just unfit to be president. Didn't have the temperament, didn't have the intelligence, didn't have the broad vision of things that Lincoln did, deeply racist. Probably the worst President ever.

Antonio Elmaleh: Did he have the ambition? You think he had the ambition?

Eric Foner: Oh, he was totally ambitious. He started out as a very poor man in North Carolina, then Tennessee. He worked his way up through politics, held many public offices in Tennessee, a very ambitious guy — as Lincoln was, of course. But somehow, and this is a question of personality, Lincoln's ambition led him to be open-minded, generous, willing to listen to criticism. Johnson was closed-minded, egomaniacal, would never listen to anybody. Once he took a position he stuck with it, couldn't imagine any criticism. He just didn't have the right temperament to be a leader.

Antonio Elmaleh: Because he was an alcoholic, too, wasn't he?

Eric Foner: Well, unfortunately he turned up drunk at the inauguration...

Antonio Elmaleh: Right. That's a famous...

Eric Foner: ...on March 4th, 1865. That was rather humiliating for Lincoln and others, I don't think he would call him a drunk. But anyway, Congress and Johnson got into this gigantic battle over Reconstruction because Johnson's policy was so clearly inequitable.

Antonio Elmaleh: I want to jump to a notion that I have and I've heard from other folks as well. And the question is this: do you share the view that a vast guerrilla war, or an insurgency if you will, promoted by planners and carried out by ex-Confederate veterans began right after the surrender at Appomattox in Durham Court House?

Eric Foner: I wouldn't put it quite that way, although the basic point is probably accurate that there never was a real peace after Appomattox. That is to say in 1865 the soldiers go home, the war is over, but very quickly sporadic violence against the former slaves breaks out. It's not organized; at that point it's much more localized, there's no organization that's doing this. It basically comes out of slavery: black people want rights, whites don't want to give it to them. They want pay for their work, they want to be able to leave and find other places to work and live. And throughout 1865 you'd get reports of what seemed to be random violence: a black guy refuses to step off the sidewalk for a white person and somehow people would start shooting at each other; someone tries to go into a church to worship and is shot dead. In other words, whenever black people try to step out of the roles and mores of slavery, they often find violent retribution.

But what happens later, once you get into what we call "radical Reconstruction" – this is 1867 where the Johnson state governments are basically overturned and Congress says, "Okay, we need new governments in the South with black men voting for the first time in American history and black men holding office" – then you get organized political violence, the so-called Ku Klux Klan and other such groups which are led by major figures in Southern society. And they're basically launching a counter-revolution or you could call it a guerrilla war against the new system of biracial government in the South.

Antonio Elmaleh: I think it's fair to point out also that it was probably Grant and Lincoln's abiding nightmare that unless they've afforded generous surrender policies and extended an open hand, that they would spark that very kind of guerrilla or popular uprising that would lead to something more organized and more protracted. And I just wonder whether that in effect is how it ended up, how it turned out.

Eric Foner: Well, first of all, Johnson's split policies were extremely lenient. Basically, the white South didn't have to do anything except admit that they'd lost the war, which was fairly evident. Yet still they were unable to come to terms with the end of slavery, really. They were unable to offer even a modicum of equal rights to former slaves. I don't think it's a vindictive punishment that leaves this violence. There was plenty of violence in 1865 when the white South was basically given a free hand by Johnson: "You guys do whatever you want as long as you admit that slavery is over and that you're part of the Union. Other than that, you got a free hand."

No, I think you have to understand this not as a matter of psychology or something like that, but as a fundamental battle over what kind of society you're going to have in the South. As I said, with the end of slavery they've got to build up a new society: is it going to be just white supremacy again with blacks having no rights – that's Johnson's attitude. Or is it going to be some vision which – not all by any means – some Northerners had of equal rights for all, of trying to get the country to live up to its supposed principles as laid out in the Declaration of Independence?

I would say Lincoln didn't have a policy of Reconstruction, but remember in the Gettysburg Address he said, "The proposition on which this country is based is all men are created equal, and let's try to see how we can implement that." But that led to violent resistance in the South.

Antonio Elmaleh: I also want to point out that the government confiscated something like eight hundred thousand acres of former planters' land. By one year after the war was over, Johnson had returned over half of that. And I think it's also safe to say that blacks were more vested in owning land as a way into liberty, self-reliance, than they were with the more rarefied issues of voting rights and the ballot. That owning a piece of the Earth ...

Eric Foner: I don't think it's either/or, but you're absolutely right. Unfortunately many people don't know much about Reconstruction even though it's still very relevant to our world today, but they have heard the phrase "forty acres and a mule" that's come down from Reconstruction. That was a kind of shorthand for the desire, as you just said, of the former slaves for land of their own. This would be the economic underpinning of freedom.

The phrase actually comes from General Sherman. After his March to the Sea and occupying Savannah, early in 1865 he met with a group of black ministers in Savannah and he said to them, "Well, what do people need?" And they said, "We need land. Give us land and we can really be free people." And he then set aside a lot of land along the coast of South Carolina and Georgia for the settlement of black families in forty acre units, and also gave them a mule if they needed one. And there is your forty acres and a mule. And by the spring and summer of 1865 many thousands of blacks were settled on that land.

As you said, Johnson ordered all that land in federal hands to be returned to the former owners. People who had been settled on what they call the Sherman land were evicted at the end of the year. And this was a considerable betrayal in the view of these people.

But I think you've pinpointed a basic problem with Reconstruction. What one might say is that the political revolution of Reconstruction went forward: the first civil rights laws, the first writing of the principle of equality into the Constitution in the 14th Amendment, the right to vote in the 15th Amendment for black men. That was a political revolution.

The economic revolution didn't go so far, particularly when it comes to this business of access to land. That was a big problem with Reconstruction.

Antonio Elmaleh: I'm sure you would agree that Reconstruction is extremely complex, dense, and unfortunately still shrouded in myth and public ignorance of its historical significance to our Republic. Is it safe to say that the fundamental clash, just to give a broad stroke so that our listeners have a fundamental grasp of what was being fought over, was a fight between Congress and the executive branch over war powers and civil rights?

Eric Foner: I wouldn't quite put it that way because to say that, you eliminate the former slaves who were also part of this battle. They're putting forward their own agenda, as I just mentioned, of rights. They're forcing the issue of civil and political rights onto the national agenda. Yes, the battle between Johnson and Congress is one of the great political set pieces of our history, but Reconstruction is much more than that. What I call it is a battle over what kind of society is going to succeed slavery. What does it mean now that there's no more slavery in the United States? Is everything else going to stay the same but no more slavery, or do other changes follow from that?

As you said, civil rights, political rights, what does it mean to be a free person in America? There are four million people moving from slavery to freedom. What comes along with that? Does it just mean that they can't put a chain on you anymore, or are there certain basic rights that come along with being a free American? Reconstruction is important for one reason: it's one of those times where they're debating the fundamental questions of the society. Normally these are not debated, but in this crisis situation they are.

I think that's why it's complicated, as you say, and difficult to understand. But it's also a dynamic and, to my mind, inspiring period in many ways. You have people really trying to get this country to live up to what it claims it believes in, that is equal rights for all.

Antonio Elmaleh: I did a show earlier and it was clear to my guest there was such an irony in the radical Republican strategy of prolonging the war on technicalities. In other words, not announcing that the war is over to forge a lasting peace. It's very ironic and it hinges on this idea of the War Powers Act and what constitutes the end of hostilities. There are all sorts of technical reasons why radical Republicans hung their hat on stretching out ...

Eric Foner: Yes, but in a way I don't think we should emphasize those issues quite so much. You're right that they are looking for legal constitutional grounds to do what they want to do. They want to make sure that there is what they call loyal government in the South, not just a bunch of ex-Confederates taking over again. They want to make sure that the end of slavery produces genuine freedom for the four million former slaves. And they want to make sure the Republican Party stays in power. In other words, there are political motivations, there are human humanistic purposes, there are national power issues.

One of the things about Lincoln that I think is interesting, in his last speech before he was assassinated when he talked about Reconstruction he said, "Look, let's make this a practical matter. Are they in the Union, out of the Union, there's no point in going and debating that. Everybody understands the Southern states are not in their normal relationship with the Union." He was a pragmatist. He didn't believe in debating how many angels can dance on the head of a pin, he said, "Let's just figure out how to get this situation resolved fairly to everybody."

The question of when the war ended is interesting, but that wasn't what was driving policy. When they figured out their policy, then they said, "All right. Well now, what does that mean for when the war ended? Did it end up at Appomattox, did it not end up at Appomattox, is the South still in what is called the grasp of war?" That's what most Republicans eventually decided: they were in the grasp of war. That is, even though there's no more fighting going on, peacetime is not really fully returned and therefore Congress can do things that it couldn't normally do in peacetime, like tell the states what they have to do.

I think Reconstruction is a giant crisis of all kinds, and I think it's important to look at it from all these vantage points, the legal, the constitutional, the social, the racial, the political, etc. etc.

Antonio Elmaleh: And try to balance all of those different trumpets.

Eric Foner: Yes, all those things were on people's minds.

Antonio Elmaleh: Yes. I want to shift to something a little bit more minute. Can you describe the effect of the panic of 1865, 1866 on US Army muster rolls, and consequently the size and strength of Union occupation forces in the South?

Eric Foner: There wasn't a panic until 1873 which led to the depression, really, of 1873 to 1878 and that had a big effect on Reconstruction because it undermined the Republican party in the North, which was the party in power. When there's an economic depression, people tend to shift to the other party and it boosted the power of the Democrats who were opposed to Reconstruction. '65, '66 it's not really an economic question, but the fact is, yes, after a war is over people want to go home, they want normalcy. You couldn't just have a giant standing army in the South, and therefore the size of the Army is reduced radically in 1865 and 1866.

I don't have the number in front of me but by the end of 1866 there's what, fifteen thousand men left in the South, and most of them are around Texas fighting the Comanche and the Apache. The picture of the South as an occupied territory is partly true and partly a considerable exaggeration. There were Union Army units stationed in major cities in the South, but most of the rural areas didn't have any military presence after the end of 1865 of any great significance.

Antonio Elmaleh: I think what I was trying to get at though is, if there was not just Johnson's racism and Rutherford B. Hayes' decisions to do what he did, but that there was an economic underpinning which was, "We can't afford, literally, to keep all these soldiers in uniform, we have to cut back."

Eric Foner: That's true enough. Remember the war had cost an enormous amount of money. There was a gigantic national debt built up in order to pay for the war. Fiscal policy, the sort of standard fiscal policy which the Republican Party pursued, was that you reduce the national debt, you pull the greenbacks, the money that had been printed during the war, out of circulation. And that meant, you're right, there were budget problems and the amount of money you could spend on the military was limited. No question about it.

Antonio Elmaleh: Much has been made of Andrew Johnson's and Edwin Stanton's clashes over Reconstruction policy. I'm not so clear on Ulysses S. Grant's attitudes and his treatment of Johnson; do you think he had his eyes on the presidency well before 1868? He doesn't really show up in terms of taking sides in the arguments. I know he's General of the Army of the United States so he has to essentially deal with whatever Johnson tells him to do, but he doesn't emerge as clearly in terms of...

Eric Foner: Grant had more political savvy than people sometimes think. He certainly knew that, when the war ended and Lincoln was no longer living, he was the most popular figure in the North. He was a man who had led the victorious military campaign and people were already talking about him for president. Johnson is president but 1868 is going to roll around, then there'll be a new election. And already very early in 1865 people were talking about Grant. Now, as you say, he's a general in the Army, he has to follow the president's policies, but he quickly becomes disillusioned with Johnson.

In 1866 Johnson travels around the North basically promoting Democratic Party candidates for the congressional elections, and he drags Grant along with him. This is the so-called "swing around the circle," and Grant is humiliated after a while. He doesn't really want to be there. Johnson is a stump speaker, as you said he drinks a little too much, he speaks in all sorts of tirades against the radicals. And Grant tries to distance himself. By then Grant is making it pretty clear that he favors Congress in the fight that's going on between Johnson and Congress, and he doesn't announce himself as a candidate but it's pretty clear that many Republican leaders see Grant as their best candidate for 1868.

By the time he is elected in 1868, Reconstruction policy has been set, new governments are in place in most of the South, the Constitution has been amended – at least the 14th Amendment – and Grant basically says, "Look, Reconstruction is settled, we've settled it." He runs on the platform "Let us have peace," which is a double-edged thing. On the one hand it's peace between North and South, but it's also a peace between black and white. And he says, "Look, if the Klan keeps operating we're going to have to go after them because you can't have a functioning society where murderers, terrorists are running around with impunity, killing people." The Klan was basically the American Al-Qaeda. They were homegrown terrorists and they killed more Americans than Osama bin Laden ever did.

Antonio Elmaleh: I think it was estimated that between 1865 and 1885 something like fifty thousand freedmen and ex-slaves were murdered.

Eric Foner: Those numbers are guesses. They're estimates, nobody knows how many, but there were certainly thousands of people killed, no question. Now the Klan was not just like Al-Qaeda. It wasn't a tightly-knit highly organized thing. It's local groups all over the place, sometimes they're called other things. But certainly there were these local terrorist groups all over the place who were committing violence against the freed people and also white Republicans. And Grant sent troops into South Carolina in 1871 to crush the Klan. He didn't particularly want to do that but he said, "Look, there's no alternative, this is like a second Civil War they're starting down there."

Antonio Elmaleh: I want to jump to a central figure in the whole Reconstruction drama, Rutherford B. Hayes. As an attorney, Hayes won two landmark civil rights cases, I believe in the 1840s or early 1850s, and by doing so, he put himself publicly in support of abolition.

Eric Foner: Or even support of black rights in Ohio, which is not quite the same thing, but still, yes, he had a reputation as favoring the rights of African Americans, no question.

Antonio Elmaleh: As president he attempted to reform the civil service and he institutes state-supported education. These are all progressive initiatives, yet his Reconstruction actions, specifically helping to engineer the removal of the final troops from the South, endangered millions of ex-slaves and freedmen and degraded and hampered progress on civil rights for at least a hundred years. How do you explain the dichotomy of somebody whose heart seemed to be in the right place but politically he was called "the man of the middle" and was so far afield in terms of a moral compass? Was he just naive to what he was doing? And unaware of the consequences?

Eric Foner: He was a little naïve. In my book on Reconstruction I say, "Hayes would never have been nominated if the Republican Party was still really committed to Reconstruction." In other words, by this point he had carved out a position as a sort of moderate who felt that the Reconstruction governments were not functioning properly and a new Southern policy was needed, but that was the way most Republicans were going in the mid-1870s. It wasn't that Hayes initiated these new policies, it's that he reflected a shift in Northern public sentiment.

In 1875, when the so-called white rifle clubs as they called themselves in Mississippi were running amuck and using violence, and eventually won electoral control of the state, John R. Lynch, a black Congressman from Mississippi, went to see President Grant and said, "Look, you've got to send troops into Mississippi or we're going to lose Mississippi. You've got to protect black people, otherwise they can't go and vote." And Grant said, "I could send troops and win all of Mississippi, but if I do that I'm going to lose Ohio."

In other words, what he's saying is Northern public sentiment no longer supports intervention in the South. Now, if that's the case and you're Rutherford B. Hayes, you're going to have to come up with a new Southern policy. Grant was already on that path toward the end of his presidency. I'm not defending Hayes as much as saying he reflects a general shift in Northern public opinion.

Now also, the withdrawal of troops was part of a deal. As you know, Hayes's election was disputed. There were multiple electoral vote counts in the three states of Florida, South Carolina, and Louisiana. There was disputes over who would carry them. Eventually it went to an electoral commission established by Congress and they certified Hayes. But meanwhile, the party leaders, in the so-called Bargain of 1877 where leaders of the two parties basically negotiated behind the scenes that Hayes would become President, agreed that he would withdraw these troops.

That was already a deal worked out before he became president by leaders of the two parties. He didn't really have much choice. Now it is true, of course, he was naive and he only served one term and when he left office he said, "I've been misled." The white Southerners who were now in control had said, "We will respect the basic rights, the political rights, the civil rights of blacks," but they didn't. And he felt that he had been lied to by the Southerners who were part of this Bargain of 1877 but he also felt that he had no room to maneuver, that the Northern sentiment and public opinion would not support further intervention in the South.

I'm not trying to defend Hayes, except to say that his position reflects a broader shift that's going on in the country.

Antonio Elmaleh: I've thought a lot about this shift in Northern attitudes and what was underlying this kind of eventual, "I've had enough, let them figure it out for themselves." Do you think that exhaustion played a role?

Eric Foner: Yes.

Antonio Elmaleh: Then we can talk about the finer points of the legal points and all that, but from the sheer humanitarian point of view these folks had fought for four years and in God knows all kinds of conditions, and they were done. They felt that they'd anted up. It's not just a moral collapse or lack of a backbone, it's just very human, do you agree with that?

Eric Foner: Absolutely. What happened after World War I? The desire for normalcy. Big wars lead people to want normalcy when they're over.

They don't want it to continue forever. And naturally there was a general sentiment – in fact, it's amazing Reconstruction happened at all, it was the intransigence of Johnson and the white South, their inability to face up to the reality of the end of slavery, that led Northerners in '66, '67, and '68, '69 to say, "We can't just let these guys do everything. Forget about normalcy for a minute, we're going to have to continue to tell them what to do down there."

But as I said before, by 1873 with the economic depression – when I was doing research on my book on Reconstruction I read a lot of letters to members of Congress, in the papers of congressmen in the Library of Congress. They got letters from constituents and that's an index of public opinion. It's not scientific but it gives you a good sense, and up through about 1872 the letters were all about what's going on in the South: "Look at this, there's violence, the rebels, etc." But after the panic of 1873 and the economic depression they're no longer writing about the South. They're writing about unemployment, they're writing about fiscal policy, they're writing about the needs of jobs, businesses closing. There's a shift in the focus of public sentiment, and that's part of this retreat from Reconstruction, that other issues just come to the fore.

Eventually that's going to happen in any generation, any circumstance. It's not simply a moral failing, although it was to some extent, but it's also just a, you're right, exhaustion. And in a certain sense, white Southerners persevered longer in their efforts to restore white supremacy in the South than Northerners persevered in their willingness to intervene to protect the basic rights of the former slaves.

Antonio Elmaleh: Can you describe what happened at the 1876 Republican Convention and describe how Hayes won the presidency. It's one of the most amazing elections I've ever read about. It just defies...

Eric Foner: Well, we did have Bush versus Gore, which was basically like that. Back in the bad old days national conventions really were places where the candidates were chosen. Nowadays, because we have primaries and everything, by the time the national convention meets it's already clear who's going to be the candidate. When was the last time the Democratic or Republican National Convention met when there was any question about who was going to be the nominee? Maybe 1976 when Reagan challenged Ford, maybe back in the 1950s, the Republican Convention of 1952? Today, the National Convention ...

Antonio Elmaleh: '68.

Eric Foner: '68? Well, but Humphrey...

Antonio Elmaleh: We didn't know...

Eric Foner: You had the delegates, they knew he was going to get nominated; they didn't know there was going to be rioting at the same time. But anyway, back then in the smoke-filled rooms they picked the candidates, and frankly they probably did as good a job or better than we do nowadays. And they were various possibilities in 1876, but Hayes was acceptable to the whole party. Hayes, as you said, had a reputation early on for radicalism. On the other hand, later he'd become more moderate, more mainstream. He hadn't alienated anybody, particularly in the party. He had won election in 1875 as governor of Ohio, which was a major swing state back then, and he represented the need for a new policy on Reconstruction, which many Republicans had failed. And, of course, let's not forget his wife, "Lemonade Lucy," who was a teetotaler and the evangelical vote, which we had back then also. The fact that he was married to a woman who didn't approve of hard liquor meant that parties at the White House when he was president were pretty boring, frankly, no liquor served, lemonade, that's it, guys. Can you imagine the French Ambassador coming to meet the president and being handed lemonade?

Anyway, as I said before. when the election took place the results were disputed. And in fact. late that night it seemed like Tilden had won. But a reporter from a Democratic newspaper called the Republican National Headquarters in the middle of the night and asked them what their count of the electoral vote was. And this led William Chandler, the head of the Republican National Committee, to say, "Hmm, they're not absolutely certain that they've won. Let's get out the figures."

And he did a bunch of calculations. He said, "If we can hold these three states, South Carolina, Florida, Louisiana, we'll have a win. Hayes will win by one electoral vote." He issued a press release: "Hayes has won. Hayes is victorious by one electoral vote." And then chaos happened a couple of months later and nobody knew who had won. The Constitution unfortunately does not tell you what to do. It tells you that, "Whoever gets the majority of the electoral votes wins." But it doesn't tell you what happens if two different returns come in from a state.

The Republicans claimed to carry it. The Democrats, too. Who decides? It went on, and on, and on until, as they said, in the waning days before the Inauguration of March 4th, 1877, the so-called Bargain was reached. And Hayes was inaugurated. Very unusual, and again, it's outside the Constitution. There's nothing in the Constitution that says there can be an electoral commission to determine who won the vote. That's just completely made up but there was nothing else to do.

Antonio Elmaleh: No other recourse.

Eric Foner: No other recourse.

Antonio Elmaleh: The narrative of the Lost Cause did not rise until well after the war ended?

Eric Foner: Yes.

Antonio Elmaleh: Is that's safe to say?

Eric Foner: Oh, yes.

Antonio Elmaleh: My question is why did it take so long? The elements: the notion the war was fought for states' rights and the right of states to choose and just salvage the Southern way of life and all this stuff – those arguments were always there. But it surprised me that it wasn't really taken up, at least by historians, with any momentum until probably what, the 1890s?

Eric Foner: Yes, 1890.

Antonio Elmaleh: Why do you think it took that long to get that kind of traction?

Eric Foner: Well, look, in 1865 the South had suffered a total disaster. There were about seventy-five thousand people killed in the war, more or less, but the proportion of men in the South killed was far higher than in the North because the South, even though there were fewer casualties all told, had a much smaller white population. And this was devastating. You were not going to go out celebrating the Confederacy in 1865; these guys have brought total disaster on the society.

And then secondly, a view of Reconstruction is part of the Lost Cause. The Lost Cause, as you say correctly, really becomes prominent in the 1890s. It has three elements: One is that slavery was a fairly benign institution and we probably would have gotten rid of it eventually but it was good for blacks to be raised up into Christianity, they were well treated, etc., etc. Two, the Civil War was about states' rights, local self-government, not about slavery, and our soldiers fought gallantly, we should respect them all, etc., etc. Three, Reconstruction was a disaster because black people were given the right to vote. It was a tremendous mistake to give black people the right to vote and therefore the violent campaign to take away their right to vote was justified.

And all that is part of the Lost Cause. The Lost Cause is a glorification of the Confederacy but it's also a glorification of white supremacy. It needed the end of Reconstruction to really put that coda onto it. It's not until the 1890s that the Lost Cause becomes really prominent in the South and that's when you get these famous monuments, statues being built which are controversial nowadays, all over the South. In 1865, they didn't have any money to build a statue. There was nothing like that. But by the 1890s they did.

Antonio Elmaleh: They picked up some traction with historians, as well.

Eric Foner: Yes, absolutely.

Antonio Elmaleh: And this is the part that's so interesting to me. It took thirty plus years for that narrative to rise and be promoted actively amongst prominent historians of the day.

Eric Foner: In 1910, let us say, if you picked up whatever was the leading American history textbook, which I don't know quite what it was, you would find pretty much the picture of the Civil War that I just described, the pro-Southern. They often say, "The South lost the war, but won the battle over the memory of the war." And David Blight, of course, in his book some years ago, the very fine book *Race and Reunion*, shows how what he calls a "reconciliation" takes hold by the 1890s in the North and South: the Civil War was a family quarrel among whites, it was brother against brother, and both sides should look back on it with pride. Really, slavery didn't have much to do with it one way or the other. And in the 1890s that becomes dominant culturally if you look at magazines and things like that, and also in historical scholarship.

Now, of course, the view of Reconstruction as a disaster comes out of Columbia University, my university. William Dunning and his students produced the so-called "Dunning School" around 1900 and then a little after that, which dominated historical scholarship on the period all the way into the 1950s and '60s. And it was a justification of Jim Crow, a justification of taking away the right to vote from blacks because if you gave them their rights, look what happened, what a disaster. If you gave them back their rights you'd have the horrors of Reconstruction again. So, it was very much a political historical argument. It was not only about the history, it was about the present. They were saying, "We were right to take away the Constitutional rights of black people because of the so-called horrors of Reconstruction."

And that lasted all the way through the civil rights movement, which finally undercut the racist underpinning of that view and then led historians to start developing new approaches to Reconstruction, which we're still doing.

Antonio Elmaleh: Do you think it's safe to say that the Union won the war, and the Confederacy won the peace?

Eric Foner: At that point, yes. If you looked around 1900 you would certainly say that, except for the fact that the South remained a backwater in the nation. The economic debate – this is the period of giant industrialization– it's almost all happening in the North. It's a period of national power. White Southerners – especially the upper classes, the planters, the merchants – control Southern government but they're really junior partners in the nation. They don't have the kind of power that they always did before the Civil War, etc. The North is calling the tune on national policy all the way through this period.

Antonio Elmaleh: I'd like you to comment on these apparent contradictions, at least they are contradictions to me, and the first one is the end of slavery helped expand the political power of the South for a hundred years after the war. That's one contradiction that I think our listeners would be interested to learn about. And the second one is that in expanding the right to vote, instead of having what I would call a purifying effect on expanding democracy, it had the unfortunate consequences of intensifying and accelerating civil violence. Can you comment on those?

Eric Foner: First of all, the end of slavery had this ironic result because the Three-Fifths Clause of the Constitution was thereby abrogated. The original Constitution said that representation in the House of Representatives, and also the number of electoral votes any state has, is based on the total number of free inhabitants plus three-fifths of "other persons," which means slaves. The word slave is not in there, but everyone knows who they're talking about. Three-fifths, but now that the slaves are free all five-fifths, all of them are going to be counted, right?

It doesn't matter whether they're voting or not, women were accounted although they didn't have the right to vote at that time, children accounted, it's the total population. The Southern population on which representation is based is expanded by the end of slavery, which means that they will get twenty or thirty more members of Congress than they would've had before the war. That's a bizarre, maybe yes, ironic as you said.

Now, during Reconstruction blacks were able to vote. The people representing the South in Congress were representing the whole population, blacks and whites. But once Reconstruction ends and then later they take the right to vote away from blacks, you get this expanded representation but they were only representing white people. Black people have no say in Southern political power at that point. Now of course, Congress in the 14th Amendment had tried to anticipate this by saying, "If a state took away the right to vote from any group of men, not women, they would lose representation in Congress." The South should have lost half its Congressmen when they disenfranchise black voters around the 1890s and early 20th century. But this was never enforced. It's supposed to be automatic, it was never enforced.

But the problem is, as I said before, the South is solidly Democratic at this point and the Republican Party is running the government pretty much up through the New Deal, although Woodrow Wilson, of course, served two terms in there. When the Democrats were in power, then Southerners have a lot of influence. When the Republicans were in power and had the presidency, then the South doesn't have very much influence because they were all Democrats. But certainly, you can look into the Wilson administration and then the New Deal, and you'll see Southern committee chairmen and members of Congress having very strong influence on national power.

What was the other irony? Oh yes, that expanding the right to vote led to violence.

Antonio Elmaleh: Yes. Instead of having a purifying effect and getting standard democracy, it created such a...

Eric Foner: There are people who don't like democracy in this country, I'm sorry to say, especially when it comes to non-whites taking part in it. As Lincoln said in the Gettysburg Address, democracy means "government of the people, by the people, for the people". But that begs the question: who are the people of United States? If you look at the original Constitution it begins with the words, "We the people." But if you read the text, you will find there are the people, and then there are other persons, the people who are not part of the people: the slaves, and then there were Native Americans who are their own sovereignty.

From the very beginning, there's been confusion or conflict about who actually is the people. And unfortunately, white Southerners could not accept African Americans as part of the people. And when the concept of people was expanded to include blacks, it led to, as you say, violent reaction. That's an unfortunate piece of our history but it is there.

Antonio Elmaleh: In studying this subject so thoroughly and for so long, what new things are you discovering about Reconstruction?

Eric Foner: One of the things that strikes me is historians have a funny way of counting. They think the 19th century ran from 1780 to World War I, the so-called "long 19th century." They now talk about the "long civil rights movement," and there's a kind of thing nowadays to start talking about the "long Reconstruction," not ending it in 1877, maybe going all the way up to 1900. Because even though we say, "All right, 1877, troops withdrawn," history never ends at one point. I'm interested in what happens after that.

Because black people still vote all the way into the 1890s. They still hold offices in some places. There were insurgent white movements in North Carolina, for example, a coalition of white populace and black Republicans come together to govern the state in the mid-1890s and they have a second Reconstruction. In other words, the ferment that happened in Reconstruction continues well into the end of the 19th century and that's, I think, something scholars are looking at now in more detail than perhaps they did in the past.

Antonio Elmaleh: As a follow-up to my last question, I'm just curious what was updated in the newer edition of your book?

Eric Foner: I wrote a new introduction. My book on Reconstruction was published thirty years ago, 1988 basically, a lot of scholarship has happened since then. I must admit my book is not the last word on the subject. Other scholars think there's something to be said and there's been a lot of work on various aspects. In the new introduction from a couple of years ago I tried to basically say, "Well, what has happened in this field since I was writing?" For example, there's been a lot more work on women's history; how did Reconstruction affect black women, white women, the family, things like that? I didn't really devote a lot of attention to that and other issues which weren't really on the radar screen as much then as they are now. But you can't rewrite a book. My book was written and to revise the book would require writing a new book and I don't feel like doing that. But the new introduction tries to give an indication of what important work has come out, then what they're saying. It was good for me, too, to try to come to grips with what the scholarship has been doing since my book appeared.

Antonio Elmaleh: Typically, I end the show by asking my guest to leave our listeners with one thought, idea, or image to take away from our discussion. Instead, with your permission, I'd like to borrow your voice for a moment and ask you to read the last sentence of your book. Would you do that?

Eric Foner: Certainly. This is what it says, page 612: "Nearly a century elapsed before the nation again attempted to come to terms with the implications of Emancipation and the political and social agenda of Reconstruction. In many ways it has yet to do so." I was writing in 1988, which was twenty years after the civil rights revolution. Thirty more years have passed, and yet the issue of race in our country has not gone away. The questions that are central to Reconstruction are still on our agenda, on the front pages of our newspapers.

Who is a citizen? That's a Reconstruction question. What exactly should the division of power between the federal and state governments be? That's a Reconstruction question. Terrorism is a Reconstruction problem. How do you deal with terrorism, the Klan and groups like that, what is the relationship? We talked about this before, between economic democracy and political democracy. That's on our agenda today, we talk about inequality and things like that.

I guess my point is simply that even though, and I have to admit it, a lot of people know about the Civil War but a lot of people don't know very much about Reconstruction. It's still, in a way, part of our world today and Reconstruction issues are still out there. And if you want to understand our society, you really should know something about that Reconstruction period after the Civil War.

Antonio Elmaleh: Thank you. And I just want to point out something and if you have a minute just to comment, that you talk about how one of the fundamental shifts of the Reconstruction efforts were focused on black socialization. That the church, the book clubs, the study groups, the desire to be educated, are a very, very intuitive and natural approach to gaining more resiliency. I'm wondering if there's any kind of a shift in the black community since the Civil Rights Acts where we're now starting to see a profound reexamination of the role of men in the society.

Eric Foner: That affects everybody, not just African Americans as you well know. We're no longer living in the era where forty acres and a mule is your economic aspiration. It's a different society, it's a different world. These basic aspirations for equality, for dignity, for opportunity are still out there and Reconstruction gave voice to them, and people are still giving voice to them. I don't know if that answers your question really, but I think it does link us back. The present should be linked back to that period of slavery and the Civil War and Reconstruction.

Antonio Elmaleh: I think we've run out of time. I'd like to thank you, Eric Foner, for coming on the show and engaging in an informative and provocative discussion. I hope our listeners enjoyed it as much as I did. Thank you very much.

Eric Foner: You're very welcome. I enjoyed talking to you.

Antonio Elmaleh: Before we sign off, tell us a little bit about your new book.

Eric Foner: Well, it's a short book called *The Second Founding*. And it's about the 13th, 14th, and 15th Amendments that were added to the Constitution during Reconstruction, how they changed the Constitution, how the courts have interpreted them over the years, and how I think they still have a latent power which has not been really utilized lately to address some of the lingering problems that maybe originated in the days of slavery and Civil War.

It's really trying to introduce people to these three Amendments, which are critically important in our Constitution and yet have never quite achieved the degree of public recognition. Like our key documents, the Declaration of Independence, the Bill of Rights, the Gettysburg Address, the Reconstruction Amendments ought to be up there because they did change what it is to be an American in terms of our rights, our liberties. It's just a book about that.

Antonio Elmaleh: Sounds great.

Eric Foner: Thank you very much for having me.

Antonio Elmaleh: You're very welcome. And as always, thanks to our listeners for taking the time and having the curiosity to listen to another episode of *Uncovering the Civil War*. Please come back again. Until then, be safe and do good.

END NOTE

This has been *Uncovering the Civil War* with your host Antonio Elmaleh. For more information about our podcast, please visit uncoveringthe-civilwar.com. This podcast is produced by Antonio Elmaleh, Chandra Years, and Joe Marich. Music by Andrew Elmaleh. This podcast is the sole property of Antonio Elmaleh. Copyright 2018, all rights reserved. No portion of this podcast may be reproduced, transmitted, sold, edited, broadcast or reposted on the internet without express written permission of the owner.

ABOUT ANTONIO ELMALEH

Antonio Elmaleh is the author of the novel *The Ones They Left Behind* and is the host of the podcast *Uncovering the Civil War*.

Antonio was born and raised in New York City. After an early exit from Duke University, he worked on such feature films as *Sidney Lumet's Child's Play*, *The Last Of Sheila*, Neil Simon's *The Sunshine Boys*, *Bang The Drum Slowly*, *The All-American Girl* and Simon's stage version of *Chapter Two*.

Antonio worked in acquisitions at World Northal Corporation, which domestically distributed independent/foreign films such as: *Bread And Chocolate*; *Cousin, Cousine*; *The Who's Quadrophenia*; Nicholas Roeg's *Bad Timing* and Peter Weir's *The Last Wave*, as well as the first Chinese martial arts movies ever seen on American television. Later he was a development executive at 20th Century Fox and a freelance story analyst for Warner Bros., Motown Productions and Vestron Pictures.

From 1986-89 he managed a co-production slate of six films in partnership with BBC-TV and was Executive Producer of *The Vision*, starring Lee Remick, Dirk Bogarde and Helena Bonham Carter. A story of American evangelicals taking control of the fledgling British satellite television industry, the film opened the London Film Festival in 1988.

Between 1989 and 1998 Antonio managed the portfolio of World-Wide Holdings Corporation, a privately-held real estate company.

During that time, he also bought and developed residential projects in New York City's Tribeca and Chelsea neighborhoods.

In 1999, Antonio began researching and writing *The Ones They Left Behind*, a novel about a Civil War veteran's one-man peace march set during the stormy days of American Reconstruction, which was published in October 2014. His next book, *A House United*, published in October 2016, serves as a companion book to *The Ones They Left Behind* and is a compilation of essays and thoughts by Antonio discussing themes of political divisiveness, war, PTS, and other issues paralleling our country's bloodiest war and today's America.

Beginning in 2017, Antonio served as executive producer and host of the popular Civil War podcast series, *Uncovering The Civil War*, which brings to life interesting, little-known, or even unknown facts about the Civil War, and how people, places, and events during the Civil War impact our lives today. The series ran for two years for a total of twenty-nine episodes. Transcripts from the podcast series of *Uncovering The Civil War* have been edited and anthologized and is now available in book form.

Antonio passed away on January 16, 2020 in Ringoes, New Jersey after a long illness.

ALSO BY ANTONIO ELMALEH

The Ones They Left Behind

A House United

Uncovering the Civil War (podcast series)

FOR ADDITIONAL INFORMATION

AntonioElmaleh.com

UncoveringTheCivilWar.com

Twitter: @AntonioElmaleh

Facebook: AntonioElmalehAuthor

INDEX

CPSIA information can be obtained
at www.ICGtesting.com
Printed in the USA
JSHW040545160421
13629JS00004B/24

9 780990 640639